A Working Life for People with Severe Mental Illness

Innovations in Practice and Service Delivery
with Vulnerable Populations

Series Editors:

David E. Biegel, Ph.D.

Arthur Blum, D.S.W.

Case Western Reserve University

Innovations in Practice and Service Delivery Across the Lifespan,
David E. Biegel and Arthur Blum

Community Treatment for Youth: Evidence-Based Interventions
for Severe Emotional and Behavioral Disorders,
Barbara J. Burns and Kimberly Hoagwood

This series is sponsored by the
Mandel School of Applied Social Sciences,
Case Western Reserve University

A Working Life
for People
with Severe
Mental Illness

Deborah R. Becker and Robert E. Drake

UNIVERSITY PRESS

2003

OXFORD
UNIVERSITY PRESS

Oxford   New York
Auckland   Bangkok   Buenos Aires   Cape Town   Chennai
Dar es Salaam   Delhi   Hong Kong   Istanbul   Karachi   Kolkata
Kuala Lumpur   Madrid   Melbourne   Mexico City   Mumbai   Nairobi
São Paulo   Shanghai   Taipei   Tokyo   Toronto

Copyright © 2003 by Oxford University Press, Inc.

Published by Oxford University Press, Inc.
198 Madison Avenue, New York, New York 10016

www.oup.com

Oxford is a registered trademark of Oxford University Press

Library of Congress Cataloging-in-Publication Data
Becker, Deborah R.
A working life for people with severe mental illness /
Deborah R. Becker, Robert E. Drake
    p.   cm. — (Innovations in practice and service delivery with vulnerable populations)
Includes bibliographical references and index.
ISBN-13 978-0-19-513121-5
ISBN 0-19-513121-5
1. Vocational rehabilitation. I. Drake, Robert E., M.D., Ph.D. II. Title. III. Series.
HV3005 .B425 2003
362.2'0425—dc21   2002013525

9 8 7 6 5 4

Printed in the United States of America
on acid-free paper

In memoriam

Carolyn Mercer and Tom Fox

Whose values, dedication, and friendship
inspired many of us in New Hampshire
for more than two decades

Preface

When we began to study employment in New Hampshire in the late 1980s, many individuals helped us to understand the field's experience. First, numerous clients and family members, many of whom prefer to remain anonymous, met with us and described their disappointing and occasionally constructive experiences in the service system when they attempted to find and keep employment. Second, Donald Shumway, Jim Musumeci, Thomas Fox, and Paul Gorman from the New Hampshire Division of Behavioral Health; Jess Turner, William Torrey, and Phil Wyzik of West Central Services; and Nick Verven, Ken Snow, Bill Rider, and Ed Bailey of the Mental Health Center of Greater Manchester gave not only their time but also their support to our efforts to study different vocational service models in New Hampshire.

Third, Bruce Archimbault, Paul Leather, and others from the New Hampshire Division of Vocational Rehabilitation met with us regularly to help us understand how the vocational services system operated and why it often did not function well for clients with mental illness. From the beginning we have found that colleagues in vocational rehabilitation departments around the country have been interested in improving services rather than protecting conventional programs.

Fourth, numerous mental health and rehabilitation professionals with experience and expertise in vocational services met with us, generously gave us advice, and assisted us in defining and studying programs. Among those who were particularly helpful were William Anthony, Marianne Farkas, Karen Danley, and Sally Rogers from the Boston University Center for Psychiatric Rehabilitation; Jana Frey, Mary Ann Test, William Knoedler, Deborah Allness, and Leonard Stein from Madison, Wisconsin; Judith Cook and Lisa Razzano from Chicago; Robert Liberman, Charles Wallace, Keith Neuchterlein, and Michael

Green from UCLA; Morris Bell and Robert Rosenheck from Yale; and Anthony Lehman from the University of Maryland. There could be no scholar more generous and helpful than Gary Bond from Indiana. He enhanced our efforts at every step, but especially by bringing his encyclopedic knowledge, enormous energy, and selfless support when he joined us during a sabbatical year (1994–95).

As Individual Placement and Support (IPS) has spread around the United States and into other countries, many others, too numerous to mention here, have joined our efforts to study its implementation and effects and to improve the approach in ways reflected in this book. We continue to be public stewards rather than owners.

We use the name Individual Placement and Support in this book, but at the same time we recognize that other approaches to supported employment are rapidly adopting the principles of IPS because they are consistent with consumer choice and good outcomes. In many ways we prefer the nonproprietary term, evidence-based supported employment, which represents the natural evolution of IPS. Our goal has always been to improve services and outcomes, not to promote or sell a model. In the National Evidence-based Practices Project, supported employment is equivalent to what is described here as IPS. For complementary information from that project, see the Supported Employment Implementation Resource Kit (Becker & Bond, 2003).

A few additional words about language are in order. People who have mental illnesses or who use mental health services are of course primarily individuals, people, and citizens. Terms that refer to their illnesses or service use should never be taken to define their identities. People who become users of the mental health system are referred to by a variety of terms, and these change over time. People who receive services in hospitals are usually called patients; in community mental health centers, they are typically called clients; in self-help organizations, they are often called consumers, survivors, or users; and in vocational research projects, they are referred to as participants. Some of these differences are discussed in chapter 2. We use these terms interchangeably in this book and apologize at the beginning for any resulting confusion. Similarly, there are many conventions for referring to a person's sex. To avoid the awkwardness of writing "he or she" throughout the book, we change back and forth, recognizing that a specific example refers to either a man or a woman and hopefully illustrating that people of both sexes use supported employment services. Finally, as the organizational structure of health services continues to change in this country, IPS services are appearing in a variety of mental health and rehabilitation programs, agencies, centers, clinics, organizations, institutes, and so on. Again, we adopt the convention of using these terms interchangeably to recognize the diversity of relevant organizations in different parts of the United States and elsewhere.

The format of the book is simple. It is divided into three sections. The first reviews the historical, theoretical, and empirical background of the IPS approach to supported employment. This section may be of greater interest to students than to practitioners. The second presents an update and substantial revision of our earlier book, *A Working Life,* which was written 10 years ago and is now woefully out of date and in need of retirement. The third section addresses some of the common questions and typical dilemmas that practitioners have raised over the years while implementing IPS. The second and third sections respond to the needs of practitioners, as we have heard them expressed over the past 15 years.

Contents

Part III
Special Issues

Appendices

Illustrations

"Still, it was the stable periods, times when I was most productive, that built my self-esteem and helped balance the down times. And so it is with so many of us who struggle with schizophrenia and other mental illnesses. That's one of the reasons I feel so strongly about the need to be given meaningful work instead of the make-busy tasks or rote assignments that make up the bulk of what we are offered. If people are treated as capable, they often surprise everyone and live up to expectations."

—Ken Steele in *The Day the Voices Stopped: A Memoir of Madness and Hope* by Ken Steele and Claire Berman (p. 103), New York: Basic Books, 2001.

Part I

Conceptual and Empirical Support for Individual Placement and Support

1

Introduction

Deinstitutionalization of persons with mental illness, which began in the 1950s, did not quickly change treatment attitudes. Mental health professionals continued for decades to treat people with mental illness as though they were vulnerable, incompetent, and in need of protection (Kiesler, 1992; Nelson, Lord, & Ochocka, 2001; Rapp, 1998). The great majority of mental health services were shaped by the perceived need to take care of dependent and severely impaired people (Rappaport, 1987). Mental health practitioners emphasized supervised and segregated settings, treatment and medication compliance, and sometimes coercive interventions; they often were pessimistic about outcomes. The dominant heuristic regarding psychopathology, called the "diathesis-stress" model, emphasized vulnerability to stress and limiting stimulation (Wing, 1978). In this paradigm, medications were conceptualized as reducing vulnerability, and psychotherapies as increasing ability to cope with stress.

Ironically, the lessons of institutional care were remarkably hazy. Although we had learned that hospitalization could have adverse effects (Goffman, 1961; Stanton & Schwartz, 1954), mental health professionals didn't take the message to heart. In fact, many clients were transferred from hospitals to other institutions such as nursing homes, and a variety of new institutions that resembled hospitals arose in the community: group homes and other supervised living situations, day treatment centers, sheltered workshops, homeless shelters, and segregated treatment facilities in the community. Nursing homes and some day programs recapitulated the close control and supervision of the hospital, while shelters, day centers, and board and care homes often offered the stultifying environments and lack of meaningful activities that had characterized large hospitals. Meanwhile, public interest in deinstitutionalization often focused on controlling the potential for violence rather than on promoting community integration (Carling, 1995).

Vestiges of all of these themes unfortunately remain as mainstream attitudes in community mental health care today. Many approaches to case management assume a developmental model in which the clinician relates to the client in a parental fashion with low expectations. Current biological models hypothesize neurodevelopmental arrest and static brain injury as a model of psychopathology. Following these models, the *Diagnostic and Statistical Manual* remains pessimistic about the potential for recovery (American Psychiatric Association, 1994). Treatment too often emphasizes stabilization of symptoms and staying out of the hospital rather than pursuing personal goals, functional roles, and quality of life. And despite evidence that substance abuse rather than severe mental illness underlies increased rates of violence (Steadman et al., 1998), public interest in violent behavior by people with mental illness remains keen. Meanwhile, we continue the trend toward reinstitutionalizing people in different types of institutions by shunting large numbers of people with severe mental illness into jails and prisons (Abrams & Teplin, 1991).

Approaches to vocational rehabilitation generally have reflected our paternalistic treatment models. According to the diathesis-stress model, competitive employment is often seen as a high-expectations stress to be avoided, at least until the individual has been stable for many years. Many mental health professionals still believe that competitive work represents a dangerous experiment, despite many studies showing that even the most assertive employment programs do not result in more relapses of illness, hospitalizations, or other adverse outcomes (Bond, Becker, et al., 2001). Sadly, the attitudes of mental health professionals are frequently cited as a barrier to implementing supported employment (Torrey, Bebout, et al., 1998; Bond, Becker, et al., 2001).

Most vocational rehabilitation programs have been anything but liberating. Just as community mental health treatment models recapitulated the hospital environment, vocational rehabilitation approaches resembled the work programs that were offered in state hospitals. Sheltered workshops and day rehabilitation programs emphasized structure, protection by close oversight, slow stepwise approaches to prepare people for the community, and low expectations. The sheltered workshop approach was recognized as "deadening" many years ago (Dincin, 1975). These programs segregated people with mental illness and kept them apart from mainstream jobs, mainstream workers, and mainstream society. In both treatment and rehabilitation settings, the explicit goal was to provide stabilization, and the implicit goal was to help people become "good patients" rather than regular citizens. Thus, people with mental illness moved to the community, but segregation and patienthood continued to define approaches to mental health care and rehabilitation (Estroff; 1981; Rappaport, 1987). Emblematic of this shift were the numerous day programs in which smoking and watching television were the dominant activities.

How did rehabilitation programs justify this level of perpetuating and reinforcing disability? Theoretically, the predominant "train-place" philosophy of vocational programs assumed that learning was very slow, that extensive preemployment training was necessary, and that a prolonged, stepwise approach was appropriate prior to competitive employment (Wehman & Moon, 1988). Pessimism about outcomes inspired extensive approaches to evaluation and assessment that were designed to identify the details of deficits and to prescribe corresponding changes in attitudes, cognitions, and behaviors that had to be accomplished prior to employment. In practice, the approach was even more stultifying because bureaucratic assessment procedures operated to preclude vocational services by defining people as lacking readiness.

In sum, even though institutionalization became viewed as a debilitating process that led to atrophy of functional skills, the mental health field quickly developed new community-based institutions, such as mental health centers, group homes, sheltered workshops, and day centers, which replicated many of the negative features of hospitals (Nelson et al., 2001). Segregated and protected environments in the community replaced hospitals, with the hope that greater stimulation could be provided in such settings but with the reality that these settings were isolating and stigmatizing in many of the same ways as prolonged hospitalization. There was little awareness on the part of professionals that activities in community mental health centers might again be socializing people into disability by segregating them and emphasizing their patienthood rather than integrating them into mainstream society and emphasizing their ability to function in mainstream adult roles. How did we get from these early failures of deinstitutionalization to the optimism of supported employment?

2

Conceptual, Historical, and Ideological Underpinnings of Supported Employment

At this point in our narrative, the experienced social science reader anticipates the epiphany. History has been painted as a straw man to contrast dramatically with and set up the new view. We all have read this story many times. Treatment was a disaster until the sudden development of the orgone box, frontal lobotomy, past life therapy, megavitamins, or some other new approach. For example, Freud fashioned the myth that he discovered the unconscious and defense mechanisms out of thin air, even though he could not have failed to encounter cultural, artistic, and popular ideas about the unconscious, and he had only to read 19th-century novelists such as George Eliot to find elegant descriptions of defense mechanisms (Schorske, 1981). Similarly, many current writers would have us believe that that all psychiatric care was morally and scientifically benighted until they developed a more compassionate approach to rehabilitation, housing, family intervention, recovery, or whatever. These accounts seriously misrepresent the recent history of mental health care.

In the truly inchoate state of community mental health care following deinstitutionalization, there has been no dominant model or paradigm. With 50 state mental health systems and numerous administratively independent mental health regions within most states, hundreds or thousands of experiments in community-based care have occurred over the past 5 decades. A plethora of theories, popular movements, practical treatments, guild arguments, personal preferences, and experimental approaches have been put forward and translated into services repeatedly. Throughout this time, the fashions of current wisdom and political correctness, the rigidity of professional dogma, and the constraints of regulations and financing mechanisms, rather than science or empirical data, have determined service offerings in most places. Moreover, while deinstitutionalization was failing to realize its goals in most areas of the

United States (Lamb & Bachrach, 2001), a number of societal plagues afflicted the poor generally and people with mental illness in particular. These included the decline of the inner cities, violence, increased incarceration, shortages of low-income housing, homelessness, drug abuse, hepatitis, and HIV infection. Many would include managed health care as another plague.

Stress has a remarkable way of challenging equilibrium and stimulating change. A variety of more positive views of treatment, rehabilitation, recovery, and community integration somehow have emerged from the shambles of deinstitutionalization, fragmented mental health care systems, and social problems. For clients, the recovery movement symbolized this sea change. For family members, the formation of the National Alliance for the Mentally Ill was pivotal. For professionals, new psychosocial approaches based on integrating services and promoting strengths rather than treating deficits, new medicines with less disabling side effects, and a focus on evidence-based medicine began to challenge traditional ways of thinking and to promote optimism regarding treatment outcomes. In sum, the convergence of many different voices encouraged change. These new ideas are no panacea, of course, and whether or not they will be realized broadly in the United States remains to be seen.

The Consumer Movement

The central figures in the drama of community mental health care are, of course, people with mental illnesses. Spurred by bleak mental health models that emphasized chronic illness and poor prognosis, inadequate community-based treatment systems, widespread stigmatization, and psychiatry's preoccupation with hospitals and medications, mental health care recipients began to organize in the 1940s to provide mutual support and to seek more effective services in the community (Dincin, 1975). Recently, they have sought not only to demand reforms in the mental health system but also to promote consumer self-help services (Capponi, 1992; Chamberlin, 1978; Deegan, 1988; Mead & Copeland, 2000). The consumer movement has taken myriad forms. As we will describe, early efforts led to the development of psychiatric rehabilitation programs. Personal stories of recovery have been a consistent and dominant theme (e.g., Deegan, 1988; Fergeson, 1992; Glater, 1992; Leete, 1993; Ralph, 2000; Steele & Berman, 2001). Recovery stories emphasize several common notions: taking personal responsibility for managing one's own illness and taking charge of one's own life, becoming hopeful about the future, having one or more close personal relationships for support, and finding meaningful activities that reinforce a sense of purpose and accomplishment. At the same time, personal accounts point to the destructive effects of some mental health treatment experiences: hospitalization, involuntary treatment, demeaning activities in segregated settings, and messages about deficits and chronicity.

The consumer movement became a particularly potent force during the 1980s and 1990s (Rapp, 1998). By emphasizing self-help, empowerment, choice of services, and recovery, consumers rejected the professional model of chronic illness that was characterized by patienthood, incompetence, dependence, and deterioration. They insisted that the mental health system provide less coercive and more respectful services that supported their goal of returning to usual adult roles in integrated settings in the community rather than being shunted to alternative settings of segregation, dependence, and make-work. They became advisers and employees within the mental health system, always relying on personal experience, learning to manage their own lives and illnesses, and developing hope, satisfying relationships, and meaningful activities. And they also initiated consumer self-help programs to promote wellness and recovery (e.g., Copeland, 1997). Although some consumer leaders understandably became mired in anger and recrimination, and some followed an earlier and now discredited generation of intellectuals in rejecting the concept of mental illness, the great majority supported constructive reforms of the mental health system based on notions of community integration and recovery.

Consumers advocate using knowledge, personal resources, coping strategies, social supports, self-help, and professional services to attain what they term "recovery." Although professionals have attempted to define recovery, consumers have insisted on varied and personal definitions. Because we can neither define the term precisely nor allude to hundreds of definitions, in this book we take recovery to encompass taking responsibility for managing one's life and illness and moving ahead to pursue a personally satisfying and meaningful life (Anthony, 1993; Mead & Copeland, 2000; Ralph, 2000; Torrey & Wyzik, 2000). For consumers as well as nonconsumers, having a meaningful daily activity is one central component of a satisfying life (Campbell, 2001; Fisher, 1994), and the great majority of consumers identify competitive employment as one important activity that they are interested in pursuing (Rapp, 1998; Rogers, Walsh, Masotta, & Danley, 1991).

There are numerous outstanding examples of the consumer recovery movement. In the New England area, Mary Ellen Copeland has been the most influential proponent. Her many books and her widespread workshops for consumers emphasize hope, personal responsibility, education, advocacy, peer support, and learning to use the mental health system effectively (e.g., Copeland, 1997).

The Family Movement

Although mental health clients ("consumers" in preceding text) have been at center stage, families have been their primary supporters and the primary political advocates for changes in the mental health system. Families long recognized that they did not deserve to be blamed for causing mental illness. New data regarding the biological underpinnings of major mental disorders (Andreasen, 1985), a new commitment to collaborating with rather than treating families (Bernheim & Lehman, 1985), and new data on the effectiveness of family psychoeducation (Dixon et al., 2001) combined with the angst of families and their latent potential for activism to produce a political movement. One cannot overemphasize the positive impact of the family movement, chiefly the National Alliance for the Mentally Ill, on the U.S. mental health care system.

With political empowerment, families have inspired numerous positive changes. We highlight here just a few of the changes that directly stimulated supported employment. First, families have been clear about the need to provide mental health services that are oriented toward helping people with mental illness to achieve independence, functioning in adult roles, and quality of life, not just stabilization of illness or living outside of the hospital. Second, families have demanded access to accurate information regarding mental illnesses and treatments, for themselves and for their client family members, and collaborative participation in the treatment process and service system planning process. Information is of course empowering, because it reveals the problems that clients have had accessing effective rehabilitative services. Families identify vocational services as their relatives' most common unmet need (Steinwachs, Kasper, & Skinner, 1992). Third, family organizations have been keenly aware that traditional vocational services have been remarkably ineffective (Noble, Honberg, Hall, & Flynn, 1997). They have insisted that federal agencies remove political, financial, and structural barriers in order to facilitate the provision of effective services. Finally, families are concerned with helping their relatives to become self-sufficient so that they will be able to provide for themselves and pursue satisfying lives when parents and other family members are no longer available (Lefly, 1996). Family organizations have recognized the potential of supported employment to promote competitive jobs, decent wages, real independence, and true community integration rather than segregation and dependence on the mental health system.

Innovative Approaches to Community Mental Health

Early in the deinstitutionalization era, approaches to community mental health were based on moving hospital staff and functions to outpatient settings in the community. These efforts naturally transferred the attitudes, philosophies, and treatment approaches of long-term hospitalization to the community. New approaches to treatment rapidly emerged, however, with more of an emphasis on helping individuals develop skills in their community living environments rather than in clinics, helping clients to pursue their own life goals rather than just to stay out of the hospital, and focusing on clients' abilities rather than on their deficits. We describe two emblematic approaches that have been particularly influential and that have demonstrated positive benefits: the Program for Assertive Community Treatment (PACT) and the Strengths Model of case management.

PACT founders Leonard Stein and Mary Ann Test recognized early in the course of deinstitutionalization that teaching skills to clients with severe mental illness in the clinic was ineffective because skills did not generalize well and clients needed assistance to learn important skills in their community living environments. Thus, PACT teams did nearly all of their work outside of the clinic or office. They helped clients to learn practical skills for riding buses, negotiating with landlords, cooking, developing friends, and for other activities in the community, in the settings in which they would actually use the skills so that transfer was not a problem. Soon this approach was extended to employment. After early attempts to broker traditional services for vocational rehabilitation, PACT leaders decided to take a direct approach to helping people find and keep jobs (Russert & Frey, 1991). Rather than helping people to prepare for work, they attempted to help clients find jobs rapidly and to learn relevant skills on the job. Thus, the Madison PACT team was among the first to apply the principles of supported employment in the mental health field. Moreover, Test (1995) showed that this shift in approach led to dramatically improved employment outcomes.

One important idea of the early PACT leaders was integrating a variety of services through a multidisciplinary treatment team. To avoid service fragmentation and diffusion of responsibility, the PACT team provided nearly all services by having clinicians from different disciplines on the team, by providing different work shifts to insure 24-hour access to clients, and by daily communication. Over time, as other components of community-based care have evolved and been refined, they have been easily integrated into the structure of the 24-hour multidisciplinary team, because the team provides appropriate services directly rather than by referral. That is, as approaches to crisis intervention, family psychoeducation, treatment of co-occurring substance abuse, supported employment, and other interventions have evolved, they have been rapidly and successfully incorporated into the multidisciplinary team model (Stein & Santos, 1998; Allness & Knoedler, 1998; Liberman, Hilty, Drake, & Tsang, 2001). For years, employment has been a central concept of the PACT approach, and Test (1995) documented that, when supported employment is consistently available over several years, more and more clients become interested in working and succeed in competitive jobs. Reviews of PACT do indicate, however, that the vocational component is often omitted from replication efforts and that employment outcomes do not improve without the supported employment component (Bond & Resnick, 2000; Mueser, Bond, Drake, & Resnick, 1998; Phillips et al., 2001).

At the same time that Stein and Test were pioneering a community-based approach to combining mental health and social services, Charles Rapp (1998) and his colleagues from the field of social work were innovating an even more radical departure from traditional approaches. Recognizing that values, language, concepts, roles, and all of the other determinants of stigma combined to reinforce the negative aspects of patienthood, they attempted to reverse the long-standing medical focus on psychopathology by emphasizing strengths—

the client's own abilities as well as the positive potential of his or her living environment—rather than weaknesses. The client or consumer now was conceptualized as the citizen with rights to be the director of services. Traditional emphasis on training, treating, and changing the recipient of mental health care was eschewed in favor of a new emphasis on integration, normalization, resilience, hope, environmental strengths, self-determination, and recovery. Among the fundamental tenets of the strengths model is the belief that people with mental illness can use their own strengths and the natural strengths of community environments to achieve their personal goals; to develop hope, confidence, and self-esteem; and to attain success, satisfaction, independence, and quality of life. This process occurs one step at a time, and people need access to resources, opportunities, and social supports to succeed. According to the strengths approach, ensuring that these facilitative elements are available should be the central task of the mental health system.

Because most people with mental illness identify competitive work as one of their primary goals, the strengths model has focused on supported employment for years. Rapp has also suggested that a small number of simple outcomes, which reflect the goals of citizens who have mental illness, should be used by mental health programs for management and supervision (Rapp & Poertner, 1992). Chief among these outcome indicators is, of course, competitive employment.

Many other innovators in community mental health have had likeminded insights and have enacted similar changes to improve community support programs and case management programs. We have described just two outstanding examples because they have been particularly clear about pointing toward supported employment, and it has been shown empirically that their approaches improve outcomes.

Psychiatric Rehabilitation

Psychiatric rehabilitation has long emphasized improving supports, opportunities, skills, and community integration (Anthony, Cohen, & Farkas, 1990; Dincin, 1975; Cnaan, Blankertz, Messinger, & Gardner, 1990; Fabian, Edelman, & Leedy, 1993; Liberman, 1992; Rutman, 1993). The psychiatric rehabilitation movement began in the 1940s with a group of ex-patients discharged from New York hospitals who met together on the steps of the New York Public Library to seek fellowship. Their meetings evolved into the formation of Fountain House, which became a club for former mental patients. Subsequently, in the 1950s, Fountain House took on professional leadership, began to emphasize returning to employment as well as social support, and developed into a national network of psychosocial rehabilitation centers (Dincin, 1975; Beard, Propst, & Malamud, 1982). Among many important innovations, the clubhouse movement spurred community integration by injecting strong ideas about optimism, self-help, personal dignity, and experiential learning in real-world settings. While the clubhouse movement spread across the United States, it also spawned a series of independent rehabilitation programs that introduced a wide range of innovations (Dincin, 1975).

As psychiatric rehabilitation has evolved over the past half century, a few trends seem apparent (Anthony, Cohen, Farkas, & Gagne, 2002; Bond & Resnick, 2000; Liberman, 1992; Mueser et al., 1997). First, rehabilitation continues to focus on the skills needed for practical purposes, that is, to live an independent adult life in the community. Approaches range from experiential learning to specific skills training, but research and clinical experience have led to a greater emphasis on specific skills for specific tasks or settings and a greater awareness that skills do not generalize well. Second, there is increasing emphasis on the specific supports that are needed to help individuals to be successful in housing, work, school, and social settings rather than in mental health treatment environments. Third, current approaches recognize that clients' goals include normalization, recovery, and community integration: that is, they emphasize culturally defined adult roles in everyday community environments with the usual rights and responsibilities of citizenship and involvement in community life. Fourth, there is increasing awareness that stepwise approaches to community integration are relatively ineffective. People typically become stalled in some of the steps that are presumed to facilitate their progress toward regular community activities and do not get to the desired endpoint. Thus, rehabilitation practice currently emphasizes early involvement in regular community activities with supports as needed. Such practices include, for example, supported housing, supported employment, and supported education. Fifth, there is recognition at the public policy level that not only general support but also individualized accommodations are sometimes needed to help people to function in community settings. Finally, there is an emphasis on involving clients as the main agents in choosing goals, approaches, and settings. Client choice is in fact one of the main driving forces behind the movement toward rapid involvement in routine community settings. That is, clients do not generally choose segregated mental health settings, such as hospitals, group homes, sheltered workshops, and day centers for people with disabilities. Rather, the great majority of mental health clients prefer to enter routine settings, roles, and communities as rapidly as possible.

Shared Decision Making

One of the seminal contributions of psychiatric rehabilitation and one of the central tenets of the consumer movement is the emphasis on client choice. The Psychiatric Rehabilitation Center at Boston University has for years championed the value of attending to clients' values, goals, choices, and involvement in decision making (Anthony et al., 1990). Curiously, however, the movement toward client education, choice, and shared decision making has received more attention and research support in general medicine than in psychiatric rehabilitation (Wennberg, 1991). In a wide variety of medical areas, such as hypertension, back pain, prostate disease, and diabetes, clinical approaches have moved away from the traditional "doctor as authority" model toward an approach that involves providing patients with up-to-date information about their illnesses and current treatments so that they can make truly informed choices regarding their treatments. Moreover, research indicates that involving patients in the process of making medical decisions leads to better outcomes, not just in terms of satisfaction and adherence but also in terms of biomedical parameters, for example, blood pressure and blood sugar levels (Wennberg, 1991). Psychiatric rehabilitation and other mental health approaches have been relatively paternalistic in the area of shared decision making, apparently because of the often erroneous belief that people with mental illness have impaired decisional capacity.

Even some approaches to supported employment have implied incompetence on the part of clients by, for example, assuming that months of counseling are needed to help the client choose a realistic work goal. As we discuss later, research shows that nearly all people with severe mental illness who express an interest in employment already have a realistic work goal. Furthermore, and in support of the shared decision-making model, employment in jobs that match clients' goals results in greater satisfaction and longer job tenure than employment in jobs that do not match preferences.

Cross-cultural and Outcomes Research

Research on the long-term outcomes of mental illness, even the most severe illness of schizophrenia, has never been totally bleak. Although it is true that Kraepelin (1971) attempted at the close of the 19th century to define the diagnosis of schizophrenia in terms of poor outcome, his logical error of circularity was repeatedly criticized. Early in the 20th century, Bleuler (1911) recognized that the course of schizophrenia was heterogeneous, that a significant proportion of clients with the syndrome experienced a complete return to preillness functioning, and that the modal course involved improved functioning after a few years of active illness. In the middle of the 20th century, before antipsychotic drugs had impacted outcomes, numerous follow-up studies showed substantial rates of complete remission and even higher rates of return of functioning (Huston & Pepernick, 1958). Thus, despite misinformation in documents such as the *DSM–III* (American Psychiatric Association, 1987), the prognosis of severe mental illness, even schizophrenia, has never been uniformly poor, except when we have removed opportunities for recovery by, for example, keeping people in institutions for decades.

Two recent lines of research underscore the potential for recovery and the importance of psychosocial supports and opportunities. First, cross-cultural studies of major mental illness show that the prevalence of major disorders, such as schizophrenia and affective psychoses, appears to be similar across different cultures (Draguns, 1980), but that the course appears to be related to the nature of the culture. Specifically, in cultures in which major psychotic disorders are less stigmatized, in which family and community supports are greater, and in which access to and return to culturally defined adult roles are expected, the course of disorder appears to be dramatically better (Hopper & Wanderling, 2000). Thus, cross-cultural studies support the notion that the expectation of culturally defined adult role functioning carries a self-fulfilling prophecy: the greater the expectation and support for community functioning, the more likely that result.

Second, as an antidote to misinformation regarding the course of mental illness, Tsuang, Woolson, and Fleming (1979), Harding, Brooks, et al. (1987), and many others have reminded the mental health field that schizophrenia, like other psychiatric disorders, has a variable course with many good outcomes and a likelihood of functional recovery for many clients. Furthermore, DeSisto and colleagues (1995) also have argued from long-term follow-up studies that an emphasis on community-based rehabilitation rather than hospital-based care substantially affects functional outcomes. That is, clients who are in systems of care that emphasize community integration, building and strengthening of familial and social supports, and access to competitive work roles have better long-term outcomes.

New Medications

The advent of a series of new antipsychotic medications, starting with clozapine, has energized the field of psychiatry with a more hopeful view of recovery (Essock, 2002). The current medications, and others to follow, have different neurochemical profiles from traditional antipsychotics and offer the promise of fewer and less serious side effects, better impact on negative symptoms (e.g., withdrawal and lack of motivation) and cognitive problems, and significant relief of positive symptoms (e.g., hallucinations and delusions) for some clients who did not respond or were unable to take traditional medications. Many clients report substantial improvements with the new medications (Mellman et al., 2001). As a result, psychiatrists seem less willing to accept partial symptomatic responses and disabling side effects with antipsychotic medications (Covell, Jackson, Evans, & Essock, 2002).

There is also the anticipated possibility that the new medications will enable people who use them to benefit more substantially from rehabilitative and recovery-oriented approaches. Unfortunately, the research on this issue is minimal. Rosenheck et al. (1997) found greater participation in rehabilitation by clients on clozapine. Noordsy and colleagues (2001), working in a mental health center with an extensive supported employment program, found that clients who elected to change to a new antipsychotic medication were more likely to attain competitive employment than those who remained on traditional medications. At this writing, however, the rehabilitation potential of new antipsychotic medications should be considered a hopeful hypothesis that needs to be studied.

Supported Employment

Traditional approaches to vocational rehabilitation involve preemployment training of various types (e.g., skills training, sheltered workshops, trial work programs, work adjustment jobs, enclave jobs, or businesses run by mental health programs) to prepare the individual for a competitive job. These step-wise approaches are termed "train-place" models. They all assume that the individual benefits from some form of training, instruction, or practice in a protected but artificial setting before entering a competitive work role. However, the stepwise approach has been criticized on several fronts. People often are not motivated in practice settings; work tasks rarely match their interests; skills do not generalize, and it is impossible to predict the skills that will be needed for a particular job; people tend to lose interest and motivation during the training; and there is little or no evidence that these types of experiences really help people to move on to competitive employment (Bond, 1992; 1998).

Wehman and Moon (1988) first described supported employment as a "place-train" approach to vocational rehabilitation in the early 1980s. Working in the developmental disabilities field, they were able to demonstrate that rapid placement in competitive employment, even for the most severely disabled clients, followed by specifically targeted job training and support, was superior to preemployment "train-place" approaches. The supported employment approach was rapidly transferred to mental health by a number of leaders in the psychiatric rehabilitation movement (Anthony & Blanch, 1987; Fabian & Wiedfeld, 1989; Mellen & Danley, 1987).

The basic rationale for a place-train approach is simple and straightforward. Without knowing ahead of time what type of job an individual will obtain, it is highly inefficient to train the person for the specific skills, including social skills, that will be needed for success on a particular job. For example, practicing food preparation skills may give little benefit to an individual who obtains a gardening job, and practicing social skills will be largely irrelevant (at least in the work environment) for another person who obtains work as a housekeeper. In other words, the idea of preemployment training assumes that learned skills will transfer to different situations and different tasks and, for individuals with major mental illness, this often turns out to be inaccurate.

Another problem with preparatory skills training is the unappealing nature of the training situation. Many preemployment training or work adjustment sites frankly are boring, unchallenging, and unrealistic (Dincin, 1975). Clients know these are not competitive jobs, not the jobs they want, and not the skills they need (Estroff, 1981; Quimby, Drake, & Becker, 2001). Hence, they appear to be uninterested or unmotivated. The situation becomes complicated because staff often misinterpret clients' behavior as representing traits rather than situational states. By contrast, it commonly happens in supported employment programs that an individual who previously showed no interest in job training situations surprises everyone by working successfully in a competitive job of her choice.

Determining needed skills and supports in the context of a competitive job is more straightforward. The individual has a job he is interested in doing, he has real demands for performance, he can see that he needs specific skills to do the job successfully, and he experiences a real social situation on the job. At this point, an employment specialist and a team can be more helpful. Along with the client, they can identify and develop the needed skills and supports.

Wehman and Moon (1988) clearly described the place-train approach as fundamental to supported employment. However, the Rehabilitation Act Amendments of 1986, which codified supported employment in law, specified competitive employment, follow-along supports, and emphasis on the most severely disabled clients without requiring a place-train approach. This led to a wide variety of programs claiming to offer supported employment, many of which continued to rely on train-place methods. Leaving aside political considerations, perhaps one intent of the legislation was to avoid prescriptiveness so that a diversity of approaches could be tried in the field for different settings and for different disability groups.

Collaborative Empiricism

As we began to implement supported employment programs in New Hampshire in the late 1980s, we received enormous amounts of help not only from the literature but also from colleagues who were already exploring supported employment. It was clear to us, however, that we often received conflicting advice. This situation is not atypical in the field of mental health services, because there is often so little solid information available to guide service developments. Our task in these situations is to clarify opposing ideas, to collect data from natural experiments, to measure outcomes carefully in relation to services, and to set up controlled experiments when the field is ready to compare specific approaches. In each of these steps, clients, families, practitioners, and mental health administrators are partners with the research team. We share the data with our partners and make collaborative decisions about next steps and needed studies. This is the method of collaborative empiricism—improving services through continuous feedback and the interplay between practice ideas and actual outcome data. This approach parallels continuous quality improvement methods, except that it is done across programs using research quality data (Dickey & Sederer, 2001).

In regard to supported employment, the field was ripe for this approach. Political pressures from many sources focused attention on improving employment outcomes for clients with severe mental illness. In New Hampshire, leaders of the Division of Behavioral Health responded to the pleas from consumers and family members by identifying employment outcomes as a priority area and providing small financial incentives to regional mental health programs to improve rates of employment (Drake, Fox, et al., 1998). Beginning in 1989, our group of mental health services researchers at the New Hampshire-Dartmouth Psychiatric Research Center was asked by the Division of Behavioral Health to help with clarifying service models, documenting changes in the vocational service system, studying outcomes, conducting controlled clinical trials, and suggesting policy changes.

Individual Placement and Support

As we describe in the following chapters, Individual Placement and Support (IPS) represents not so much a unique approach to supported employment as an attempt to standardize the approach by combining the information on services and outcomes from many research studies. Our goal has been to review clinical and research experience continuously and to synthesize the principles of supported employment that are empirically related to successful outcomes for clients. In describing IPS, we begin with a brief chapter on theory and then proceed rapidly to describe the principles of IPS and the research that underlies these principles.

3

Theoretical Underpinnings of IPS

As the previous account clarifies, the Individual Placement and Support (IPS) approach to supported employment arose from a variety of theoretical, ideological, clinical, and empirical perspectives. For us—as a rehabilitation specialist (Becker) and a clinical services researcher (Drake)—the basic aim has been to improve services to help people reach their own goals. Because the majority of people with severe mental illness, like most others in this society, are interested in competitive employment, we have tried to help them reach that goal. The method, as described in chapter 2, has been collaborative empiricism, an iterative process of testing ideas and using feedback from clients and other participants for further refinements and testing. Many of these ideas rest on theoretical underpinnings. In this chapter, we describe briefly some of the theoretical notions that led to supported employment in general and to the IPS approach specifically.

The basic theory of psychiatric rehabilitation is that a person's functional adjustment can be enhanced by (1) finding or creating supportive environments and (2) improving the individual's skills or abilities (Anthony et al., 1990; Liberman, 1992). And the basic theory of recovery is that people can move beyond illness and pursue meaningful life goals such as work (Deegan, 1988; Mead and Copeland, 2000; Surgeon General, 1999; Ralph, 2000). But theory also provides explanations as to why rehabilitation and recovery are so critical for people with severe mental illness.

Severe mental illness is defined in part by functional difficulties in culturally prescribed adult roles (American Psychiatric Association, 1994). Many theorists have described how the combination of illness and displacement from adult roles can lead to a vicious downhill spiral via stigma, segregation, disculturation, diminished self-esteem, and institutionalization (Foucault, 1965; Goffman, 1961; Scheff, 1967). The essence of these ideas is that disability is a conferred status, not an inherent part of illness but a secondary problem created largely by how society (individuals and institutions) responds to the person with an illness. People who suffer an illness can easily be isolated, devalued, persecuted, and socialized into thinking of themselves as defective when opportunities for healing, recovery, growth, and success are not available. Goffman (1961), Scheff (1967), and many others described this process years ago in relation to treatment in mental hospitals. More recently, the ethnographer Estroff (1981) as well as many other critics of community mental health (Chamberlin, 1978; Fisher, 1994; Rappaport, 1987) have delineated the deleterious effects of mental health treatments and policies in the era since deinstitutionalization began. According to these arguments, having a mental illness not only results in cognitive, emotional, and social disruptions but also may lead to a series of disempowering, deflating, and generally destructive learning experiences within the mental health system. These experiences adversely affect one's sense of self as one internalizes the views of mental health professionals and others in one's environment. To cite one pertinent example, people in segregated work programs often learn to believe that they can only work in such settings. One can easily become socialized into disability, and also find that external and internal reinforcements to maintain disability are plentiful. This has resulted in what Rapp (1998) calls the spirit-busting impact of mental health treatments that emphasize deficits and mental health policies that emphasize control, protection, and segregation, for example, in day treatment, sheltered workshops, and group homes.

Conversely, many social, ecological, and behavioral theories have been offered in attempts to counteract the disabling propensities of standard mental health practice. Rappaport (1987), Carling (1995), and Nelson et al. (2001), for example, have pointed out the positive and healthful possibilities of community environments. Similarly, Anthony et al. (2002), Liberman (1992), Rapp (1998), and others have created interventions that emphasize the internal strengths and learning abilities of people with mental illness. One central theme in these innovations is the emphasis on finding environmental niches that are consistent with growth and health (Rapp, 1998). Community environments can stimulate recovery by, for example, providing opportunities for work, education, spiritual expression, recreation, and affiliation with families and friends—in other words, inclusion in all of the healthful activities that a citizen of a community usually experiences. Treatment systems can promote recovery by shifting the focus from segregated or institutional settings to integrated, normalizing settings in the community. This assumption constitutes the fundamental theory underlying supported housing, supported education, supported employment, and community integration.

The notion of healthful environment invokes the concept of goodness-of-fit. Mental health treatment settings or segregated environments are rarely if ever a good fit for any client, because they promote activities, feedback, and self-concepts that are inherently segregating. People who live in group homes or nursing homes, who work in segregated work enclaves, or who socialize only with others who have similar illnesses are influenced to believe that they do not have a place in routine society and that they need to be isolated, cared for, supervised, and watched over. By contrast, the community offers a multitude of healthful niches. Even in the world of competitive work, which often is characterized as uncaring and "business-like," there are an almost infinite number of niches for people with different interests, abilities, and preferences. As we describe later, helping a person to find the optimal job match can be enabling, normalizing, and health-promoting in many ways.

Theories are often in conflict or incorrect and must be tempered by empiricism. Aristotle, for example, got many ideas about science and psychology quite wrong because he failed to make observations and collect data. Similarly, the mental health and rehabilitation fields are replete with examples of interventions that thrive for years without testing and turn out to be incorrect. Consider one brief example to illustrate this point. When we began studying vocational services, one theoretical perspective that we heard repeatedly was the principle of parallel services. According to this view, clinical services and rehabilitation services needed to be separated physically for the sake of maintaining the healthful, nonstigmatizing attitudes and expertise of the rehabilitation setting apart from the clinical environment with its customary emphasis on psychopathology. This reasonable theory had become the conventional wisdom of psychiatric rehabilitation, and of course it was strongly reinforced by all of the vested interests built up around operating separate systems of care. Because it conflicted with theories about the importance of service integration, we and other researchers tested the theory.

In practice, every time researchers have compared integrated services (treatment and rehabilitation in the same setting, delivered by the same team) and nonintegrated services (parallel services in separate settings, agencies, and teams), clients reported a more coherent experience in the integrated system, and the integrated services were more successful in helping people to find and keep jobs (Bond, 1998). The reasons that parallel services encounter difficulties also were obvious when one observed actual practice settings closely. In nonintegrated systems of care, the client had difficulty going back and forth between two agencies with disparate philosophies and messages; the practitioners in the two agencies tended to disagree at times and failed to share their expertise and coordinate services; and the mental health program maintained traditional and unhelpful views of employment (e.g., viewing work as a stress that might undermine the client's clinical stability). Integrated teams had a relatively easy time combining treatment and rehabilitation, helping the client with a consistent message, and transforming the views of mental health practitioners so that they were more favorable toward competitive employment (Drake, Becker, Bond, & Mueser, 2003).

In sum, there is no shortage of theories in psychology and rehabilitation, and many of the existing theories regarding recovery, community integration, and strengths lead us in the direction of current ideas about supported employment. As we explain in the next chapter, IPS incorporates principles that are supported by not only theory but also by empirical outcome studies.

4

Introduction to the Individual Placement and Support (IPS) Approach to Supported Employment

IPS provides a standardized approach to supported employment for clients with long-term impairments due to severe mental illness (Becker & Drake, 1994). IPS is based on eight empirically derived principles: (1) rehabilitation is considered an integral component of mental health treatment, rather than a separate service; (2) the goal of IPS is competitive employment in integrated work settings, rather than prevocational, sheltered, or segregated work experiences; (3) people with severe mental illness can obtain and succeed in competitive jobs directly, without preemployment training; (4) vocational assessment is continuous and based in competitive work experiences, rather than in artificial or sheltered settings; (5) follow-along supports continue for a time that fits the individual, rather than terminating at a set point after starting a job; (6) job finding, disclosure, and job supports are based on clients' preferences and choices, rather than on providers' judgments; (7) services are provided in the community, rather than in mental health treatment or rehabilitation settings; and (8) a multidisciplinary team approach, rather than parallel interventions in separate agencies or systems, promotes the integration of vocational, clinical, and support services.

In practice, employment specialists typically combine with mental health treatment teams, implement the IPS program, and provide liaison with other agencies. The IPS unit includes a vocational supervisor and two or more employment specialists who work with 20 to 25 clients each. This caseload size appears to be optimal in the IPS programs studied so far, because different clients are in different stages of rehabilitation, with some requiring only a minimum amount of assistance over time. The vocational supervisor typically has a master's degree and experience in vocational rehabilitation. The employment specialists come from a variety of educational and experiential backgrounds. More important than background is personality; employment specialists must be optimistic, energetic people who enjoy working in the community with clients, employers, and mental health clinicians.

Unlike some vocational programs, IPS does not exclude clients with severe symptoms, poor vocational histories, or uncertain readiness for competitive employment. Instead, IPS employment specialists assist all clients who express interest in competitive employment because the underlying value is self-determination.

IPS is fundamentally a "place-train" model, which means that employment specialists rapidly engage with clients in the task of finding jobs in the community, even if for only a few hours a week or for a limited time. The client is encouraged to take the lead as much as possible in all of these decisions, but if the client prefers, the employment specialist initiates activity. The key is finding a job that matches the client's interests, skills, and unique qualities rather than changing, preparing, or training the client prior to looking for a job. For example, a client with poor hygiene might be employed in a recycling center or another outdoor job rather than trained to bathe and wear new clothes to prepare for an indoor job. Another client who is restless and spends a great deal of time walking might be employed delivering advertising fliers for a restaurant rather than trained to be less fidgety. A third client with anxiety and fearfulness around people but comfort around animals might be helped to find a job in a veterinary clinic, in a pet store, or on a farm rather than trained to control feelings.

When the client is working, the employment specialist provides follow-along support to the client and, with the client's permission, to the employer. In addition, practicing performance skills and social skills might be appropriate and can be more specific and meaningful once the client has a job. Although on-site job coaching is available, most clients prefer and benefit from support away from the job site.

Another central task of the employment specialist is to coordinate services with the clinical team. Otherwise, the client may get contradictory messages from clinical and rehabilitation counselors, and the clinical team may inadvertently undermine the employment plan or become engaged in an unhelpful miscommunication with the vocational provider (Drake, Becker, Xie, & Anthony, 1995). Employment specialists coordinate clinical and vocational efforts by joining the clinical team in regular meetings, by developing plans in conjunction with clinicians as well as clients, by dividing up responsibilities for supporting the employment plan, and by regular communication. As a simple example of this process, when a client who has been unemployed returns to work, new clinical issues as well as vocational issues will emerge. Just as the employment specialist must understand the job tasks in order to help the client with skills and supports, the clinician must understand how the new job creates interpersonal and performance anxiety and help the client to cope with these new feelings (Torrey, Bebout, et al., 1998). In other words, all members of the team must be consistent in supporting the client's vocational efforts.

IPS is not intended to be a unique vocational service. It merely adapts and standardizes principles of supported employment for persons with severe mental illness that are emerging from several areas (described earlier) and that are supported by empirical research (described later). In this sense, IPS attempts to be synonymous with evidence-based supported employment. We expect that IPS and other models of supported employment will continue to evolve as the field of psychiatric rehabilitation continues to move into an era of evidence-based practice and recovery.

5

Research on IPS

Supported employment has been implemented for people with severe mental illness in different ways, but research indicates that several specific principles of practice are associated with better employment outcomes (Bond, 1998; Bond, Becker, et al., 2001; Cook & Razzano, 2000). IPS combines the empirically validated principles that are consistent across various approaches. Furthermore, the details of the IPS approach are intended to evolve rather than remain static as more information becomes available. Of course, any model must be held constant temporarily so that it can be clearly defined, implemented, measured for fidelity, and studied in relation to outcomes. But the process of testing, reassessment, feedback, and revision is continuous. Thus far, the iterative process of refinement has not in any sense deterred implementation, because research findings have been relatively consistent and changes have accumulated slowly.

Within the IPS model, employment specialists join the treatment teams in a mental health program and collaborate directly with the clinicians to ensure that employment is part of the treatment plan for every client who is interested in working (Becker & Drake, 1994). (In some programs, the same specialists also can help clients who have related instrumental goals, such as supported education, but the emphasis is on competitive employment because that is a primary goal of most mental health clients and the area of expertise of employment specialists.) IPS employment specialists on each team provide the full range of supported employment services to a discrete caseload of clients. As described and illustrated in later chapters, IPS specialists emphasize integration of vocational and clinical services, minimal preliminary assessments, rapid job searches, competitive work settings, matching clients with jobs of their choice, and ongoing supports.

The IPS approach has several practical advantages over other ways of organizing vocational services (Bond, 1998). In many settings, typical problems include lack of service integration, diversity of team approaches, and allowing clinical and financial crises to undermine efforts to support employment. Separation of mental health and rehabilitation services into different agencies is the norm in most settings, but research shows that separation leads to miscommunication, poor coordination, and high rates of dropout (Drake et al., 1995; Drake et al., 2003; Harding, Strauss, Hafez, & Liberman, 1987). IPS overcomes these problems by combining mental health clinicians and employment specialists in regular team meetings within the same program.

Although many mental health programs are shifting toward multidisciplinary teams for clients with severe mental illness, the types of teams differ greatly. Some team models, such as assertive community treatment, prescribe service structures and levels of intensity that rarely exist or are appropriate for only a minority of clients. IPS does not depend on specific types of mental health teams; instead, the employment specialists usually join more than one clinical team, and the teams can be of different types or levels of intensity. IPS supported employment can be implemented in many kinds of agencies and programs. The key is that vocational and clinical practitioners work together with the client on the same team.

Another problem that commonly afflicts rehabilitation is the short-term, crisis orientation of many mental health programs. When there is a clinical emergency, a shortage of staff, or some other crisis, employment specialists often are redirected to provide clinical services (Meisler, Williams, & Kelleher, 2000). This is the primary practical disadvantage of models that require all staff to address vocational issues. IPS employment specialists, by contrast, do not provide clinical services themselves and thus cannot be reassigned when short-term exigencies arise to threaten long-term goals. To prevent diversion from critical activities, IPS has a clear and simple training manual, fidelity scale, and training procedures (Becker, Torrey, et al., 1998), which have been successfully used in numerous implementations. Finally, as we explain later, IPS has the strongest empirical support of any model of vocational services for people with severe mental illness.

The purpose of this chapter is to review several aspects of the research on IPS, including vocational outcomes, nonvocational outcomes, costs and economic impact, and some future directions. We begin by discussing vocational outcomes in two specific types of studies: (1) those in which clients are transferred from traditional rehabilitative day treatment programs or sheltered workshops to IPS, and (2) those in which IPS is compared to other models of vocational services. We then review research on nonvocational outcomes, such as clinical status and quality of life, to understand how these are related to competitive employment. Next, we examine the limited data on costs of IPS and on the economic impact of supported employment. Finally, we suggest directions for future research.

Vocational Outcomes when Programs Convert to IPS

The initial study of IPS arose as a natural experiment in New Hampshire. For financial and other reasons, the leaders of one mental health center decided to close their rehabilitative day program for clients with severe mental illness and replace it with a supported employment program, which subsequently became known as IPS. To evaluate this experiment, a nearby day treatment center that did not plan to change its operations was recruited to serve as a comparison program.

The first day program that converted was already active with employment efforts prior to conversion, but improved within 1 year of the change. Their yearly rate of competitive employment outcomes for the former day treatment attenders improved significantly from 33% to 56%, while the comparison day center showed no significant change in employment (Drake et al., 1994). Satisfaction with the program change was high among clients, families, and clinicians, even for clients who were not interested in employment, virtually all of whom preferred the new emphasis on finding active niches in the community rather than in day treatment (Torrey, Becker, & Drake, 1995). The surprising results of the first conversion induced the clinicians and clients in the comparison day program to try a partial conversion to IPS themselves. The staff continued to operate day treatment in the mornings but offered IPS supported employment services in the afternoons. Within a few months, however, all clients dropped out of the morning program, and greater numbers steadily arrived in the afternoons seeking supported employment services. Accordingly, the participants agreed to close the day program and to complete the conversion to IPS. When clients involved in this second conversion were followed up 1 year later, the results were similar to the first conversion: a dramatic increase in competitive employment from 9% to 40% (Drake and Becker, 1996). See figure 5.1.

Following this initial study, many day programs, sheltered workshops, and rehabilitation programs throughout New England and elsewhere in the United States converted to supported employment. In every instance of which we are aware, employment outcomes have improved. Even clients who have been in day treatment or sheltered workshops for many years have benefited from IPS. For example, in one program conversion, a group of 32 clients with lengthy tenure in a sheltered workshop (more than 5 years), who were considered unable to work competitively by staff, volunteered to try IPS-supported employment. Within 1 year, 74% obtained competitive employment, several times higher than a comparison group of less disabled clients who were matched for age, diagnosis, and sex (Bailey et al., 1998). These conversions demonstrated that the potential for competitive employment with the IPS supported employment approach was much greater than had been expected. Many clients who were stalled for years in rehabilitation programs and sheltered workshops

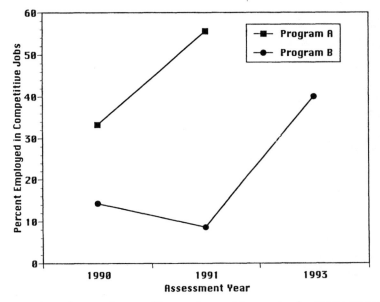

Figure 5.1 Annual rates of competitive employment for regular day treatment participants in Programs A and B in the conversion study

because staff did not believe they were capable of competitive employment clearly were able to go to work in competitive jobs.

At the beginning of a statewide implementation of supported employment in Rhode Island (McCarthy, Thompson, & Olson, 1998), two mental health centers closed their day rehabilitation programs entirely and converted to IPS. In both centers, rates of competitive employment among unemployed former day treatment clients with severe mental illness increased substantially to 44.2% and 56.7%, while similar clients in a comparison program showed no change over the same time interval (Becker et al., 2001). Because the argument had been made that clients in these day treatment conversions may have succeeded because of preparation for competitive employment by their prior experiences in rehabilitative day programs, we followed a group of clients assigned to IPS in one Rhode Island program who were new to the mental health center and had never been in day treatment. These clients increased their rate of competitive employment to over 50% even more rapidly than the former day treatment clients, confirming that spending time in a day program was not a prerequisite for attaining competitive employment. Indeed, clients who have been involved in these rehabilitation program and sheltered workshop closures consistently report that their experiences in segregated programs have been a hindrance to obtaining competitive employment. Like others with psychiatric disabilities (Estroff, 1981; Quimby et al., 2001), they report that participation in preemployment programs led to boredom and demoralization rather than employment.

To summarize, several studies of shifting clients with severe mental illness from rehabilitative day treatment settings or sheltered workshops into IPS show that the potential for competitive employment is much higher than previously believed. People tend to start work in small amounts and build up to 20 to 25 hours per week. Similar results were obtained for clients with quite different amounts of training and socialization in rehabilitation programs of various kinds. But what happens to clients who are not interested in competitive employment? We consider the issue of potential adverse effects of closing day programs later, under nonvocational outcomes.

Vocational Outcomes in Randomized Controlled Trials

In a second type of study, IPS has been compared experimentally with other vocational programs in five completed studies. This approach represents the gold standard in medical research, the randomized controlled trial. We next review these five trials.

In an initial experimental study in two New Hampshire cities, we compared IPS with the leading rehabilitation agency in the state (Drake, McHugo, et al., 1996). Unemployed clients who desired competitive employment were randomly assigned either to an IPS supported employment program within the local community mental health center or to a rehabilitation program that offered 8 weeks of vocational skills training followed by job finding and follow-along support services. All clients were followed closely for 18 months. The results of this study were quite dramatic. Clients in the IPS program obtained competitive employment faster, were more likely to be employed throughout the follow-up, worked more total hours, and earned more wages than those in the rehabilitation agency. The magnitude of differences was generally 2:1 or greater. For example, the overall employment rate for IPS clients was 78%, compared to 40% for the program that offered a stepwise approach; during most months about 40% of the IPS clients were competitively employed, while only 20% of those served by the rehabilitation agency were working. Both clients with some work history and those with no recent work experience did better in IPS. See figure 5.2.

One interesting aspect of this study was that both programs described themselves as state-of-the-art supported employment services and had relatively good outcomes. Nonetheless, the programmatic contrasts and the outcome differences were quite clear and meaningful in helping to understand the principles of supported employment. The New Hampshire study provided a contrast on two dimensions. Although both programs offered supported employment approaches, the private vocational agency was separate from the mental health agency and, hence, its services were not as closely integrated. In addition, the private agency provided 8 weeks of preemployment counseling and skills training. The two contrasts appeared to account for the differences in outcomes. We were able to rule out most other factors because the private

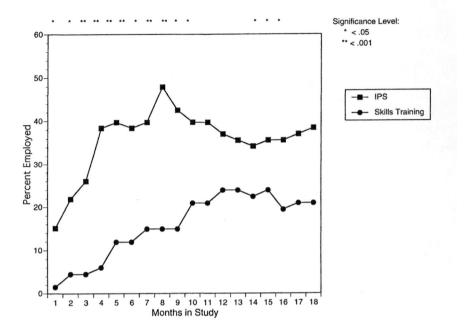

Figure 5.2 Rates of competitive employment for the Individual Placement and Support (IPS) and the skills training groups in the New Hampshire Vocational Study

agency had an experienced, well-trained staff, received grant money to support their efforts that was equivalent to the IPS program, showed high fidelity to their model, and actually obtained good outcomes, much better than the norms in the field and equivalent to their own published outcomes from an earlier study in Boston (Trotter, Minkoff, Harrison, & Hoops, 1988). Both dimensions of contrast influenced outcomes. In the first case, the research team was able to observe repeated examples of miscommunication between the private rehabilitation agency and the mental health centers (Drake et al., 1995). That is, in the brokered model of supported employment (separate agencies), clients often reported different aspects of their ambivalence to staff in the two separate agencies, leading to disagreements about plans and decisions. These discrepancies did not appear in the IPS programs, because clinical staff and employment specialists were in the same meetings and communicated regularly. Regarding the second difference, the preemployment training offered in the comparison program was reported as tiresome and irrelevant by many clients. One third dropped out during this phase and never got to the job finding phase of the program. We found no evidence that the preemployment counseling conferred any advantage in terms of better, higher paying, more satisfying, or longer lasting jobs. Thus, both clinical-rehabilitative integration and rapid job search without preemployment training appear to be critical aspects of success.

The New Hampshire study was conducted under relatively optimal circumstances: in a state with excellent mental health services, in two relatively small cities, using only a single private vocational program, and with clients who had relatively good work histories and minimal amounts of the background features that are considered barriers to working, such as homelessness, co-occurring substance use disorder, and minority status. Although these factors might be considered limits to generalizability, the New Hampshire study has now been replicated and expanded in four randomized controlled trials: three in urban settings—Washington, DC, Baltimore, MD, and Hartford, CT—as well as one in rural South Carolina. Each of these studies has added new and important information to our understanding of supported employment.

The Washington, DC, study was conducted with very high-risk clients to test the limits of IPS supported employment (Drake, McHugo, et al., 1999). In the Washington study, IPS was implemented in an urban case management program that served clients from homeless and institutional settings. The clients were predominantly African-American, with high rates of homelessness, co-occurring substance disorders, HIV infection, and other complicating features. They had very poor vocational backgrounds; most had not worked at all in the previous five years. Nonetheless, over one half attended informational groups and volunteered for a study of vocational services. Clients were randomly assigned to IPS within the case management agency or to their choice of vocational vendors in Washington, DC. The case management agency that implemented IPS had essentially no history of providing or brokering vocational services of any kind, because their clients had always been considered unemployable. The alternative condition included guaranteed services from a wide range of vocational providers. Clients who were randomly assigned to the alternative group were allowed to choose their vocational agency, and they also could change providers during the study, which many did. Over an 18-month follow-up period, the competitive employment results dramatically favored IPS, with employment differences even stronger than in the NH study. IPS clients obtained competitive employment at a rate of 61%, versus only 9% for the comparison group clients. During an average month, about 25% of IPS clients were competitively employed, versus less than 5% of the comparison group clients. The comparison group clients had a high rate (71%) of working in sheltered settings over 18 months, but they rarely transitioned to their goal of competitive jobs. Although both groups earned similar amounts of money, the IPS clients expressed greater satisfaction with their vocational program and with their progress toward meeting their goals. See figure 5.3. We will discuss differences in nonvocational outcomes later in this chapter.

The basic findings of the Washington study have recently been replicated in two other urban settings—Baltimore, MD, and Hartford, CT—in which clients from minority backgrounds are served. In the Baltimore study, Lehman and colleagues (2002) found that 2-year competitive employment outcomes among

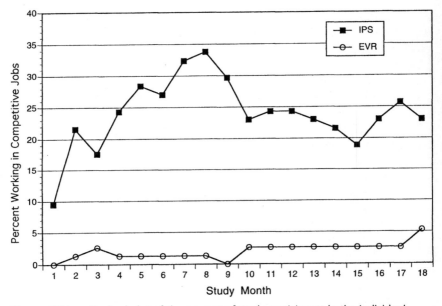

Figure 5.3 Longitudinal plot of the percent of study participants in the Individual Placement and Support (n=74) and Enhanced Vocational Rehabilitation (n=76) groups who worked in competitive jobs in each study month in the Washington, DC, Vocational Study

inner-city residents with mental illness and high rates of co-occurring substance abuse were much higher for clients in IPS than for clients in a traditional psychiatric rehabilitation program. However, the overall rates of competitive employment in this study were disappointingly low (27% in IPS vs. 7% in the psychosocial rehabilitation program), in fact substantially lower than has been found in other urban settings. Low rates of employment may have been due to the comorbidities of the clients in this study, the quality of IPS implementation, the unrelated financial difficulties of the mental health system during the time of the study, or the recruitment of clients who had little interest in vocational services. The researchers attempted to recruit a wide range of clients, not just those interested in working. As a consequence, only 33% of those assigned to the psychosocial rehabilitation program expressed interest in even a single contact regarding employment. Thus, IPS was superior to traditional approaches, but various aspects of recruitment, services, and context led to lower rates of employment than have been found in other studies.

The Hartford study was more straightforward and consistent with earlier results (Mueser et al., 2002). This study included inner-city residents from diverse backgrounds (including African Americans and Hispanic Americans) with very poor vocational histories but who nevertheless expressed interest in working. Clients were randomly assigned to three programs: (1) IPS within a large regional mental health center, (2) a psychosocial rehabilitation program that provided specific work units and transitional employment, and (3) standard rehabilitation vendors offering supported employment and other vocational services within the Hartford area but outside of the mental health center. Over 2 years, the clients in IPS had substantially superior employment outcomes that were four times and three times higher, respectively,than the comparison programs. Moreover, the overall rate of competitive employment (74%) was similar to the high rate found in New Hampshire. Employment rates were similar for Hispanic-American, African-American, and Anglo-American clients. As in the New Hampshire and Washington, DC, studies, clients with some work histories had greater success than clients with no or minimal work histories, but both groups benefited from participating in IPS rather than in the comparison groups. As in the New Hampshire study, clients who received supported employment integrated with clinical services (IPS) did much better than those who received supported employment outside of the mental health center (standard services).

The Hartford study demonstrated a number of interesting findings in addition to the superiority of IPS for various ethnic and work history groups. The comparison with a typical psychosocial rehabilitation program offering work units and transitional employment was unique, and the comparison with a supported employment program outside of the mental health center reinforced the finding that close integration of mental health and vocational services is critically important.

The differences between the Hartford, Washington, DC, and Baltimore studies of inner-city residents could be due to myriad factors related to the clients, the IPS programs, the mental health agencies, the mental health systems, and the local communities. Although it would be impossible to sort these out, the Hartford study did establish that inner-city residents of different ethnic and racial backgrounds are capable of attaining high rates of competitive employment.

The basic comparison of IPS supported employment versus standard rehabilitation services also has been replicated recently in rural South Carolina with predominantly African-American clients. Although this study has not yet been published, the basic findings have been presented (Meisler et al., 2000). The results are quite similar to the preceding four clinical trials discussed, with statistical and clinically meaningful differences favoring IPS.

Additional experimental and nonexperimental studies of IPS supported employment are currently underway in several other locations in the United States, Canada, Europe, and Asia. These studies are in early stages but are expected to clarify further aspects of delivering IPS-supported employment and expected outcomes under different conditions and with diverse clients. At this point, however, several aspects of IPS-supported employment seem clear (Drake, Becker, Clark, & Mueser, 1999). Competitive employment outcomes are relatively high in all available IPS studies, including quasi-experimental studies and experimental studies in different settings and with different types of clients. For clients who express interest in competitive employment, even those with very poor work histories, the majority of clients in IPS programs can obtain competitive jobs and ongoing rates of employment that are higher than in various other rehabilitation programs that use traditional, stepwise approaches to employment. This appears to be true for clients from diverse backgrounds, for those living in severely disadvantaged communities, and for those with various co-occurring conditions and other complications.

These studies also support several consistent findings about the type of work, the amount of work, and job preferences among clients in IPS supported employment. Most clients start in entry level jobs, most often service sector jobs, working 5 to 10 hours per week, for wages that are slightly above minimum wage. The jobs are commensurate with their educational and vocational histories. Over the 1st year, clients often change jobs to find more satisfying work and typically expand their average hours of work to 20 to 25 hours per week. (Many clients would prefer to work a greater number of hours per week but fear losing Medicaid health insurance.) Clients are generally very satisfied with the jobs they obtain, and they tend to be more satisfied and stay longer in the jobs when the jobs are consistent with their preferences (Becker, Drake, Farabaugh, & Bond, 1996; Mueser, Becker, & Wolfe, 2001).

Understanding Vocational Outcomes

Why are competitive employment outcomes so high in IPS supported employment compared to traditional vocational rehabilitation approaches? The simplest explanation is that IPS is based in part on outcomes research. IPS explicitly incorporates the principles of effective vocational services that have been synthesized from other practices and from empirical research. The fundamental principles—competitive employment as a primary goal, rapid job searches, integration of rehabilitation with clinical mental health services, attention to clients' preferences, continuous assessment through trying competitive jobs, and follow-along supports as long as needed—are each grounded in research from IPS and also non-IPS studies (Bond, 1998).

Many studies show that *competitive employment is a realistic goal for the majority of clients who express interest in working*, and that the overall potential for employment in the population is much greater than the 10% that we have settled for in the recent past. For example, the overall rate of competitive employment has improved to more than 30% in New Hampshire after supported employment began to be emphasized in 1990 (Drake et al., 1998), and some mental health centers achieved over 40% overall rates of competitive employment. Statewide improvements also have been documented in Rhode Island and Vermont, confirming that supported employment is an effective strategy in large systems, not just in small research demonstrations. This overall finding suggests that traditionally low rates of employment may be a result of low expectations and ineffective programs rather than clients' limitations. In many areas of the country, the vocational programs that receive the bulk of vocational funding have no record of producing good outcomes.

Similarly, several studies support the effectiveness of conducting *rapid job searches* without preemployment training (Bond and Dincin, 1986; Bond, Dietzen, McGrew, & Miller, 1995; Shafer & Huang, 1995). Clients who desire work appreciate early attention to their goal, and most find a first job within 3 or 4 months if the search begins right away. Research consistently shows that the great majority of clients know what type of job or job area interests them and that their preferences are realistic (Becker et al., 1996; Becker, Bebout, & Drake, 1998; Mueser et al., 2001). There is currently no evidence of which we are aware that preemployment training of any kind leads to longer, more satisfying, or higher paying jobs.

In addition to the IPS studies reviewed above, other non-IPS studies support the effectiveness of *integrating clinical and vocational services* (Chandler et al., 1997; McFarlane, Stastny, & Deakins, 1995; Test, Allness, & Knoedler, 1995). Integration in these studies means combining services at the level of interaction with the client. Programs that are in separate agencies have difficulty doing this, because the burden of integration is left on the client's shoulders.

Anthony and colleagues (1990) have argued for years that paying *attention to clients' preferences* is critically important to achieving rehabilitation goals. Recent studies have confirmed that helping clients find jobs consistent with their work preferences leads to greater satisfaction and longer job tenure (Becker et al., 1996; Mueser et al., 2001). Moreover, it is also clear that the great majority of clients have realistic work preferences and do not need professional counseling to help them choose an appropriate job.

We need more longitudinal evidence on helping clients to find satisfying, long-lasting jobs, but *continuous assessment* based on trying different jobs rather than on preemployment assessments and work trials is consistent with most of the research currently available (Bond, 1998). Preemployment work trials and other forms of assessment lead to diminished enthusiasm for work and do not seem to help clients find more appropriate jobs. Clients often learn about the world of work and their talents, interests, and needs the same way that most others entering the work force do—by trying different jobs (Alverson, Becker, & Drake, 1995, Quimby et al., 2001).

Time-unlimited support reflects the consistent observation that mental health clients often need supports beyond typical closure points imposed by rules of the Department of Vocational Rehabilitation (Cook & Razzano, 2000). Most clients in supported employment need help not only to adjust in initial jobs but also to transition out of first jobs appropriately and to find second and third jobs that are more satisfying and long lasting. Because there are so few long-term research studies, we know little about clients' long-term needs for supports, but there is evidence from one study that when job supports were substantially reduced after 18 months because grant support ended, clients maintained their relatively high rate of employment (McHugo, Drake, & Becker, 1998). Thus, time-unlimited support may mean longer than an arbitrary limit of 60 days but much less than years; it certainly makes sense that supports are flexible and tailored to the individual's needs rather than eliminated at a specific point for all.

Consistent with IPS principles, the details of implementation almost certainly make a difference in competitive employment outcomes. IPS prescribes specific structural elements, such as having one employment specialist on a clinical team take responsibility for all aspects of supported employment for a discrete group of 20 to 25 clients (Becker & Drake, 1994). These principles can be expressed as concrete guidelines, trained, and assessed in detail (Bond, Becker, et al., 1997; Bond, Becker, et al., 2001). One study showed that a better implementation of IPS produced better vocational outcomes (Drake, McHugo, et al., 1996). A survey of 10 employment programs across the state of Vermont showed that those adhering more closely to the critical components of IPS, such as outreach and zero exclusion, had better employment outcomes, even if the programs did not define themselves as IPS (Becker, Smith, Tanzman, Drake, & Tremblay, 2001). A study in Kansas by Gowdy (2000) also supported the principles of IPS.

Nonvocational Outcomes Related to IPS

The field has been strongly influenced by two diametrically opposed hypotheses about the effects of vocational services on nonvocational outcomes. According to one view, many clinicians, rehabilitation professionals, and family members have expressed concerns about eliminating sheltered, low-expectations rehabilitation programs that appear to provide a safe, structured day setting for clients, even if they do not lead to competitive jobs (Scheid & Anderson, 1995). Their concerns assume, first, that clients will not be able to find another safe place to spend their days and will therefore incur negative outcomes, such as boredom and getting into trouble; and, second, that the increased expectations of supported employment will be stressful and will thereby produce negative consequences, such as relapse and rehospitalization. On the other side, many advocates for vocational services have made just the opposite claim: that since clients want to work and since work is a healthy adult role, participating in a vocational program will confer positive benefits in terms of self-esteem, management of symptoms, new relationships, and quality of life (Bell, Milstein, & Lysaker, 1993; Brekke, Levin, Wolkon, Sobel, & Slade, 1993). Because IPS exemplifies a high-expectations approach and several studies of IPS have involved simultaneous elimination of day programs, research on IPS should shed light on these competing hypotheses.

What does the evidence show? In the first place, the research consistently demonstrates that negative clinical outcomes and other serious adverse consequences do not increase while clients are participating in IPS, working in competitive jobs, or leaving day treatment settings (Bailey et al., 1998; Becker, Bond et al., 2001; Drake et al., 1994; Drake, Becker, et al., 1996; Torrey et al., 1995). That is, there are no measurable negative effects on symptoms, hospitalizations, homelessness, suicide, treatment dropout, self-esteem, or relationships. The only concern that has been attributed to closing day centers is that a small minority of clients express loneliness (Torrey et al., 1995). For this reason, drop-in centers, consumer-run programs, and other types of social clubs have been instituted as replacements for day treatment to meet social needs (Torrey et al., 1998).

Surprisingly, the lack of negative outcomes on closing day treatment programs applies to nonworkers as well as workers. For example, after one day treatment program closed and converted to IPS, even those clients who were not competitively employed expressed greater satisfaction with their involvement in routine community settings, such as senior centers, athletic clubs, volunteer jobs, and meeting friends at restaurants (Torrey et al., 1995). Similar findings have occurred in other states (Becker, Bond, et al., 2001) and in England (Goddard, Burns, & Catty, 2001). These results suggest that long-term day treatment may be more harmful than helpful.

What about the stress of actually working in a competitive job? Again, there is no evidence that clients who go to work suffer relapses or other negative clinical outcomes. Clients themselves often question professionals' assumption about work and stress, sagely suggesting that unemployment may be more stressful than employment. And, indeed, there is robust evidence that unemployment is stressful for most people. Furthermore, the IPS approach prescribes specifically that an appropriate job match should fit with a client's needs for support, interpersonal contact, coping strategies, and interests so that it should strengthen one's resistance to illness and other threats.

The evidence for positive effects on nonvocational outcomes is much less clear. At this point, it appears that clients who participate in vocational services of various types do sometimes improve modestly over time in nonvocational areas of adjustment, but the areas, the amount of work needed to induce these changes, and the time course are unclear. Common areas of improvement are those proximally related to employment, for example, satisfaction with finances (Drake, McHugo, et al., 1996) or with life goals (Drake, McHugo, et al., 1999), whereas improvements in clinical areas are less common. Small but significant correlations are often found between current work status and positive changes in self-esteem or quality of life, but these could be because of bidirectional effects or underlying third factors, such as the natural course of illness (Mueser et al., 1997). When improvements do occur, they usually appear among active workers in both IPS and comparison programs.

One possible explanation for the lack of strong relationships between IPS and nonvocational outcomes is that only a minority of clients in most programs are working at any one time, thereby obscuring short-term benefits in nonvocational areas that are related to work. A related hypothesis is that nonvocational benefits accrue only over time as clients become successful workers and begin to think of themselves as workers rather than as mental patients. The clearest evidence on this point comes from an IPS study by Bond, Resnick, et al. (2001). They found that clients who worked a substantial amount of time (greater than the median) in competitive jobs experienced significant gains in several areas: reduced symptoms, greater satisfaction with finances and leisure, and improved self-esteem. Meanwhile, clients who did not work, who worked only in sheltered jobs, or who worked only minimally experienced none of these gains. Because all of the groups were similar at the start of the study, it is possible that the nonvocational benefits were due to the greater community integration and functional demands of competitive employment.

Costs and Economic Impact

The cost of the IPS intervention to providers was approximately $2,000 to $4,000 per client per year in two studies (Clark, 1998). In these studies, IPS costs were similar to the costs of rehabilitative day treatment (Clark, Bush, Becker, & Drake, 1996) and of stepwise rehabilitation programs outside of the mental health center (Clark, Xie, Becker, & Drake, 1998). Because IPS produced better vocational outcomes at a similar cost, it was considered a cost-effective alternative to traditional vocational services in these studies and may be in many settings. Costs of traditional vocational services vary widely across locations, however, leading Clark (1998) and Latimer (2001) to conclude that the net effect of IPS supported employment on service costs is highly dependent on context. In other words, adding IPS in a setting where few vocational services have been provided will almost certainly increase costs, whereas substituting IPS for an expensive day treatment or sheltered workshop program may lower costs.

Some have speculated that supported employment might produce a "cost offset," which means lower overall service costs (inpatient, outpatient, and vocational), because some individuals might leave the patient role and spend more time in employment. The evidence thus far indicates that a significant cost offset does not occur, at least over the short interval assessed during 12- to 18-month research studies. Instead, supported employment tends to be associated with nominally lower service costs (Latimer, 2001).

Concerns about the costs of supported employment should be tempered by two considerations. First, it is clear that ineffective services can be provided at a very low cost and certainly more cheaply than effective care. For example, we have evaluated programs that provide rehabilitation services at a very low cost by failing to engage most of the clients referred to them, by excluding clients with multiple problems, or by insisting that clients find jobs on their own. An ineffective program can appear cost-effective if clients become frustrated and drop out, and a few subsequently find their own jobs.

Second, cost estimates from research programs are subject to several artificial constraints that may lead to inaccuracy. For example, during a research project, employment specialists may only be allowed to work with clients who have been assigned to them through the research study, resulting in unrealistically low caseloads, and may continue working with these same clients for longer than necessary for the same reason. In addition, they may be atypical employees in terms of having more degrees, higher salaries, and unusually costly supervision. The result is that their efficiency is low compared to routine practice conditions. Moreover, program administrators have no incentive to manage these positions and costs when staff and supervisors are paid for by research grants (Latimer, 2001). To illustrate this point, in one of the New Hampshire programs that we studied during the early 1990s, the cost of providing supported employment services was approximately $4,000 per client per year. Adjusting that figure to 1999 dollars, the annual per client cost of supported employment would have been approximately $4,700. However, the same mental health program was in fact providing supported employment services to nearly 500 clients as part of usual care by 1999, and they calculated their actual per client costs at below $1,500. Our point is not that $1,500 per client is the correct figure; service costs are likely to vary considerably across the United States. Rather, the point is that mental health programs and state and county mental health authorities need accurate data on what it costs to provide evidence-based practices, including IPS, under conditions of routine practice rather than under research conditions (Goldman et al., 2001). It also should be obvious that we must confirm the finding of good employment outcomes under routine practice conditions, which has to some extent been done (Becker, Bond, et al., 2001; Becker, Smith, et al., 2001; Drake et al., 1994; Drake et al., 1998).

What about the economic impact of IPS supported employment on individuals themselves? According to Latimer's (2001) review, the average net improvement in total income (increased wages minus lost benefits) tends to be small, although some individuals who become consistent workers may increase their incomes considerably. Because we know that many of these consistent workers limit their work hours to preserve Medicaid insurance, recent Federal legislation (the Ticket to Work and Work Incentives Act of 1999) is expected to improve this situation, but we have no data on these effects as yet. At this point, individuals with mental illness report that the psychological (e.g., self-esteem) and social (e.g., community integration) gains from supported employment are more significant than the economic gains. Meanwhile, concerns about losing benefits due to temporary employment remain the largest barrier to supported employment programs.

Understanding costs from the perspectives of government and society are more complex discussions, involving values, politics, advocacy, and other factors. No answers are as yet clear, but the interested reader should consult Latimer's (2001) thoughtful review of these issues.

Separate from the issue of economic impact is the question of financing. Who pays for IPS supported employment services and how? The issue here clearly involves the separate organizational and financing structures of mental health services and vocational services. IPS does not fit easily into the usual guidelines that the Rehabilitation Services Administration uses to fund rehabilitation agencies. Therefore, state mental health administrators, rehabilitation authorities, financing directors (e.g., Medicaid authorities), and local providers need to synthesize funding mechanisms to support the IPS approach (McCarthy et al., 1998). The need for specific contracting with health maintenance organizations to include vocational services is also clear (Clark, 1998). An alternative is to combine staff from different organizations on the same teams without blending funding (Johnson and Johnson, 2002). Many states currently continue ineffective day treatment and sheltered workshop programs because they are easy to finance and, in some cases, pay for other programs. This situation is clearly detrimental to clients' vocational aspirations. All of the incentives must line up to facilitate the implementation of evidence-based practices (Goldman et al., 2001; Surgeon General, 1999; Torrey et al., 2001).

Concerns and Future Research

Several current randomized controlled trials in the field, which compare IPS with other approaches to vocational rehabilitation, should shed further light on relative effectiveness. Additional studies in effectiveness situations should yield new data on the generalizability of IPS outcomes in other regions and other populations, for example, with first-episode clients. Several IPS studies that have been initiated in other countries also will shed light on issues of cultural influences on vocational services. However, the field of supported employment for people with severe mental illness is still in its infancy. Fundamental issues remain to be investigated and numerous problems need to be solved.

Several concerns have been raised about IPS specifically and supported employment in general. Among them are criticisms that IPS is too expensive, that it is difficult to implement, that it is not for everyone, that jobs do not last, and that the impact on clients outside of work is minimal. We have addressed many of these concerns earlier in this book, and other concerns will be addressed in the practice guidelines to follow. In general, however, we agree that these are important issues and that more research is needed. As more information becomes available, IPS and other mental health services should evolve. The goal is not to develop a name brand but, rather, to continue to improve services to help people in their recoveries.

One key issue involves the diversity and choices of service offerings and goals: key philosophical concepts among service providers and clients. At this point, we really do not know how many clients with mental illness want to be competitively employed, how many and which clients will benefit from supported employment, and what other service choices might be helpful and for which clients. In part, these questions are unanswered because they have not been studied in a service system that removes financial barriers and emphasizes recovery and community integration consistently for a substantial period of time. We know that more and more clients become interested in competitive employment as barriers, such as poor insurance coverage and stigma, are reduced, and as recovery rather than patienthood becomes normative within a system of care. But these changes are in flux and may not be stabilized any time soon.

Another key unknown involves the long-term course of jobs and of vocational careers in relation to IPS and other forms of supported employment. Consistent with their educational and vocational backgrounds, most IPS clients begin with entry-level jobs. They typically work about 20 hours per week in order to maximize their incomes and protect their medical benefits. Initial jobs typically last only 4 to 6 months and often have negative job endings (Becker, Drake, et al., 1998). Although many individuals move on to other jobs, little is known about what happens to these individuals' vocational careers over time. Do they find satisfying jobs and stay for longer job tenures or fall out of the workforce? Do they continue in entry-level jobs or increase their hours, get off benefits, and get job promotions? Does becoming a consistent worker over time affect other areas of adjustment, as Bond, Resnick, et al.'s (2001) study purports to show? And what about their use of mental health and vocational services and the costs of supported employment over time?

There are, however, some hints regarding positive outcomes. McHugo and colleagues (1998) found a persistence of competitive employment for three and a half years as IPS support services were phased down. Bond and colleagues (1995) found a similar long-term effect with another rapid-job-search program. Test and colleagues (1995) reported that there was a long-term, gradual increase in the overall employment rate with another consistent approach to supported employment over 10 years. Salyers and colleagues (submitted) found remarkably good outcomes, including greater job tenure, on a 10-year follow-up study of IPS-supported employment. Thus, the long-term view appears to be very favorable. But we need more studies of these issues under optimal circumstances to make sure that long-term outcomes reflect clients' goals and the development of satisfying careers. We also need much more data on how moving into competitive jobs affects people's community integration, self-concepts, and quality of life over time. At this point, supported employment appears to help many people begin a healthful trajectory and obtain satisfying outcomes that are consistent with the goals of recovery, but only longitudinal data will enable us to be certain.

Part II

Practice Guidelines for Implementing Supported Employment

6

Introduction to IPS

In IPS, services are delivered by a multidisciplinary treatment team that includes the client, case manager, psychiatrist, employment specialist, and other staff members who relate to the client. The client chooses whether family members and other friends are part of the team. Through the team process, treatment and rehabilitation are individualized, coordinated, and integrated at the level of service delivery. Because agencies are organized differently, IPS is designed flexibly so that employment specialists join different types of teams, from assertive community treatment teams to other case management teams.

In IPS, employment is viewed as therapeutic and normalizing. It is an integral part of the treatment process. Some employment programs require clients to participate in mental health or substance abuse treatment before they are considered ready to begin vocational rehabilitation. But in IPS, employment support occurs simultaneously with other mental health services. *IPS is based on the premise that working in regular community jobs with people who don't have a severe mental illness enhances people's lives, promotes wellness, and reduces stigma.*

Work and mental health are interactive. Work, on the one hand, often motivates and helps people to manage symptoms of mental illness and substance abuse. Mental health issues such as failure to use medications effectively and interpersonal difficulties, on the other hand, often are impediments to long-term employment. Improvement in these areas enhances the effectiveness of rehabilitation. Many mental health providers, families, and people with severe mental illness believe that work is central to what really helps people regain control of their lives. "I'm an ordinary person," is how one person described what it has meant for her to become a worker again (Bailey, 1998).

In IPS, clients of a mental health agency who express interest in competitive employment are assigned to work one-on-one with an employment specialist throughout the employment process. The employment specialist begins to build a trusting and collaborative relationship with the client.

During the engagement process, the employment specialist gathers information that is used to identify a job that matches the unique interests, abilities, and challenges of the person. Traditional assessment and evaluation tools such as standardized tests, work samples, and work adjustment activities are not a part of IPS. Instead, the employment specialist taps many sources of information, including conversations with the client, and with permission from the client, family members, and previous employers. The employment specialist reads the clinical record and consults with the other members of the team. The client and the employment specialist draw up a plan that seems most likely to help her obtain a job based on all of this information as quickly as possible. *The best assessment and training for getting a job is often getting a job.*

Vocational assessment is a continuous process based on regular work experiences in the community. Each job experience provides new information about the person as a worker. In this vein, all work experiences are viewed positively. There are no failures in IPS. No matter what the outcome of a particular job experience, something is learned about that person as a worker that informs planning for the next job. For example, one person who was fired from a job in a retail store after 3 days learned that he has paranoid thoughts when he works around a lot of people. In his next job search, he looked for quiet, uncrowded work settings in which he is able to control these thoughts.

Some people want to move directly into jobs. Others are hesitant and want to take slower steps. And still others benefit from encouragement, step by step, to consider the idea of a regular competitive job. Some people have difficulty seeing themselves as workers. And possibly no one else has had this expectation or hope for them either. IPS is based on the belief that nearly every person with a severe mental illness can benefit from working in a job that matches their interests, skills, and experiences. Most people start in part-time jobs. Positions ranging from 5 to 10 hours a week are not uncommon.

Fear of losing entitlements is the biggest barrier to employment for people with severe mental illness. The employment specialist, therefore, becomes fully knowledgeable about the impact of work on entitlements and communicates this information clearly to clients and families. With accurate information, clients choose how many hours per week they want to work. For many clients, the greatest fear is losing medical insurance. People with severe mental illness are able to work and keep medical insurance. *The employment specialist helps clients understand the rules regarding benefits so people have good information to make optimal decisions.*

Clients make the decision about whether to disclose to employers about having disability. Some people want to negotiate their own jobs with employers, and do not want to disclose their mental illness because of stigma and fear of rejection or being treated differently from other employees. Others have difficulty in the job search process and want the employment specialist's involvement. With disclosure, the employment specialist may help directly in the job search by contacting potential employers about job openings. Although the client assumes as much responsibility as possible in the job-seeking process, the employment specialist assists as needed in securing employment. *In IPS, the goal is to help people start working and not let the job search and interviewing process become barriers to employment.* The employment specialist and the client identify each of their collaborative roles in the job search process.

When a person starts a job, supports are provided to enable her to maintain work. The supports are provided as long as needed and individualized according to the desires and challenges of each person. Family, friends, mental health providers, and supervisors and coworkers at the job site may all be part of the support plan. The psychiatrist may adjust medications based on how the person is functioning on the job. The case manager and clinician may talk with a client about managing interpersonal difficulties at work. The employment specialist often stays in touch with the employer (with the client's permission) and offers the client whatever support is necessary, from initially helping with transportation to meeting frequently after work to review job progress. The employment specialist and the rest of the team members update each other frequently about the client's progress, work to resolve problems as they occur, and celebrate achievements.

Seeing clients go to work is ultimately what convinces people of the benefits of supported employment. Psychiatrists and case managers who have assumed that many clients were not "job ready" begin to see people shift their identity from mental patient to productive worker and citizen. Positive changes occur as individuals find that they can work in competitive, community-based jobs beside other people without disabilities. Their confidence builds. And, after IPS has been operating for a while, ripples of those changes move throughout the mental health center, reflecting a general change in attitude toward work among clients and mental health providers alike. The expectation that people with severe mental illness can work and should have the opportunity to work begins to become the norm, rather than the exception. *Work increasingly becomes the focus of team meetings so that staff members address what is important and meaningful to people with severe mental illness.*

Illustration 1: Janet, a Person Using IPS Support

Janet is a 58-year-old woman who began experiencing symptoms of mental illness when she was in her late 20s. Trained as a secretary, she had been moving steadily through positions of greater responsibility in a small firm. But by the time she was 30, reoccurring symptoms of paranoia and anxiety began to affect her work performance. After a 3-month hospitalization she found the door closed to her old job.

Over the next 15 years, she worked a series of short-term secretarial jobs, initially performing well and earning the respect of her supervisors. But in each job she would begin to feel persecuted by her employer. She accused her coworkers of trying to make her work look bad, and she developed symptoms of anxiety that led to several hospitalizations.

With the end of each job and the onset of a new cycle in the illness, she experienced increased feelings of desperation and failure, and eventually, in her late 40s, gave up any further attempts at working.

For the past 10 years, she has been living a relatively stable life and has managed to put all the supports she needs in place, from living with an understanding roommate to collecting monthly disability insurance payments. Over the past year, however, she has been thinking more and more about working. She has missed the sense of purpose and positive self-esteem that work brings. She has wanted to regain the feeling of connection with her community and the rewarding social contact that she remembers from her first 10 years of working.

Janet was vaguely aware of the vocational rehabilitation program at the community mental health center where she receives psychiatric services, but thought that such a program was for people with little or no work experience. She didn't know how, by herself, she could ever find a job and pick up her career where she'd dropped it 10 years ago.

Janet's case manager supported the idea of Janet starting to work again but also was reluctant to encourage changes that might threaten the hard-won stability in her life. The case manager discussed Janet's interest in work with the other members of the treatment team, which included an employment specialist.

Two days later, Janet, her case manager, and the employment specialist met for the first appointment. Janet described her interest in secretarial work but was worried that she hadn't worked in a long time. The employment specialist asked her about how many hours a week she wanted to work. Janet was surprised by this question as she had assumed that working meant a full-time job as it had in her previous jobs. During this first meeting, Janet talked about her interest in working but also conveyed a lot of self-doubt. She explained that she was worried mostly about trying to set up job interviews.

When the team met the next day, the employment specialist described Janet's interest in considering a part-time secretarial position. The goal was to find a situation that wouldn't feel overwhelming and put her back into the cycle of losing jobs and feeling unsuccessful, which had been her experience with work in the past. Remembering that Janet had accused coworkers of trying to make her look bad, the psychiatrist suggested that the employment specialist have regular contact with the employer about her work performance. The case manager said that Janet found it helpful when she was given regular, direct feedback. She suggested that the employment specialist talk with the employer about giving Janet daily feedback on her work performance.

The employment specialist and Janet discussed looking for a part-time job as a way of reentering the work world. They talked about Janet's interests, skills, and the type of work environment that she would like. In light of her work history, she wanted to avoid situations that might be anxiety-producing. Janet agreed that a part-time secretarial job was probably a good way to get started again. They talked about how relationships with her supervisor and her coworkers would be important.

Janet decided that she was comfortable letting an employer know that she has a disability. Because Janet was willing to disclose her illness, the employment specialist was able to contact employers on Janet's behalf to develop job opportunities. Janet and the employment specialist agreed that they would both look for job openings. Within a couple of days, the employment specialist found a lead on a part-time secretarial position, 12 hours a week, in the office of the city arts center. The employment specialist was aware of the opening, because his sister was the director of the center. Janet asked the employment specialist to arrange the interview but said she wanted to go to the interview by herself.

Janet's biggest fear about the interview was how to explain the lengthy gap in her work history. By role-playing and rehearsing with the employment specialist, Janet developed a response to the dreaded question.

The interview went well and Janet was hired to work 4 hours a day, 3 days a week. At the end of the first work day, she called the employment specialist in a panic. She said the day had been a disaster. Everything had gone wrong. She was certain that the administrative assistant, who had gone on vacation, had left incorrect instructions just to confuse her and make her look bad.

The next morning before work Janet and the employment specialist met for coffee to talk about what happened and how to manage the problem. He accompanied Janet to her office, and reviewed the job with her and the office manager. It became clear that Janet was confused by the phone system along with the fast pace of business in the office at different times of the day. With written instructions for the phones and an agreement with the manager to hold some of the word processing for the next day, Janet went back to work and finished out the first week. Janet was convinced now that her skills were not up to a 40-hour-per-week job, as they had been 15 years ago.

Over the past several months, Janet has continued to improve her office skills and ability to work with others. The employment specialist talks with her weekly to give her support and encouragement. Knowing that the anniversary of Janet's divorce was coming up and that she has a pattern of severe despondency at this time every year, the employment specialist scheduled a lunch meeting with her to celebrate her work accomplishments.

Janet's treatment team continues to review her progress. The psychiatrist has reduced Janet's medication and is encouraged by how good Janet feels about working again. Janet and her case manager talk about social interactions at work and identify situations when she feels anxious. The case manager conducts social skills training on an individual basis with Janet to help her learn different ways of managing interpersonal relationships at work.

And Janet has decided that she wants to begin looking for a 20-hour-per-week job. The employment specialist is talking with her about how the job will affect her Social Security benefits. The case manager and the employment specialist agree with Janet that a job similar to the secretarial position in which she could work at her own pace in a small office is desirable. Janet is revising her résumé and working with the employment specialist to develop new job leads. She has decided that this time she will set up job interviews on her own.

Janet's story is actually drawn from the experience of several people in IPS programs. IPS is designed to help people with severe mental illness move into paid, community jobs of their choice as rapidly as possible. *Each person gets the support that she wants at every step of the way to ensure that success builds on success and that difficulties can be resolved as part of living and learning.*

In IPS, all aspects of the employment process are individualized. Much of the success in helping people work in competitive jobs results from recognizing the unique character, talents, and challenges of each person. The IPS method has grown out of the recognition that individualized services help people with severe mental illness achieve their goals. A plan that worked for 25-year-old Ben yesterday may be terribly wrong for 25-year-old Dave tomorrow.

The purpose of Part II of this book is to provide an overall description of how IPS operates and what is required to set up and run a program step by step. In the same way that individualized programs are designed for different people, however, the concepts presented here must be adapted to different community mental health agencies. This training part, therefore, should be used as a guide, rather than a blueprint, to help create an IPS program. By understanding the concepts, community mental health center providers will be able to put together a version of the program that works best for their setting and remains faithful to the evidence-based principles and practices of supported employment.

7

The Structure of IPS in the Mental Health Agency

Two Methods of Implementation: Add-on or Conversion?

Community mental health agencies have implemented IPS programs in two different ways. In one way, IPS is added to the current menu of services offered to clients (e.g., case management, psychiatric services, residential services, substance abuse treatment, etc.). An employment specialist joins a multidisciplinary treatment team to integrate supported employment with mental health treatment. In the other way, IPS replaces another service, such as rehabilitative day treatment. Resources are shifted from one program (e.g., rehabilitative day treatment) to pay for another one (supported employment). In this arrangement, day treatment counselor positions are converted to employment specialist positions.

Both ways of implementing IPS have different ramifications vis-à-vis costs and funding, staffing, services, organizational structure, and training. The decision makers at a mental health agency weigh the advantages and disadvantages to determine which method of implementation is best for their agency.

There are several basic considerations that need to be reviewed when deciding which implementation method is most feasible for a mental health agency. Studies have shown that, when IPS is added to an agency, overall costs increase. Alternatively, when converting another program to IPS, costs do not increase. IPS sometimes offsets other costs (Clark, 1998). When resources from rehabilitative day treatment, for example, are shifted to implement supported employment, overall costs stay about the same.

Mental health agencies are challenged to find ways to pay for effective supported employment services. Traditionally, fee-for-service plans have not provided reimbursement for vocational services. Agencies are reluctant to give up day programs that receive lucrative Medicaid reimbursement. In a capitated environment, however, supported employment may be an effective substitute for other psychosocial services such as rehabilitative day treatment. In many states, portions of the employment service are paid by different state agencies, and typically the reimbursement plan is not coordinated.

Strategies that have helped to solve the funding dilemma include shifting resources from day treatment programs and sheltered work settings to pay for supported employment services. In some states, directors of behavioral health, vocational rehabilitation, and Medicaid offices have collaborated to ensure resources are configured in a way to finance supported employment programs. Additionally, in some states, Medicaid rules have been designed to allow reimbursement for parts of the supported employment service.

The costs of supported employment programs vary widely. Costs vary in part because of local wages of employment specialists, and how much indirect costs and costs of clinical services are included. *Solving the funding problem is a basic first step toward implementing supported employment.*

Special staffing issues must be addressed when IPS is implemented through a program conversion. In a day treatment conversion, the day treatment counselor positions are converted to employment specialist positions. All day treatment counselors do not make good IPS-supported employment specialists, however, as the job duties are different. On the one hand, day treatment counselors facilitate group activities that are usually agency-based. On the other hand, IPS employment specialists provide individual services that occur mostly outside of the agency. Not all day treatment counselors enjoy or are good at conducting assertive job searches. In these instances, program managers look for other positions within the agency that are more suitable for the day treatment counselors, and hire candidates more suited for the employment specialist positions.

If an agency considers converting a program such as rehabilitative day treatment to IPS, the impact on clients must be assessed and anticipated. Studies have shown that when rehabilitative day treatment programs are converted to IPS, some clients miss the socialization aspects of the former day program. Community mental health centers are helping to develop ways to meet socialization needs by supporting consumer-run drop-in centers and peer support programs.

To implement IPS, whether adding it as a new service or establishing it through a program conversion process, the agency must have an organizational structure of multidisciplinary treatment teams. Employment specialists join treatment teams to integrate employment services with mental health treatment. Through a team structure, services are comprehensive, individualized, consistent, and seamless at the delivery level.

Agencies that attempt to implement IPS with a structure of individual practitioners, instead of with teams, quickly experience difficulties. One problem involves sharing information. Individual practitioners are trained to keep information that is discussed within individual sessions confidential. They are not accustomed to sharing what they know about a person. IPS, however, is based on a team approach, in which information about a person is shared among the team members for the purposes of coordination, planning, and integrating services. For example, an individual practitioner may know that a client feels fearful around men. This information is key for the employment specialist when helping to conduct an individualized job search. On receiving IPS services, clients are educated about the team structure and how information is shared to improve services.

A second problem with an organizational structure that is not team-oriented is that individual clinicians are usually not reimbursed for time they spend with employment specialists. Employment specialists are hindered in their jobs by not having access to individual clinicians for planning and service coordination.

A third problem is that individual clinicians often do not provide case management services. If there is no one addressing case management issues, IPS employment specialists feel compelled to carry out nonvocational tasks that support a client's work efforts. For example, if there are problems with housing, the IPS worker may be tempted to solve the problem because there is no other staff person to do it. Stable housing contributes to a person's ability to work. Carrying out case management duties, however, prevents employment specialists from focusing directly and exclusively on clients' employment goals. *In IPS, the support services that case managers and other team members provide are critical to making the work effort possible.*

All team members are trained about supported employment when putting a team structure in place. To provide seamless services at the delivery level, everyone on the team must understand and embrace the principles and practices of supported employment. *Elements of a good implementation of IPS include a comprehensive financial plan, a team structure with skillful leaders who value and monitor IPS, and a training plan with ongoing supervision for the staff.*

Treatment Team

Planning for people to have productive work experiences takes time and often much coordination. "We have found that the most successful way to help clients is through a team approach. Everybody at the center needs to understand about IPS to make it work," said Barbara, an employment specialist at a mental health center in a small city. Some vocational programs are set up separately from mental health treatment services but, in IPS, supported employment is integrated with mental health treatment. Case managers, nurses, psychiatrists, residential workers, and others must understand and support the same approach to help someone in her work efforts.

Employment specialists join one or two multidisciplinary treatment teams to assist clients served by the teams in considering work possibilities. IPS uses a team approach so that all services are coordinated and complement each other. Working in teams, staff members communicate regularly to support a client in achieving her goals.

The term *treatment team* here refers to, at minimum, the core group of people who provide and coordinate treatment, rehabilitation services, and support for clients who are recovering from the effects of mental illness. In most situations, a person with severe mental illness who is a client at a mental health agency meets regularly with a case manager, a psychiatrist, and perhaps a nurse or therapist. Staff members from other mental health agency programs such as housing, health care, substance abuse treatment, peer support, and recreation may be a part of the team. Other providers outside of the agency are also part of the team. For example, if a client is receiving services from Vocational Rehabilitation (VR), the VR counselor is part of the team and attends team meetings.

Traditionally, each of the people who provide services has tended to act like a specialist, concerned more or less exclusively with providing her particular service to the client. Individual providers often are uninformed of the other services that a client is receiving. For the client, it's like not having a family doctor, and therefore having to go to a different specialist for each complaint. Although each doctor may be an expert in the field, none has an overall understanding of the patient's health. The client receives different and often conflicting messages and is left to coordinate her services.

In IPS, the treatment team works with a group of clients, meets regularly (at least weekly) to discuss each client's situation, and generally makes recommendations as a group on all aspects of each client's service plan. Each team member sees the client from a different perspective, and each brings that perspective to the other members. None of the individual members of the team has to be all things for the client. Yet, all team members are aware of what each member is working on with a client and supports that effort. All team members, therefore, must be knowledgeable about IPS.

The size of multidisciplinary teams varies from one community mental health agency to another. Some agencies have teams that serve 100 to 200 people. And other agencies have smaller working teams or mini teams within teams. A mini team may be composed of a psychiatrist, a case manager, and an employment specialist. *Employment specialists work with clients on teams and have discreet caseloads of up to 25 people.*

Meeting frequency within teams also varies. In some teams, the staff members meet on a daily basis, such as in the program of assertive community treatment. Other agencies have team meetings to discuss clinical and rehabilitative issues less frequently, one or two times during the week.

The employment specialist attends all the team meetings and participates as an equal team member with shared decision making. In other vocational programs, the employment supervisor attends the team meetings as a representative. Employment specialists, however, cannot function as team members if they do not attend and participate in meetings. In IPS, therefore, the employment specialists attend all the meetings.

Team meetings provide a forum for people to work in concert for the benefit of clients rather than as individuals delivering separate services to people. Communication is an overall goal of the team. Teams that meet only one time a week must rely on notes, telephone contacts, voice mail, and informal meetings at the mental health agency to share information and solve problems.

Team members share information on a timely basis. For example, if a client shows increasing signs of delusional thinking at work, the psychiatrist, the case manager, and the other team members need to know about it right away. The case manager may know that this client's delusions often are exacerbated when he drinks heavily and uses marijuana. The team discusses what interventions and supports have been tried with this person in the past. The client is asked what he wants to do and what may work best for him. Together, the client and the team put a plan in place. This may be a new way of doing business for clinicians who have functioned as individual practitioners.

Traditionally, multidisciplinary teams have focused on illness and treatment. Teams may have difficulty incorporating employment into case reviews and treatment planning. But, as teams pay greater attention to clients' strengths and goals, work becomes a larger part of the discussion. Because most team members have not been trained in supported employment, it is the responsibility of the employment specialists and team leader to educate the team about supported employment practices. Team leaders and influential front line clinicians openly support the employment specialists' efforts.

Just naming the members of a treatment team, however, does not automatically create a working team. It is important to put as much time as needed into making sure that case managers, psychiatrists and other team members, and even the employment specialist, fully understand and support the way IPS works. The staff is educated about the principles of IPS and the specific tasks and activities of helping clients in the employment process. The role of the employment specialist needs to be understood as well as the roles of the psychiatrist, case manager, clinician, and residential counselor in supporting a client's work efforts. *Staff support and understanding usually develop as the team works together over time and they see clients becoming more independent, working competitive jobs with permanent status, and doing better.*

The employment specialist helps to keep the team focused on employment. Linda, a case manager from a mental health center, said, "In helping people go back to work, it has been crucial to have a full-time employment specialist on the team. As a case manager, I cannot address employment issues satisfactorily because I often have to attend to other issues such as housing, medication, and crises. Our full-time employment specialist focuses only on employment issues, and this has made all the difference. I am still involved in supporting clients' work efforts, but another staff person is available to make it happen when extra supports are needed." *In IPS, employment specialists provide only employment-related services. They do not carry out other staff roles such as case management or day treatment.* Programs that require employment specialists to carry a case management caseload, for example, often find that the focus on vocational services and work diminishes over time. The pressing issues of case management override employment. All activities of the employment specialists are therefore employment-related.

It is not unusual for agencies to assign case management caseloads to employment specialists when there are staff resignations, vacant positions, or budget cuts. One specialist, Carmen, said, "My supervisor suddenly assigned me a caseload of five people for case management. I had to start spending time doing case management and I got frustrated because I couldn't follow through with job leads that I had been developing. My clients started getting angry with me because I didn't have the time to help them find jobs. I started not liking my job."

The way agencies define case management is key to understanding the different staff roles and responsibilities. Supervisors must guard against employment specialists shifting their attention to case management activities for the sake of convenience. Employment specialists may receive requests to carry out case management tasks that are in the community (e.g., delivering medication, transporting clients to appointments, resolving housing problems) if case managers are providing office-based services. In fact, it may be practical for an employment specialist to transport a client to an appointment if the employment specialist is already scheduled to meet the client. Furthermore, the employment specialist wants to be a team member and help out in certain situations. It becomes a problem, however, when the employment specialist is providing other services that take time away from the employment support.

Moreover in practice, it sometimes is difficult to decide what is a case management activity and what is an employment activity. If role responsibilities are unclear to team members, they will undoubtedly be unclear to clients as well. So, the client who seeks out the employment specialist to help resolve a housing issue needs to be redirected to the case manager. Probably there will always be some overlap between the two roles. Supervisors help the team work out role responsibilities and boundaries and keep the employment specialist focused on employment.

As an ongoing member of the team, the employment specialist attends team meetings regularly and establishes working relationships with the same group of people. In this manner, the employment specialist becomes familiar with all of the team's clients and promotes employment options, even when other staff members may not identify candidates for work and when clients themselves are not yet expressing a desire to work. This process helps to prevent some clients from being overlooked, especially those people whose multiple treatment issues and crises overshadow their work potential. Some clients do not have a work goal. *The team must be sure that it is the client's choice not to work rather than a failure of the team to provide encouragement.*

Full-time employment specialists join one or, at the most, two teams. This is an efficient way for employment specialists to hear about the same clients and share information with team members. When IPS employment specialists join more than two teams, they find that their days are spent mostly attending different team meetings rather than being out of the office helping people find and keep jobs.

Illustration 2: Doug, a Person Seeking Work and Receiving Team Support

Doug is in his early 30s. He is articulate and energetic, but hasn't been able to find a job that he feels suits him. He last worked in retail sales as an assistant manager about 4 years ago.

When the mental health center, where Doug is a client, held several informational meetings about the new employment service called IPS, Doug asked his case manager to refer him. During the first two meetings with the employment specialist, Doug expressed eagerness to work and described his interest in working in retail sales again. His résumé looked good, and he said that he'd already lined up several interviews.

During the week that Doug interviewed for jobs, the employment specialist talked with Doug's case manager, and found out that the case manager had been getting a very different story from Doug. She had a long conversation with Doug, during which he talked about his fear of working and of the stresses piling up because of interviews with employers. He said he was terrified about losing his benefits, was worried about recurring symptoms of his bipolar illness, and felt the employment specialist was forcing him to find a job.

After speaking with the case manager, the employment specialist, with Doug's permission, met with one of the employers with whom Doug had just interviewed. The employer said that Doug did not interview well, and had made a bad impression.

The treatment team met that afternoon, shared information, and put together a common understanding of the difficulties that Doug was facing. The previous week he'd learned that the house in which he was renting a room was being sold, and that he'd have to move. This, and some other difficulties, appeared to put him under a lot of stress. The case manager suggested that the team make a recommendation to Doug to stop his job search, but the employment specialist reminded her that to do so would risk creating a setback for Doug. The psychiatrist agreed with the employment specialist, and said that he was in the process of adjusting Doug's medication and expected to see Doug's symptoms of anxiety stabilize in the next several days. The team's recommendation was that the case manager, the employment specialist, and Doug meet to go over what Doug wanted to do.

They met 2 days later and Doug was able to speak a little more openly about his fears. He said that he wanted to work but probably needed more help from the employment specialist in finding a job.

During the next 2 weeks, the employment specialist worked closely with Doug around his job search. Doug provided several job leads for retail sales positions. The employment specialist visited each of these employers and introduced himself as a job developer. He described Doug's work history in sales and his other strengths. The employment specialist was able to set up three interviews. Doug chose to go to the interviews by himself.

At the third interview, Doug was offered a part-time sales position. The employer explained that there were opportunities for advancement and this appealed to Doug.

Doug's story illustrates the importance of teamwork. People who feel ambivalent about a situation sometimes tell different sides of the story to different team members. Open communication among everyone, therefore, is necessary to better understand what is happening with a client, which results in better services and support. *Right from the start, the employment specialist explains to the client that the employment specialist is part of a team that shares information to improve treatment and rehabilitative services for the benefit of the client.* To promote clear communication, it is good practice for the employment specialist, case manager, and client to meet together periodically to discuss the client's employment goals and plans.

Programs with good outcomes demonstrate that clients benefit when services are integrated and individualized, and when the client is the center of decision making rather than a passive recipient of services. Services are organized to promote communication among service providers in order to reduce potential conflicts between staff members and to give the client a sense of holistic rather than fragmented support. Clearly, if a new service is offered to the client, the person who provides it needs to become part of the treatment team.

The IPS method of supported employment requires close and ongoing communication and a degree of shared decision making among the core group of people who support a client. Everyone on the team must be invested in the employment plan and supportive of the client's goal of going to work. Services become ineffectual if clients receive mixed messages from team members. Case managers, for example, may see competitive employment as a threat to hard-won benefits (e.g., Social Security Income, Medicaid). The employment specialist needs to be an expert on benefits and informs others about how people can work and still have their benefits. Team members gradually become accustomed to the idea of clients having competitive jobs. Over time, clients who are working become the norm rather than the exception.

Members of the treatment team need to work closely together, particularly when there are problems. When a client has difficulty at work, the psychiatrist initially may want to encourage him to quit the job, thinking that the stress is not productive. The employment specialist, by contrast, may view the work stress as an opportunity for the client to overcome a difficult situation and to build confidence. In other words, team members have different orientations and must talk to each other and agree on a plan. Over time, the members of a multidisciplinary team educate each other and work together more easily. Sharing successes helps staff members develop a common outlook. A few positive employment experiences are usually sufficient to help team members see the benefits of work.

Illustration 3: John, a Worker Benefiting from the Case Manager's Support

When John started drinking at his job as a groundskeeper, the employer called the employment specialist. The employment specialist knew that John usually drank heavily when he was having difficulties at home and therefore contacted the case manager. Meeting with John, the case manager learned that John's father was visiting him. John's father had physically abused him in the past and had continued to abuse him verbally.

The case manager increased his contacts with John, and they talked about ways to deal with his father. The employment specialist met John before work more frequently over the next few weeks and telephoned the employer to be sure John was working to the employer's satisfaction. John reduced his drinking and kept his job as a groundskeeper.

The case manager shares information with the employment specialist that may impact on the job, and the employment specialist may be able to provide important support.

Illustration 4: Lisa, a Worker Benefiting from the Employment Specialist's Support

Lisa was working as a sales clerk at a department store. She had lived with her parents for the past 2 years. Because she was working successfully, she wanted to move into her own apartment. Lisa had a history of getting into trouble using cocaine when she lived on her own. She would spend all her money on cocaine, and end up homeless. The case manager informed the employment specialist of Lisa's plans to move.

During this change in housing, the employment specialist provided extra support around work and watched for any changes in Lisa's behavior that might relate to the stress of moving or to cocaine use. Lisa agreed to a plan that would discourage her from buying drugs. On payday, the employment specialist transported Lisa from work to the bank to deposit her paycheck. She gave herself a weekly allowance to cover living expenses. The balance of her paycheck was put toward buying a car.

These examples highlight the need for timely, ongoing communication between team members to provide individualized supports.

The psychiatrist who is part of the team supporting clients' work efforts should attend team meetings. Some mental health agencies excuse psychiatrists from team meetings, as they are an expensive resource. Other programs have psychiatrists participate only in the portion of the team meetings that are devoted to crises. The psychiatrist, however, needs to hear how the client is functioning in everyday life, such as at a job, in order to provide effective treatment. One psychiatrist was able to confirm a diagnosis of paranoia when she heard from the employment specialist at a team meeting how a client was functioning at work. The psychiatrist had been unsure if the person had been experiencing social phobia or paranoid thought disorder. She adjusted the medication accordingly and the client improved.

In many instances, it is the employment specialist who is most knowledgeable about how a client functions outside of the community mental health agency. The psychiatrist and other team members rely on this information and use it in treatment planning. The psychiatrist, in turn, provides information to the employment specialist that is helpful in understanding symptoms and medication side effects that affect how a client performs a job and interacts with coworkers and a supervisor. For example, an employment specialist learned from the psychiatrist at a treatment team meeting that a client (whom the employment specialist had considered unmotivated) was in fact suffering negative symptoms from schizophrenia. The psychiatrist educated the employment specialist about symptoms and the need for the employment specialist and the team to think about the nature of someone's symptoms in terms of different types of jobs, different work environments, and different coping strategies.

By definition, members of multidisciplinary teams come from different backgrounds and training. They come to the team process with different values, and different ways to understand problems and find solutions. As team members work together, they learn from each other. Employment specialists learn about mental health treatment from the mental health clinicians, and the clinicians learn about supported employment and the world of work from employment specialists.

People who are not used to this approach, but who understand its importance and support it in theory, may need practice to make it work. Much of the staff communication occurs in regular team meetings, but staff members also need to interact on an individual basis to share information. A psychiatrist may have to put a note on his desk saying, "Remember to call employment specialist when making a medication change." And the employment specialist may have to drop by the case manager's office quite a few times to share some information about a client before the case manager starts dropping by *her* office.

The measure for how successfully the team functions is often the frequency that each team member talks with the other members and how well that shared information actually benefits the client. *Turf problems and bruised toes are inevitable, but a treatment team that begins to feel like a team will place good decisions and judgments in support of the client above the team members.* One team leader said, "Look, there are no 'right' answers here. We are all going to be wrong sometimes, but we need to get everybody's ideas on the table so that we have some different options to offer."

Teams mature over time. Team members talk through their different points of view. As they help clients gain competitive employment and see the benefits that clients experience, doubting staff members become believers. Teams provide effective services when they focus on clients' goals and follow the principles of supported employment.

Supported employment is one of several elements in a client's service plan. All members of the team must recognize that fact. Acquiring a job is not something the client does after her case manager and therapist agree that she is ready. Instead, getting a job is part of treatment and will usually bring about the need for changes and adjustments in other aspects of her service plan. When to look for a job and what type of job to pursue are the client's choices.

Rehabilitation is a part of treatment and, through work, people make gains in many areas of their lives, for example, financial, social, and personal. Oftentimes, because of the many benefits of working, people assume greater responsibility in managing their illness. Because rehabilitation and treatment are intertwined, it is essential that different practitioners work together. And, through a team approach, treatment and rehabilitation are integrated at the level of service delivery.

Planning

Putting an IPS program in place in a community mental health agency may be a big change from the way the employment program has been running. Careful planning and preparation are crucial to the success of such a program. Starting an IPS program affects the way other programs operate in the agency, so planning for changes is important.

Illustration 5: South River Valley Center, an Agency Starting IPS

South River Valley Center serves around 500 clients. Two years ago, the director of rehabilitation services, Nancy, made the decision to develop a vocational program within the center. South River Valley had no organized in-house vocational program, and Nancy and the other department directors at the center felt that the practice of referring clients to independent vocational programs outside of the agency simply wasn't working well.

Nancy explained, "Some of our clients were involved in a transitional employment program," said Nancy. "But the problem with that approach was that clients would learn the job, develop a good relationship with the employer, and then have to leave the job after 6 months or a year because the time allotted for the position had ended. It didn't make sense. So we began looking for a new direction."

Nancy put together a committee of a dozen people including a member of the board of directors, a psychiatrist, a member of the South River Alliance for the Mentally Ill, several clients from the agency, a prominent business person, a local VR counselor, and the department directors from the agency. The group looked at different vocational rehabilitation programs and their relative success.

They decided to adopt the IPS approach to supported employment for two reasons. First, the concept of individually designed services made a good fit with the center's overall philosophy. The center tries to "wrap the services around the client," rather than trying to make the client fit existing programs. Second, they wanted an employment program that had empirical support. The principles and practices of IPS are consistent with those of evidence-based supported employment.

The next step was to assess how implementing IPS would affect the other services that the center offered. Nancy reviewed the service needs and goals of the 500 clients at the agency by leading focus groups with staff members, clients, and families and learned that over 100 clients were interested in participating in the program in the first year. But she knew that she could only get funding for two full-time employment specialists, each with a caseload of no more than 25 clients at any one time. In the first year, the employment specialists would gradually increase their caseloads to 25 people. By reading about IPS, Nancy knew that if a client becomes ambivalent about working, she usually remains on the employment specialist's caseload for at least 6 months. People are more likely to overcome their ambivalence if they are meeting at least occasionally with an employment specialist (i.e., once every 3 to 4 weeks). Nancy estimated that, in the first year, between 40 and 60 clients would be active in the IPS program. Nancy next talked with the other program directors about other services.

She found that in order to continue receiving services such as group counseling, some participants in the IPS program would need evening or weekend sessions to avoid conflicts with their daytime work schedules. Case managers and therapists would need to schedule evening hours. The agency had reorganized into five treatment teams in the previous 6 months, so the organizational structure was in place to implement IPS.

Funding the program required creative planning. Nancy submitted a proposal to the agency's executive committee. Timing was just right, as the agency was negotiating its biennial contract with the state Division of Behavioral Health. They were able to secure two 1-year positions as part of a pilot project. The division was very interested in supporting programs that were outcomes-oriented and consistent with clients' goals. Competitive employment was one of the three major areas in which the division wanted to improve outcomes.

Within the center, it was anticipated that some programs would lose a portion of their funding as clients started working and using less services overall. Nancy had foreseen the problem of losing Medicaid revenue when clients stopped attending the day treatment program as they went to work.

Nancy's plan included converting two day treatment counselor positions to supported employment positions. The lost revenue from the Medicaid billings would be made up by the additional funding from the Division of Behavioral Health for the next year. She knew that she would need to begin planning immediately for the following years if the IPS program was to survive longer than 1 year. She already had discussed ideas with the state Division of Vocational Rehabilitation about financing. Although there were some significant changes to make, the study committee felt confident that the IPS approach to supported employment would work at South River Valley.

Nancy knew that the most important concept of IPS—that work itself could be part of a client's treatment—would also be the most difficult part for many clinicians to understand. So she spent time putting together a clear presentation on IPS including the theory, principles, research, and practice guidelines. A series of meetings was scheduled with clients, families, and agency staff to provide information about IPS and discuss ways to implement the program. During these meetings, Nancy fostered a culture of change in which people could express their doubts and fears in a supportive environment.

Nancy knew that she needed a strong advocate from the clinical staff who people respected. She identified the agency's medical director as that person. He understood the concepts, carried a high level of enthusiasm, and had the energy to keep making the rounds of key staff people and agency board members, explaining the IPS program and gradually winning positive support. Meanwhile, other members of the committee also carried the word back to their constituencies.

Nancy met with individuals and small groups of the center's executive staff and upper-level managers. She met with clients and family members. She hosted a meeting of community and business leaders, and created a series of training meetings for the clinical staff. She invited an experienced IPS supervisor from another agency to assist with a couple of the training sessions. She found that many of the questions and concerns raised at these meetings helped her sharpen her own understanding of the best way to implement IPS at South River Valley.

This example illustrates the importance of careful planning and early involvement of all stakeholders who will be affected by the new program. *During times of change, people are more likely to help if they are included early on in the decision-making and planning process.* This is often called consensus building. Staff members from mental health agencies that have implemented IPS say that it is important to encourage all people to speak up early on about their concerns and fears about supported employment. This has been particularly true for programs that converted their rehabilitative day treatment program, sheltered workshop, or previous vocational program to supported employment and changed staff members' job descriptions. The conversion process goes most smoothly in agencies that encourage everyone to talk about the transition and give input.

Putting Work in the Agency's Mission Statement

Implementing IPS at a community mental health agency may mean that the people who set policy at the center have decided to make a basic change in treatment and rehabilitation philosophy. IPS is not just another vocational service. When a center's board of directors decides to adopt a supported employment program such as IPS, they really are acknowledging that work should be a major aspect of the service plan for many clients. Most people with severe mental illness have employment as one of their recovery goals. Working is one way that people can move forward in their lives.

If IPS is introduced to a center as "just" a vocational program, the wrong message is sent to everybody involved, from clients to the center's executive director. The message that people need to hear is that clients want to work, that work is therapeutic, and that everyone in the community mental health agency needs to participate fully for a supported employment program to succeed. Work is a way that many people with severe mental illness are able to develop normal adult roles within the community, reversing the patient role that is so debilitating.

At the beginning of the planning process, the center's mission statement is reviewed to be sure that the guiding document is consistent with supported employment philosophy, principles, and practices. The mission statement should emphasize helping clients to develop independence through employment.

Committing the Resources

The overall goal of IPS is to help people with severe mental illness become more independent in their lives and less dependent on the services that the mental health agency provides. With increasing degrees of independence come, for many clients, a greater sense of self-esteem, better understanding and control of symptoms, and more satisfaction with life in general. In IPS, treatment and rehabilitation are directed toward maximizing independence and autonomy as much as possible and, as such, contrasts with other approaches that emphasize client stability over growth. *People with severe mental illness can learn to manage their illness and develop a greater level of independence and happiness. Work often is the vehicle to achieve this.*

The basic method employed in the IPS approach involves helping people obtain a competitive job of their choice through an individualized job search as quickly as possible and providing supports as needed to build positive work experiences. Unlike many domains measured in mental health, work is an outcome that is easily measured. *The main outcomes used to measure and monitor*

*the success of the IPS program over time are the percentage of people competitively
employed and the average number of weeks worked.*

How does measuring outcomes apply to committing the resources of a
community mental health agency to implement IPS? In the ideal world, one
could write a budget for 5 years for an IPS program and get it funded. In the
real world, there are limited resources to finance a variety of programs. Funding proposals often require a thorough description that includes a clear picture
of the expected outcomes and an evaluation plan. Preparing a solid case for
ongoing commitment to the program is also an important part of the planning
process. Converting rehabilitative day treatment programs to supported employment programs such as IPS is one way agencies are shifting resources.
Consumer-operated drop-in centers and peer support programs are replacing
expensive day treatment programs and providing opportunities for socialization, which clients say is the valuable part of day treatment programs.

Some states have begun combining resources across their state systems.
Leaders from the Divisions of Behavioral Health and Vocational Rehabilitation are figuring out ways to combine resources along with rewriting Medicaid
reimbursement regulations to finance supported employment. *Funding dic-
tates the types of services delivered, so administrators at the state and local level
must figure how to finance supported employment.* IPS is designed to become an
ongoing part of treatment, and bringing a client into an IPS program that ends
after a year because of lack of financial support is not wise.

Anticipating the Effects of IPS on Other Programs

By the end of the 1st year of operation, an IPS program will have created visible changes in the ways clients use services. For example, in one study evaluating day treatment conversion to IPS, over half of the regular attenders of the
former day treatment program held at least one competitive job during the 1st
year. In the early stages of planning, as many of these changes are anticipated as
possible so that staff members and other program managers can adjust their
programs and budgets. The overall amount of change will depend in part on
the number of employment specialists working with clients and will multiply
as more clients get involved.

If the program is successful, the first change that staff members will see is
that a client who used to be available during the day is now at work. Clients will
be moving out of the structured daytime programs and into part-time or, occasionally, full-time jobs. No one can predict accurately who will be working a
6-hour-per-week job, and who will be working full time. *But the majority of
people who participate in the IPS program will gain competitive employment,
gradually increase their work hours, and spend less time at the mental health
agency.* And that most likely will mean that some of those people will leave
openings in the community mental health agency's day programs.

Illustration 6: Small City Agency, How IPS Impacts on Other Programs

A community mental health center serving a city of 100,000 began running an IPS program a year ago. The program was successful during its first year, with two employment specialists helping clients obtain competitive jobs. Three clients worked in full-time jobs, and 35 others were either in part-time jobs or in active job searches.

Ten of those people had been working previously in the center's sheltered workshop. Because the workshop normally employs around 40 people, those 10 unfilled positions have reduced the workshop's productivity by 25%, and the workshop director will have to either fill the positions or reduce the amount of work she contracts from local businesses.

Ten clients who are now working are no longer attending the day program, which has resulted in decreased Medicaid billings. The director is concerned about how he should handle the situation. He is considering starting up a small evening program. He is realizing that the goals and objectives of the program need to be reevaluated.

More than half of the people working at jobs during the day used to attend group therapy sessions at the center. The therapists who run those sessions are frustrated and concerned about how working clients have missed sessions or dropped out of the program entirely. Scheduling evening appointments has become a necessary alternative to accommodate clients' work schedules.

It is difficult to predict exactly how supported employment will affect other programs. Agencies try to identify the programs that may be affected and develop plausible scenarios for each. It is helpful to discuss this with the other program managers to produce a picture of how the changing schedules and needs of working clients will affect service delivery and funding.

Staff Attitudes and Training

From the start of the planning process, key staff members from all areas of the project are brought together. It can take time for people to understand that work is a central component of treatment and the recovery process. Some people tend to think of a vocational program as an auxiliary service that operates outside of mental health treatment. Even worse, some staff hold the old-fashioned and discredited idea that work activates mental illness. Sessions are scheduled to discuss the principles and practices of evidence-based supported employment. Each person needs to understand his role and how his role interfaces with others.

The IPS method of supported employment is a relative newcomer to the field of mental health and contrasts rather sharply with some of the more established approaches to vocational rehabilitation. When teaching staff about IPS, remember that each individual has his own ideas about what is effective, not only regarding vocational rehabilitation but also regarding treatment guidelines in general for people with mental illness. Each person has built a set of beliefs through formal education, work experiences, family background, personality, values, and the opinions of people he respects. Introducing him to a new approach will almost certainly contradict some, if not many, of the ideas he has accepted as correct.

By introducing IPS, people will be asked to learn about supported employment, and perhaps change some of the ways they work and think about their own work. For example, a senior clinician of a community mental health center had a deeply held belief that her clients needed extensive vocational training and preparation before they entered the work world. She had difficulty with the IPS emphasis on rapid job search. A case manager may have invested much of his career in helping to establish a sense of stability in his clients' lives, all the way from obtaining Social Security benefits to establishing a predictable daily schedule. He may be alarmed by a program that actively strives to *change* a client's life, to create added complexities.

A key component of initial staff training is using values clarification exercises. Supervisors encourage staff members to identify the role that work has played in their lives. Would work play any different role for them than it would for people with disabilities?

Developing a plan for educating and training staff about IPS is key to a good implementation. It can take weeks or months for people to really understand a new idea. And it may take a year or more of applying the principles and concepts of IPS in their daily work before they really embrace the new ways. Training may include inviting an expert on supported employment to the center. A person experienced in implementing evidence-based supported employment can help to guide leaders of the agency, supervisors, frontline staff, clients, and families. Some agencies send a small group of four to six staff members to a training site where they can learn about IPS and observe how it is implemented in another setting. It is advisable to send the IPS employment specialists and the IPS coordinator, a case management supervisor, and an executive management person. The case management supervisor plays a key role in ensuring that the case managers learn how to participate in IPS and support clients' work efforts. An agency administrator who oversees the overall implementation of IPS needs to obtain firsthand knowledge of how IPS operates.

When visiting another site, we recommend that the trainees visit for a couple of days. They receive a general introduction to IPS and observe how it is implemented in that agency. During the visit, it is helpful to: (1) attend the weekly IPS employment specialists' group supervision meeting and a treatment team meeting; (2) meet with a psychiatrist who embraces supported employment and can describe her role in the process; (3) meet with one or two case managers who can describe their role; and (4) shadow employment specialists out in the community, meeting clients, conducting job searches, contacting employers, and so on. These visits provide plenty of opportunity for trainees to get their questions answered.

Educating people about supported employment and developing an implementation plan takes time. To keep the process on track, the agency assigns at least one person to oversee the implementation effort. As Nancy, the director of rehabilitation services from South River Community Mental Health Center, said, "I go from my executive staff to my middle managers to my front line staff, and then back again to the middle managers. I just keep bringing the ideas back to people." The person or persons who champion IPS ensure that the implementation process moves forward and the agency stays focused on supported employment.

The plan should involve more than just a round of single presentations to all the key people. A series of regular training sessions and meetings spaced in intervals of a few weeks are helpful. Forty-five-minute programs work well. Each session focuses on a different aspect of IPS and how it will work at the center. At each session, people are encouraged to respond openly to the material and discuss it. Using existing meeting times will increase attendance and reduce the feeling by staff of "another meeting."

During the time before the new program begins, the discussions are introductory, dealing with general concepts, case examples, and questions around planning and procedures. *IPS principles and procedures are incorporated and reinforced in the everyday work of the staff and through regular supervision and team meetings.*

Training sessions create a consistent overall picture of the program across all the departments and teams in any given community mental health agency. Basic practice guidelines are maintained: (1) integrating mental health treatment and employment services; (2) helping people rapidly begin to seek community jobs that pay at least minimum wage and are consistent with their job preferences and skills; and (3) providing long-term supports. Without sharing an understanding of a common conceptual framework, people begin working at cross-purposes, and the resulting conflicts affect how much benefit clients receive from the program. Supervisors are responsible for ensuring that the program implementation is faithful to evidence-based supported employment.

Locating Offices

The key word to remember about office location is proximity. *The employment specialists need to be near the other treatment team members.*

In IPS, employment specialists work most closely with the case managers. The easier it is for case managers and employment specialists to get together, the more information they will exchange about clients. As one might guess, a lot of this information flows informally between people if their offices are close and if they meet for coffee in the same area. This kind of proximity becomes particularly important when a client is in need of extra support and attention. When Jim's mother calls the case manager to say that Jim has been passing out from alcohol every night for the past week, the case manager can stop by the employment specialist's office for a quick face-to-face discussion about how Jim's performance on the job may suffer and to develop a plan for addressing his problem with alcohol. Better still, they can share this information if they have the *same* office.

We recommend that the employment specialists share office space with the other treatment team members rather than sharing space with the other employment specialists. The employment specialists, therefore, may have offices located on different floors or different wings of the center from each other, depending on where the case managers and treatment team members are located. Colocating treatment team members reinforces the principle that IPS is integrated with mental health treatment. Some centers have located the employment specialists in offices with each other, reinforcing communication within the IPS unit of employment specialists. In this design, however, service integration is often compromised. The employment specialists are at risk of not developing good working relationships with the other team members. This structure can also foster an "us" and "them" division. The employment specialists are viewed by the clinicians as being separate. And this attitude is likely to be present during disagreements among the treatment team. When sharing office space with the treatment team members, employment specialists have opportunities to communicate with other employment specialists at least twice weekly on a formal basis during IPS group supervision meetings.

Staffing

The typical IPS unit is staffed by an employment coordinator and at least two employment specialists. Each employment specialist carries a discrete caseload that increases gradually up to 20 to 25 clients. There are several advantages to running an IPS program with at least two full-time employment specialists. The employment specialists provide backup for each other. If one of the employment specialists is out of the office, the other can help a client who unexpectedly needs some support. Working together as a unit gives the employment specialists the chance to support each other and to provide cross-coverage for clients. They also have the chance to brainstorm together for new ideas and unload the inevitable frustrations that come with the job. We do not recommend using part-time employment specialist positions, particularly if the people can work only certain days of the week. Effective job searching requires employment specialists to be available to connect with employers on the employer's schedule and not the schedule of a part-time employment specialist. Missed opportunities occur when employment specialists are around only half the week.

Employment Coordinator

The IPS coordinator, who has a degree in rehabilitation counseling or a related field, supervises the work of the employment specialists and handles referrals.

One mental health agency, because of its particular organizational structure, assigns administrative supervisory responsibilities of the employment specialists to the treatment team leaders. The IPS coordinator provides vocational supervision and input in the employment specialists' yearly evaluations. For this agency, having the team leaders as administrative supervisors is a way to enhance the integration of services. Because of their supervisory responsibilities, the team leaders are able to oversee how the employment specialists become true members of the teams. With this supervisory structure, the IPS coordinator and the team leaders, who are organizationally at the same level, communicate regularly about the employment specialists' work performances.

Alternatively, the employment coordinator supervises the employment specialists and the team leaders provide input into the yearly performance evaluations. What works well for one agency, however, may not work well for another one. In either case, everyone needs to be clear who the supervisor is.

The IPS coordinator conducts two weekly group meetings with the employment specialists. One meeting is devoted to supported employment supervision in which the employment specialists discuss different clients. We recommend several elements to the meeting agenda. A first item is announcement of good news. Highlighting successes reminds the employment specialists of the gains that clients are making and that progress occurs even when it sometimes seems slow. For example, employment specialists announce when someone is offered and accepts a job, or when someone has held a job for a month, 6 months, or a year, or when someone has been able to get through a rough time and keep her job.

A second agenda item for the weekly IPS supervision meeting is discussing problems that employment specialists are encountering with individual clients. The IPS unit brainstorms about different ways to approach problems. When presenting a client, the employment specialist identifies the problem and reviews what strategies have been tried in the past. The employment specialist describes the most recent plan and looks to the group for problem-solving strategies. The supervisor makes sure that specific next steps are identified and that progress in the action steps is reviewed at the next meeting.

The last agenda item for the IPS supervision meeting is client presentations. The employment specialist presents new clients, including information from the vocational profile that she has been putting together over the 2 to 3 weeks from the time of referral, so the unit can help with planning. It is helpful to make presentations periodically on all clients to review overall progress with their employment goals. The IPS coordinator or one of the employment specialists takes notes at the weekly meeting so there is a record of the discussion and the identified action steps. An important aspect of the coordinator's job is to help ensure that recommendations are followed.

The IPS coordinator is responsible for making sure that the employment specialists are implementing IPS. During the weekly supervision meetings, the coordinator ascertains whether the principles and components of IPS are being followed. Are the employment specialists talking with their team members about employment issues? Are they eliciting suggestions for job leads from the treatment team members? What is the case manager's input about a client's situation? What is the psychiatrist's recommendation? How can the family be involved in the employment effort? Is the job search based on the client's job preference? Is the employment specialist helping clients contact employers within one month of referral to the program? Is the employment specialist spending at least 65% of her time out of the office setting? Is a client receiving individualized, long-term job supports? Some IPS programs put large posters with the IPS principles, briefly listed, on the wall of the meeting room and in individual staff offices. The posters remind people of the IPS principles as they carryout their daily work. And the employment coordinator can refer to the poster during group supervision to help the group stay on track.

The second weekly IPS unit meeting is devoted to job development. During this meeting, the employment specialists share job leads. When employment specialists conduct job searches in the community, they also keep in mind the jobs that the other employment specialists are pursuing for clients. The employment specialists aim to expand their network of contacts for employment opportunities.

Having a mechanism to keep track of employer contacts is helpful. An employer log includes the employer's name, date of contact, name of person who made the contact, nature of contact, and recommendations for follow up. Organizing this information in a computer database or in a loose-leaf notebook are helpful ways to access easily the information. We recommend that the IPS coordinator reviews the employer contact list in the group meeting with the employment specialists once a month. Employment specialists need to make return visits to employers to develop working relationships. *Developing employer networks is the most effective way to create job opportunities for clients. One of the main responsibilities of the IPS coordinator is making sure the employment specialists are broadening their employer network.*

IPS coordinators usually provide weekly individual IPS supervision to newly hired employment specialists and to those employment specialists who are having difficulties with their performance. Thereafter, the employment specialists may receive individual supervision on a biweekly basis.

The IPS coordinator must work closely with the employment specialists to know they have the skills to carry out their job. We recommend that the IPS coordinator go out with the employment specialists to observe job development. Are they presenting themselves professionally to employers? Are they confident in their presentation of potential workers? Are they finding out the needs of the employer? What an employment specialist reports that she is doing in relation to employers may appear very different to the supervisor when he is present observing the interactions.

The employment coordinator monitors how well the employment specialist collaborates with the other members of the treatment team. Is the employment specialist advocating for client choice and the principles of IPS? The employment specialist needs to participate regularly and assertively in team meetings, rather than quietly observing. The IPS coordinator periodically joins the employment specialist at treatment team meetings. The IPS coordinator models for the IPS worker how to advocate with the rest of the team members, which is helpful particularly for new employment specialists.

The employment coordinator teaches the employment specialists good time management skills. *The general duties of an employment specialist include: engaging clients around their work interest; conducting job searches; meeting with clients, employers, and family members; participating in regular team meetings; contacting team members as needed; and completing documentation.* To complete these tasks efficiently, the employment specialist must have a plan for using his time wisely. In describing a typical workday, one employment specialist said, "I attend my team meeting first thing in the morning. Right after that I get in my car and do job development. I keep a phone book in my car along with my cell phone, pager, city map, daily newspapers, and my business cards. Clients and employers can reach me anytime. My car becomes my office. This way I don't have to waste time traveling back and forth to the office. I usually connect with clients after lunch. I return to the office for the last hour of the day to complete paperwork and seek out team members that I may need to talk with." The IPS coordinator reviews the daily work schedules of the IPS workers so they develop a routine schedule that is efficient and effective. Laying out a daily plan helps employment specialists to be thoughtful in how to use their time.

The employment coordinator is informed about everyone's schedule also for safety reasons. Because the bulk of IPS work is community-based, someone should know where the employment specialists are at all times. On certain occasions, employment specialists make contacts in pairs for safety reasons.

The IPS coordinator is also responsible for hiring and training new employment specialists. The treatment team leaders may help with interviewing candidates for the employment specialist position, too. The team leaders screen for people who are team players and who will fit into the treatment team structure. In like fashion, the employment coordinator helps to screen candidates for case management and other clinical positions to choose people who value principles of supported employment and recovery-oriented services.

The IPS coordinator arranges for new IPS workers to receive an orientation to the agency at large and to the IPS program. The coordinator arranges for new employment specialists to shadow one of the experienced employment specialists to have a good role model.

The IPS coordinator makes sure that all clinical and rehabilitative staff members receive training on evidence-based supported employment at least once a year. There is usually staff turnover and people can always use a reminder about the goals, values, and practices of the program.

The IPS coordinator is the person who oversees the supported employment referrals. He determines the timing of when a client is assigned to an employment specialist based on the rate of referrals and the openings on the employment specialists' caseloads. The coordinator attempts to link the client and the employment specialist as soon as possible to build on the client's interest in working. If there is more than one employment specialist assigned to a team, the coordinator makes the decision as to which employment specialist the client will be assigned. Factors taken into account in the decision include whether an employment specialist expresses an interest in working with the person, whether the client tends to do better with a female or male worker, who has room on the caseload, and recommendations from the treatment team.

The IPS coordinator keeps track of staff morale. If an employment specialist is feeling overwhelmed with her job responsibilities, the IPS coordinator provides guidance and support around how to manage work challenges.

In addition to general administrative responsibilities for the employment program, the coordinator works as the liaison between the IPS program and other agency programs and services. She attends management meetings representing the IPS program.

While the supervisory and administrative responsibilities of the coordinator do not usually require a full-time position, we recommend that the coordinator carry a small IPS caseload (e.g., 5 to 10 clients). Doing the work of an employment specialist allows the IPS coordinator to model expected work performance. Supervisors who do not have a caseload sometimes lose a sense of the real work and the difficulties and frustrations that come with it. Carrying a caseload may legitimize the employment coordinator in the eyes of the employment specialists as they see her doing the same work.

The coordinator needs to have a thorough understanding of the way IPS operates and its overall goals. And, most important, she must believe that supported employment is the best way to help people succeed in competitive jobs. If a candidate for the coordinator position has a traditional vocational rehabilitation background, she may be inclined to emphasize preparation over rapid job seeking. For example, she may encourage her employment specialists to do skills training around job interviewing before helping clients look for a job. She may talk about the importance of clients being "work-ready." And, after 6 months, the IPS program may look suspiciously like a conventional vocational rehabilitation program. In this example, the employment specialists are devoting too much of their time to assessing how well clients perform in prevocational experiences and in different trial job situations and not enough time in helping people to find regular jobs with permanent status.

In summary, the person who supervises the employment specialists, either an employment coordinator or a case management team leader, is in a key position that will largely determine how well IPS is implemented. Good supervisors are critical to providing effective services. When choosing a candidate for the supervisory role, the agency looks for someone who wants to embrace this approach to supported employment. A successful candidate may not have previous training in supported employment but can learn the necessary skills and concepts to supervise employment specialists. We recommend that supervisors who are newly assigned to the position visit an IPS program that has high fidelity to the model or other evidence-based supported employment programs, which incorporate the critical components of IPS.

Employment Specialist

The job description for the position of employment specialist could read, simply, "Help people find jobs appropriate for their skills and interests as soon as possible, and provide ongoing support as needed." The most important aspect of a good employment specialist is the belief that people with severe mental illness can work if the right situation is found and the right supports are put in place. If a person decides he wants to work, it is the responsibility of the employment specialist and the team to help him do it. The role of the employment specialist is to support the client in her efforts and not take on the role of deciding whether people should or can work.

The tasks of the employment specialist are as varied as the skills needed to complete them. IPS workers must have counseling skills, skills to engage clients, business skills to conduct job searches, and excellent overall interpersonal skills to work effectively with team members, employers, clients, and family members. The employment specialist needs to enjoy working in the community. *IPS workers spend at least 65% of their time in the community, away from the mental health office, engaging with clients, developing jobs, and providing supports to clients and employers around maintaining jobs.* He should be the kind of person who enjoys knocking on doors, talking to people in the business world, putting people and ideas together, and doing whatever it takes. This will most likely be entirely new for those people who have worked as rehabilitative day treatment counselors. For programs that are converting day treatment to supported employment, supervisors and planners need to be aware that not all day treatment counselors have these skills and interests.

Employment specialists must be knowledgeable about the major mental illnesses and substance use disorders including: (1) psychotic disorders of schizophrenia and schizoaffective disorder; (2) mood disorders of recurring major depression and bipolar disorder; (3) severe personality disorders, such as borderline personality disorder; (4) anxiety disorders of obsessive compulsive disorder and posttraumatic stress disorder; and (5) alcohol and drug use disorders. Employment specialists need to be educated about psychiatric symptoms, medications and side effects, and different coping strategies. Employment specialists help clients identify work situations that are not likely to exacerbate symptoms. *For many people with severe mental illness, work is their coping strategy for managing symptoms of the illness.*

IPS employment specialists provide only employment services. They do not serve as case managers or carry out case management tasks. Employment specialists have only vocational responsibilities. Vocational programs that assign case management duties to employment specialists find that the emphasis on work is diluted when case management needs are pressing. As a treatment team member, however, the employment specialist may carry out a case management task in her daily schedule when it does not take away from providing employment services and improves efficiency of overall service delivery. For example, the employment specialist may deliver medications to a client if she is already scheduled to meet the client at her home to discuss her job.

Employment specialists are generalists who provide all phases of the employment process. The client establishes a working alliance with one employment specialist. Some vocational programs partition the different tasks of the employment service across several people. For example, one person provides vocational counseling, another person conducts job development, and another person provides follow-along support. Yet, many clients who are required to meet different staff members for different phases of the employment process drop out of the service during transitions. In IPS, employment specialists learn the skills of the overall employment service in order to maintain an ongoing relationship with the client.

Good candidates for the employment specialist position generally come either from the business community or from positions in vocational or rehabilitation programs in which they have worked very closely with employers. Applicants who come from other kinds of vocational programs may not be good candidates for IPS. If they have training and experience in vocational programs that use a stepwise approach that includes prevocational activities, vocational evaluation, and sheltered workshop experiences, they may be uncomfortable with the rapid job search approach to IPS. Desired qualifications for an employment specialist include:

- general knowledge and successful experience in job development, job marketing, and job securing;
- demonstrated ability to relate positively with employers in the community;
- working knowledge of a broad range of occupations and jobs;
- ability to identify clients' interests, strengths, skills, abilities, coping styles, and unique challenges, and match them with jobs;
- ability to identify and arrange long-term supports and job accomodations to help clients keep jobs;
- knowledge of severe mental illness, including diagnosis, treatment and medication, and the impact on vocational functioning;
- knowledge about benefits;
- ability to advocate effectively for clients with other team members, employers, and families.

People who become good employment specialists do not usually come to the job with all the above qualifications. Some of the knowledge about mental illness and work occupations can be learned on the job. Agencies have advertised the position under the heading of "employment specialist" or "job developer." IPS coordinators develop contacts with schools that have rehabilitation counseling programs to recruit employment specialists. The IPS program can serve as a training or internship site for students and an employment opportunity for graduates.

Successful employment specialists tend to be mature, high-energy, positive-thinking, enthusiastic, and persistent people who see the bright side of situations—people who see challenges where other people see problems. Oftentimes they are outgoing, assertive, and have the ability to engage all different types of employers. Typically, they are task-oriented people. Above all, each employment specialist develops his own style of working in what is a complex position in which personality and the quality of interpersonal relationships can contribute greatly to success with employers and clients. The people chosen for the job need to fit in well with the other members of the treatment team as well as with the other employment specialists. It is helpful to have a balance of male and female workers. If some clients speak a language other than English, hiring someone who can speak that language is necessary. Hiring employment specialists who live in the community and are well connected where they will be conducting job searches is important. Candidates who have lived in the area for years are familiar with the local businesses and employers and already have numerous contacts that can be used for networking in job searches.

During the job interview, the employment coordinator describes scenarios common to employment specialists and asks how the job candidate would approach the situations. Through this process, the IPS coordinator elicits information about whether the candidate is a problem solver, a team player, a positive and creative thinker, a person who thinks about solving problems out in the community with employers rather than counseling, and a person with values that are consistent with IPS. In addition, the interviewer asks the job candidate to describe examples from her past experiences when she used these skills.

When hiring employment specialists, the IPS coordinator makes clear that the employment specialist's job performance is evaluated by how well he helps people obtain and keep jobs. She describes how the majority of their time is spent outside of the agency helping people find and keep jobs and developing relationships with employers. *Within the first year of hire, the employment specialist is expected to have at least 40% of the people on his caseload working at any time.* The IPS worker who goes for months without helping any client obtain work is not doing her job. She may attribute poor outcomes to clients who are not motivated, to employers who will not hire people with mental illness in their community, or to clients who have more problems than clients in other communities. However, the evidence shows that good employment specialists are able to help people with severe mental illness secure employment that is based on the person's preferences, strengths, and experiences. *Clear job expectations, training, and good supervision along with the lessons learned through day-to-day experience help most employment specialists develop the skills and confidence to do a good job.*

Not everyone, however, becomes a good employment specialist. If, over time, the supervisor determines that a person does not match well with the employment specialist position, she will begin to counsel the employment specialist to think about other work opportunities. Keeping an employment specialist in his position when he continues to perform poorly is not helpful. Treatment team members, other employment specialists, clients, and family members become frustrated by the lack of outcomes. Job descriptions for the IPS coordinator and employment specialist positions are in appendix 3.

Keeping Records and Measuring Outcomes

The success of IPS shows up in the patterns of work and the types of jobs clients hold over a long period of time. Any particular client may show a pattern of working a job briefly and then taking some time off, perhaps because of difficulties with symptoms or because the job ended. But, in the long run, many clients work consistently.

Agencies need to set up good recordkeeping procedures to keep track of clients' employment progress. *Tracking employment outcomes and using the information in supervision keeps the agency focused on helping clients gain competitive employment.* Tracking outcomes shows the benefit of IPS and the reason for continued funding.

The main outcome to track is the percentage of people in competitive work. A common definition of competitive employment is:

- it pays at least minimum wage;
- the employment setting includes coworkers who are not disabled;
- the position can be held by anyone, that is, one does not need to be a member of a population with a disability to hold the job;
- the person is supervised by the employer.

Supervisors remind staff of the definition of competitive employment when tracking outcomes.

We recommend that the data are collected on a prospective basis for purposes of accuracy. An easy way to update the data is during regularly scheduled team meetings. Recording the data in an Excel spreadsheet is a simple way to manage it. At minimum, the agency keeps track of the start date of the job, the number of hours worked each week, and the end date. The agency also may want to report wages earned each week, yet wages earned and hours worked are highly correlated. We recommend collecting a few outcomes carefully. Agencies that ambitiously track many outcomes usually find the data are incomplete and inaccurate. Clinicians tend to resent reporting increasing amounts of information, especially if they are not given meaningful reports about the data.

The spreadsheet allows for calculations for percentage of people who worked during a specific period of time and the average number of weeks worked during that time.

Illustration 7: Tracking Employment Data

1. Start and end dates of each competitive job.
2. Weekly hours worked for each competitive job.
3. Hourly wage or weekly wages earned for each competitive job.

In addition to collecting weekly data, the employment specialist writes a monthly note in the case chart describing the client's efforts in reaching her vocational goals and objectives and includes all jobs held. For example, details about how a job was obtained, the name of the employment site, the job title and description, the nature of the job ending, the person's strengths on the job, and the challenges encountered are documented.

The employment coordinator reviews the employment outcomes with the rest of the team on a routine basis. The employment coordinator uses outcomes-based supervision when meeting individually with the employment specialists to keep people focused on the overall goal. In addition, some IPS programs display monthly outcomes on a large chalkboard. The chart lists by month the number of clients working by employment specialist, the number of job starts and job endings by employment specialist, and the overall totals for the IPS unit. The board also shows the number of people (and percentage) working competitively in a month as well as the total number of people (and percentage) who have had at least one job in the past year. The employment coordinator and team supervisors review the range of jobs and quality of job matches. *Outcomes-based supervision helps the employment specialist and the team members focus on how successful they are with helping clients achieve their work goals.* For programs that have operated for at least 3 to 4 months, a monthly average of 40% of people working in competitive jobs is realistic.

Fidelity Measurement

Monitoring the implementation of supported employment with the Supported Employment Fidelity Scale (see appendix 5) provides information on elements of the program that have good fidelity to the model and those that need adjusting. Fidelity refers to the degree of adherence to the principles of evidence-based supported employment. Programs that are rated as high fidelity have been shown to have greater effectiveness than programs with lower fidelity in assisting clients to achieve competitive employment. Completing regular fidelity ratings provides objective and structured information about program development.

The Supported Employment Fidelity Scale has 15 items that are drawn from the principles and core practice components and are scored on a scale of 1 to 5. The highest rating of 5 indicates full implementation. The scale can be administered by anyone who has a general knowledge of supported employment (see Bond, Becker, et al., 1997). The fidelity measure is completed on a quarterly basis until the program achieves a rating of high fidelity. Thereafter, the scale is completed semiannually. The scale is scored by obtaining objective information from a variety of sources. (See appendix 5 for a list of suggested questions for eliciting information on each criterion.) We recommend obtaining information from agency records, client records, interviews with employment specialists, case managers, supervisors, and clients. The rater also attends a treatment team meeting, vocational supervision meeting, and shadows several employment specialists in their daily activities. The goal is for the rater to gather information on all aspects of how vocational services are provided. Measuring fidelity occurs over 1 or 2 days. Supervisors use information from fidelity measurement to improve the level of implementation over time. Graphing the fidelity scores depicts progress and can reinforce the agency's efforts.

8

Getting Started

Eligibility Criteria

Eligibility guidelines need to be explicit. *The guidelines should be simple and designed to include the widest possible range of clients rather than exclude those people who have severe disabilities, co-occurring substance use disorder, legal problems, or those with poor work histories.* The goal is to create job opportunities for all clients who want to work. Minimal eligibility criteria include people who: (1) have a major mental illness (i.e., psychotic disorder, mood disorder, or severe personality disorder) that qualifies them for services in the agency's community support program; and (2) express interest in obtaining competitive employment. Some vocational programs exclude people who have a substance use disorder, have a history of violence, or appear not ready to work. In IPS, all clients are encouraged to think about employment and the possibilities working may hold for them. All members of the treatment team are responsible for developing this culture of work and belief in peoples' potential.

Referral

A referral procedure is developed so that all interested clients can access IPS services. *Educate referral sources about the program so that people are given accurate information from the beginning.* If the people who make referrals understand how IPS works, chances are better that clients will come with accurate expectations. Clients can self-refer or be referred by a community mental health center staff person. Typically, the case manager makes the referral after a client expresses interest in working. If case managers are not referring people to the program, they may not know enough about IPS or simply are not encouraging clients to consider competitive employment.

Occasionally a client will enter the office of an employment specialist and say, "I've heard you can get me a job! When do I start? I'm ready and I can't wait to work!" But, in most cases, clients benefit from a series of suggestions and encouraging remarks, and, finally, a referral to bring them to that first meeting with the employment specialist. People vary in how quickly they want to go to work and their level of confidence and comfort to do it. One client told his case manager that he was ready to visit the Social Security office and stop his monthly Supplemental Security Income (SSI) check because he had decided to go to work full time. Another person had difficulty seeing herself in the worker role as she was more accustomed to the role of mental patient. In all cases, anyone who expresses interest in working is eligible for IPS and should be introduced to an employment specialist.

To broaden the referral base, to inform as many people as possible, and to stimulate interest, the IPS unit advertises its services, making the program and work visible within the agency and with referral sources. Posters, pictures of clients working, brochures about IPS, and job opportunities are displayed throughout the agency in waiting rooms, conference and meeting rooms, and staff offices to build a culture of work with staff and clients alike. Employment specialists introduce IPS at meetings for state chapters of the National Alliance for the Mentally Ill (NAMI) and at the agency's board meetings. They meet with referral sources, such as hospital social workers, VR counselors, community psychologists and psychiatrists, and consumer organizations and peer support groups, and provide written materials about IPS and referral procedures.

Case managers help clients to get started in the employment process. To apply for employment, people need documents—usually two, including a driver's license, State ID card, U.S. Social Security card, or birth certificate—that establish their identity and employment eligibility. If the person is from another country, she needs a green card, passport, and Social Security card. People may need to apply for and purchase a worker permit that lasts for 6 months. If people do not have these documents, the case manager helps the client to secure them.

Agencies sometimes have to set up waiting lists as the demand for supported employment increases. During the waiting time, case managers encourage clients to think about the types of work they want to do. Some people do not have a broad knowledge of the work world and benefit from visiting work sites and observing workers in different types of jobs. These activities help to keep people focused on work, but waiting for more than a few weeks to start the supported employment program may interrupt the person's desire to work. Agencies try to solve the problem of a waiting list in order to serve people in a timely way.

Everyone is encouraged to think about the possibility of working. As quickly as possible, the team engages clients who express an interest in working. *Supervisors and team leaders encourage clinicians and other team members to help all clients think about the possibility of working.* The client is always the one who decides if she wants to work. But some people do not automatically believe that they can work, so they need encouragement and support. Psychiatrists and case managers encourage clients to consider the opportunities and benefits of employment. Many people express interest when they understand that an employment specialist can help them find a part-time job. A job that is less than 12 hours a week is not uncommon for a person who hasn't worked recently. Clients also show more interest in working when they learn that an employment specialist will help them find a job of their choice. People often develop motivation for working through ongoing discussions with case managers. Benefits counseling often helps clients make up their minds about seeking employment, since that is the most common concern. Clients are referred to supported employment after they have decided that they are interested in obtaining a competitive job.

During individual treatment planning, the team addresses with the client the major aspects of her life including employment. Over time, many people begin to see the value of work in their own lives, and decide to try a job, particularly if they are steadily encouraged to consider work.

For new clients of a mental health agency, the treatment team addresses work right from the start, focusing on health and normal adult roles rather than on disability and a patient role. In this way, the staff members discourage clients from developing and accepting the self-image of "disabled person." They encourage clients by focusing on talents, abilities, and preferences. For people who are newly referred to the agency, employment is often a more attractive goal than day treatment. By addressing what the people referred want, the mental health agency is more likely to engage clients and help them with their personal goals and increase the number of people served.

Employment is sometimes the key for engaging people with severe mental illness and co-occurring substance use disorder. The opportunity to earn money and take on a worker identity motivates some people to change their pattern of substance use. The positive feelings and the increased self-esteem achieved from work can help a client to decide to reduce her use and over time can lead to abstinence.

Illustration 8: Cindy, a Person with Dual Disorders Taking the First Step Toward Work

Cindy is a 27-year-old woman who was referred to the community mental health center by the psychiatric unit in a general hospital. She has paranoid schizophrenia and a history of homelessness, discontinuing medications, unemployment, and substance abuse. During the first team meeting, which included the psychiatrist, the case manager, the nurse, the employment specialists, and Cindy, treatment goals were identified. When asked about work, Cindy replied that she did not know what she wanted to do and that no one had ever talked to her about working. She explained that she was too "messed up" to work. The employment specialist pointed out some positive qualities in Cindy and explained that there are jobs for people with these attributes. Cindy agreed to meet with him if he thought she was able to work.

The role of the team is to provide hope and support for people to move beyond their illness, and competitive employment is part of recovery.

When encouraging people to consider employment, remember that everyone has a different idea about what work is. Some people immediately think that working means a 40-hour-a-week job. *In IPS, people are helped to find jobs that are consistent with their preferences and for the number of hours a week that makes sense to them.* Some people have not worked in a long time and may want to start slowly. Sometimes people start working 3 or 4 hours a week. They may gradually increase the number of hours they work each week and may never work a 40-hour-a-week job. Some people want to work 5 days a week for 2 to 3 hours a day. Others want to work 2 to 3 days a week for 4 to 5 hours a day. As case managers and other clinicians encourage people to think about employment, it is helpful for them to ask clients to describe what work means to them. As clients begin to consider work, don't forget that they need good benefits counseling so they can make good decisions.

The referral system needs to be simple. Typically, the case manager completes a brief referral form that includes the person's name, contact information, and a description of the person's interest in work. Long forms will deter referrals. Clients, of course, may speak to the IPS coordinator directly. Sometimes candidates are identified during team meetings. If the treatment team sits down to review a person's housing, medication, daytime activity, and therapy status, work is also one of the items on the list.

The IPS employment coordinator is the person who receives the referrals and makes assignments to employment specialists. If there is more than one employment specialist on a team, the IPS coordinator gathers information from the team leader, case managers, and employment specialists to decide which employment specialist will work with the client. The goal is to link the employment specialist with the client within a day or two of the referral.

The employment specialist and the client meet face-to-face within the first week of the referral. Sometimes the case manager is present at the first meeting to introduce the client to the employment specialist. The goal is to build on the client's interest in working, and timing can play a key role. People get discouraged if there are long delays after expressing their interest in work.

As the IPS program begins to run, the IPS coordinator and team leaders make sure the referral process is working smoothly. Are people who want to work getting referred? Are people beginning to meet with their assigned employment specialist within a couple days of the referral? If necessary, adjustments are made to the referral procedures. Surveys show that about 70% of the

people with a severe mental illness desire work. If people are not getting referred at a reasonable rate, the agency evaluates the discrepancy. Are case managers and team members screening for work readiness and therefore excluding
potential work candidates? Are case managers and team members talking
about work possibilities with all of the clients they meet? *Access is an important
part of the program. If administrative procedures and clinical practices exclude
people from accessing supported employment, the agency is not implementing IPS
effectively.*

Engagement and Building a Relationship

The engagement process is individualized. The nature of the first few meetings
between a client and an employment specialist depends in part on what the
client brings to them. If a person feels overwhelmed about job interviewing,
the employment specialist's task is to find a way of helping him obtain a job
without the traditional job interview. If he works in that job successfully for a
couple of months, he may be closer to being able to interview for the next position. The goal is to help the person become a worker, and that can be accomplished without the person becoming good at job interviewing. Some people
have difficulty advocating for themselves and the interview could be a barrier
to gaining employment without assistance.

   *In the first few meetings, the employment specialist and client spend time get-
ting to know each other and identifying what the client wants to do.*

Illustration 9: Meg, Engaging with an Employment Specialist Outside the Mental Health Center

Meg is 45 years old and lives with her husband. During her 20s, she worked in
a number of jobs, from travel agent to furniture salesperson, but psychotic
episodes almost always occurred after several months on the job, and she
eventually gave up on trying to hold a job. In the past 5 years, her relationship
with her husband has deteriorated badly. On several occasions, she went on
spending sprees, which sometimes included purchasing extravagant travel
packages.

   She has been a client at a community mental health center in a midsized city
for 4 years and treated for schizoaffective disorder. Last year, she worked for a
few months in the center's sheltered workshop. Although the workshop experience initially boosted her self-esteem, because she saw that she was more
skilled than many of the people in the workshop, she still experienced the same
type of increased symptoms that had always followed within a few months of
beginning any of her jobs in the past.

   Periodically, Meg's case manager would ask her about the possibility of a
part-time job. She usually replied that she was not ready. But, on one occasion,
she agreed.

The employment specialist contacted Meg and suggested that they meet somewhere outside of the mental health center, at her home or another place where she felt comfortable. Meg suggested the park near her home. They began meeting in the park that was located in the center of the city's shopping district. The goal was to get to know each other, and establish a relationship outside of the agency. For the next month the employment specialist and Meg met once or twice a week. They talked about Meg's interest in working and her skills and strengths, thereby slowly building Meg's confidence and developing trust. As a result of these discussions, the employment specialist suggested a job in one of the small clothing boutiques among the stores and shops surrounding the park.

Meg memorized the stores they passed during their walks in the park and started to memorize the products and clothing in the window displays. She began to talk about the type of job she wanted and, perhaps even more important, the types of jobs she didn't want. It turned out that she was not interested in the employment specialist's suggestion of working in a clothing boutique. Instead, she was interested in an import furniture store that they passed on their walk. Meg wanted to inquire about job openings on her own and try to arrange interviews. She discussed with the employment specialist what she would say and possible questions she might be asked.

Two weeks later, Meg was working as a sales assistant in the import furniture store. She continued to have difficulties with symptoms, but was able to keep working by her own determination and the support she received from her treatment team and husband.

In this example, the employment specialist met with Meg away from the mental health center and focused on goals at a pace that was comfortable for Meg.

The employment specialist and the client build a working relationship that supports their collaborative efforts toward employment. The employment specialist takes cues from the client about how quickly she wants to proceed in actually securing a job. Some clients choose to investigate different types of jobs before directly trying to obtain a job.

The key to vocational engagement is getting to know the client as she is. The employment specialist listens carefully to what the client wants. In order to understand the client's world, the employment specialist, with the client's permission, may visit her home, family, and friends. The employment specialist and the client often meet in the community so that the employment specialist can learn how the client lives and relates to others. Observing a person outside of the mental health center leads to important insights about what motivates her and about the barriers that may stand in the way of employment. These insights help in vocational planning. In addition, the employment specialist's willingness to leave the clinic and enter the client's world demonstrates respect and helps the client to feel understood. The employment specialist spends many hours each week visiting her clients around their jobs, in their homes, in public places such as restaurants, coffee shops, parks, malls, libraries, and museums.

This is not meant to suggest, of course, that the employment specialist never meets with clients in the office. There are times, particularly when the employment specialist and the client are in the midst of a job search, when the need for telephones, computers, and paperwork makes the office the logical place to meet and do business.

Typically, the first couple of appointments are held at the office. This is particularly true when clients are new to the agency. The employment specialist consults with the team members to find out if anyone has visited the client in her home and whether there are any safety issues. To visit people in their homes, outside of the agency, the employment specialist needs to be aware of basic safety practices. The spouse of one client, for example, became angry and irritated when someone from the mental health center visited their home. In general, employment specialists meet with people whom they do not know well in public places. The employment specialist asks the client about suggestions where to meet and visits the meeting site in advance to be sure that it is a location that is safe and where conversation can be private.

Maintaining the relationship is important throughout the employment process. If a client begins to miss appointments or appears to lose interest in seeking work, the team and the employment specialist assess whether he is still engaged with the vocational service. They evaluate what is happening. For example, the client may feel that the employment specialist is not listening to what he is saying or what *his* goals are. If the client disappears or disengages, outreaching to the client is often helpful. An outreach plan is developed that could include telephone calls, letters, home visits, and community outreach. The employment specialist attempts to locate the client and find out what has happened. Was there a misunderstanding or a miscommunication, or was there another reason for disengaging? Finding out the reason can be difficult, especially with clients who are inarticulate and unassertive. People with poor communication skills sometimes have difficulty with engagement and, likewise, may be vulnerable to disengagement. If the employment specialist is unable to locate the client, other members of the team may know what is going on and be in a better position to talk to the client. It is a good idea for employment specialists to discuss with clients in advance what they want the employment specialist to do if they seem to be disengaging.

Some programs discontinue services after a client misses a certain number of appointments—three or four, for example. In IPS, the employment specialist continues to reach out to the client. Engagement is especially important during difficult periods when motivation appears to flag or relapse occurs.

In IPS programs, staff members never say, "We can't help him any more. He is not motivated." The employment specialist never says, "I can't provide services to her because she is drinking alcohol every day." The IPS employment specialist and treatment team continue to help the person with work despite the symptoms a person is having. We assume that working is what helps some people gain greater control over their symptoms. Even while the person is experiencing difficulties, the team looks at the positive aspects of the person and builds on her successes.

The employment specialist and the treatment team help the client to clarify his life goals and barriers to achieving them. For example, one person was able to see that when she did not take medication, she had increased auditory hallucinations that told her she was a bad person and should not work. She wanted to work and therefore decided to take the medication.

One clinician remembered that one of the people on her caseload periodically experiences increased anxiety and paranoia. Although she appeared to function poorly when she visited the community mental health center, the employment specialist reported that at work she was able to concentrate and remain focused on her work tasks during these periods of increased symptoms. The message to the client is, "We are interested in your abilities and in what you can do and want to do." The team conveys hope. Many clients have lost hope for the future and what they can do. The role of the team is to develop hope for that person. The goal is to listen for what a person wants to do and his ideal job and then help to identify small, doable steps that the person can achieve.

Sometimes a client will say he wants to take a break from working. He may feel frustrated from a job experience and not want to jump into another job. At these times, many clients say they want to maintain some contact with the employment specialist, but less frequently, perhaps once every month or two. Clients say that they are much more likely to reengage around work if they continue to meet with the employment specialist. Some contact, even when infrequent, still sends a message that the employment specialist believes that the client can work.

Interviewing Skills

Interviewing skills that the employment specialist brings to the process affect the nature of the alliance between the client and the employment specialist as well as the process for gathering relevant information. The following section describes basic elements of good interviewing.

Good interviewing begins with active listening, asking open-ended questions, reflecting back, reframing, and pointing out the person's strengths. Through interviewing, the employment specialist develops a respectful, collaborative working relationship with the client, gathering information and facilitating vocational planning. The employment coordinator provides training and ongoing supervision for the employment specialist to learn effective interviewing skills. There are numerous texts that cover interviewing skills. *The Skilled Helper* (Egan, 1986), *Motivational Interviewing* (Miller & Rollnick, 1991), and *The Strengths Model: Case Management with People Suffering from Severe and Persistent Mental Illness* (Rapp, 1998) are resources that describe these ideas in detail.

An effective way to begin an interview and build rapport is making positive statements about a person. When making genuine statements that compliment an individual about an achievement, a personal style, or way of presenting, the employment specialist conveys a sense of appreciation for the person and sets a tone of respect and optimism. Throughout the working relationship, the employment specialist routinely points out positive efforts and experiences to give the person encouragement and hope. Especially when a person is feeling overwhelmed, fearful, or hesitant, a reminder of what he has done well can offer a big boost.

Personal disclosure (i.e., the employment specialist provides personal anecdotes and thoughts) is generally not recommended when interviewing clients. Although it sometimes is helpful, it usually redirects the focus of the interview away from the client and on to the employment specialist. *Employment specialists instead use a more generalized approach to disclosure, remarking that the client's experience is similar to that of others.* For example, when discussing fears about working with a new supervisor, the employment specialist could say, "Many people feel anxious when they start working with a new supervisor. They don't know what to expect."

During an interview, employment specialists want to avoid asking questions that elicit a "yes" or "no" response that provides limited information. Instead, employment specialists ask open-ended questions that encourage a person to give a more elaborate response. For example, instead of asking "Did you like working as a cashier?" the employment specialist asks, "Please tell me about your job as a cashier? What aspects did you like about the job and what aspects did you not like?" These sets of questions elicit more information. It often helps to ask for additional information, such as, "Would you tell me a little more about that?" and "What else would you like to tell me about that?" Open-ended questions are valuable because the response reveals whether the question was understood.

Reflective listening is used to build a relationship as well as to validate that the interviewer/employment specialist has heard correctly what the person is saying. *Reflective listening involves repeating back or paraphrasing to an individual what he has just said.* Another advantage of reflective listening is that it allows the interviewee to hear what he has said and gives him an opportunity to clarify further what he means. For example, a man described angrily how his boss had criticized his work in front of his coworkers and the man didn't like it. The employment specialist responded, "You didn't like how your boss made comments about your work performance in front of other workers." The client then clarifies, "That's right. I don't mind that he is commenting on how I can do my job better. But I don't like him doing it in front of my coworkers." In this example, the employment specialist used reflective listening by paraphrasing what he heard the client say. The client clarified further for the employment specialist that he was upset about being corrected in front of other workers more than the criticism itself.

The employment specialist responds to how a person is feeling with empathy. An empathic statement includes feeling words that describe the emotion that the person is experiencing. In the previous example, the employment specialist could say, "You feel angry because you don't like being criticized in front of others." The interviewer identifies the emotion that a person is *currently* feeling about what he is saying. Empathic statements help to communicate that the interviewer understands the situation and how the person is feeling. These statements can lead to problem solving. Continuing with the example above, the client might say, "To prevent this situation from happening again, I will thank my boss for his advice and ask him if we can meet privately to discuss how I am doing at my job."

Employment specialists avoid giving advice. Direct advice tends to shift the focus from the client coming up with his own solutions to those offered by the employment specialist. When offering advice, expectations are established that the client may not want to follow. The client may resent these expectations, particularly if the advice was unsolicited. Advice-giving tends to foster dependency, whereby the client relies on what the employment specialist recommends. The employment specialist instead wants to encourage the person to find solutions. She helps the client to identify different options for resolving the problem and the advantages and disadvantages of the options.

The employment specialist may disagree with a client's plan. The employment specialist tells a client why she disagrees but continues to show that she values and supports the person. In the exceptional situation when someone's safety is at risk, however, the employment specialist takes necessary actions to keep people safe.

Disagreements should never lead to conflict. The employment specialist avoids struggling with a client over issues when they disagree. Conflict occurs when emotions rise and the disagreement is not resolved. People learn best from their own experiences rather than from advice. For example, the person who wants to be a telephone marketer, but has poor verbal and speech skills, may be persuaded more by feedback from a potential employer than by what the employment specialist recommends. Even when the employment specialist believes she is correct and is looking after the client's best interest, the employment specialist recognizes the client's right to make mistakes and learn from her own experiences.

The employment specialist helps to keep the interview focused. She redirects the discussion if they stray from the general topic. But, at the same time, she is always listening for cues from the client about areas of interest that could relate to job choices. Her responses encourage the person to elaborate on expressed interests. For example, "You seem interested in animals and pets. What experiences have you had with animals and pets? How might you be more involved with animals in terms of a job?"

Interviews take place in many different settings because employment specialists meet with clients mostly outside of the mental health office. If the employment specialist drives a client to visit job sites, conversations they have in the car can reveal information about the client that relate to job possibilities. For example, a client started talking about the construction equipment that he noticed at a building site as he drove by with his employment specialist. The employment specialist inquired about his knowledge of construction equipment, which led to a discussion revealing a work experience the client had forgotten to tell the employment specialist. This small clue eventually led to a job offer at a construction equipment company.

Closing the interview and identifying the next steps helps the employment specialist and the client to review how they are using their time toward the client's goals. The employment specialist or the client summarizes what they discussed during their meeting. They decide when they are going to meet again, how they will spend time during the next meeting, and what each of them agrees to do related to the client's employment goals before the next meeting.

Utilizing good interviewing skills, employment specialists develop positive alliances with clients that foster growth. An overall effective counseling method is *motivational interviewing.* The goal of motivational interviewing is to help the person identify what she values and her goals. The interviewer/employment specialist asks questions that help the client clarify what is important to her and the barriers that are interfering in achieving her goals. Motivational interviewing was originally described as a method for helping people with addictions make changes in their life (Miller & Rollnick, 1991). Employment specialists and treatment team members use motivational interviewing as a way to help clients clarify their goals and begin to make plans on how to achieve the goals. If someone shows a lack of interest or initiative in the employment process, the employment specialist and the client review the meaning of work for the client. If the case manager, employment specialist, and family members are the ones who believe the client would benefit from work, but the client does not, the job search may be premature.

Strengths assessment is another approach for identifying what a person does well and relating it to employment. The goal is for the client and the practitioner to collect information on personal and environmental strengths. An excellent resource for all community mental health staff is *The Strengths Model: Case Management With People Suffering from Severe and Persistent Mental Illness* (Rapp, 1998).

Overall, when working with individuals, the person is viewed and treated as a whole person. The person is not the illness. She is not "a schizophrenic." Instead, the person is someone with skills and strengths who also has an illness. Language plays a large role in influencing the stigma around mental illness. Employment specialists use person-centered language. When talking to a client or family member, they try to avoid mental health jargon, instead speaking in plain language that is culturally sensitive. The employment specialist must have knowledge about cultural factors that affect language, beliefs, and types of support. Hope is always encouraged. The employment specialist encourages people to have dreams and to help make those dreams happen. A good check for the employment specialist is to ask herself, "Is this how I would want to be addressed? If she was one of my loved ones, is this language that I would want her to hear?"

Linkage with State Vocational Rehabilitation

When starting an IPS program, the employment specialists establish a relationship with the local Vocational Rehabilitation (VR) office. Vocational Rehabilitation is referred to in different states by different names, such as the Office of Rehabilitation Services, Bureau of Vocational Rehabilitation, or Division of Vocational Rehabilitation. Through the authority of a federal program, people who have a barrier to employment caused by a disabling condition are eligible for VR services. The 1973 Rehabilitation Act emphasized serving people with the most severe handicaps, that is, people who were previously seen as unlikely to benefit from VR services. Eligibility for services ends when a person demonstrates the ability to stay employed.

VR counselors can purchase services, arrange services from other agencies, and provide guidance and counseling, Clients in the IPS program can benefit from a variety of VR services. For example, training, situational assessment, job shadowing, job-related equipment and supplies, tuition, placement, planning, and support are available for people with a psychiatric disability who have a work goal. Services are individualized.

Some mental health agencies obtain vendorship status with VR and portions of the IPS service are paid for and coordinated with the VR counselor. *One of the most effective ways to create a working relationship with VR is simply to have a VR counselor meet every week or two with referred clients and the employment specialists, preferably at the mental health center, so staff and clients become familiar with the VR counselor.* In some cases, the employment specialist is co-hired by the mental health agency and VR (Johnson & Johnson Community Mental Health Program, 2002) to join the treatment team and provide coordinated services.

VR and mental health agencies share the same goal of helping clients find and hold jobs, and thereby increasing their independence and ability to be productive members of society. Although historically the two state systems (VR and Mental Health) sometimes have had difficulty collaborating, there are many collaborative initiatives that show positive outcomes. Developing positive working relationships between the employment specialists and the VR counselors promotes coordinated and seamless employment services for clients.

When planning an IPS program, consider ways of building a relationship with VR, a relationship that will emphasize the understanding of shared goals and collaboration. Inviting a VR counselor and VR supervisor to attend planning meetings for starting an IPS program begins to establish a way of working together. Mental health agency staff members are able to build positive working relationships if VR counselors are assigned to work with the agency. The VR counselor helps educate the employment specialists and the treatment team about VR referral procedures. The VR counselor meets with clients, the employment specialists, and other staff to review clients' progress. Employment specialists find that there are many ways to collaborate with VR, and that a productive relationship can open up numerous opportunities.

Illustration 10: Arthur, Receiving IPS and VR

Arthur was referred to the IPS program for support in obtaining a competitive job in the area of retail sales of men's clothing. After an initial meeting with the IPS worker and the case manager, the client and the IPS worker met with a VR counselor and developed a plan in which the IPS worker would help Arthur to contact employers. When Arthur and the IPS worker met with the employer of a leading men's clothing store, the employer expressed interest but some hesitation in hiring Arthur. The VR counselor suggested offering a situational assessment to the employer. In a situational assessment, wages for the employee are paid by VR for 2 weeks with the understanding that the employer has a position for the client if the client demonstrates the skills necessary for the job. Arthur completed the 2-week situational assessment period, proved his ability to carry out the job duties competently, and was hired for the job.

When working with other agencies, such as VR, the Department of Employment Security, or home health care agencies with visiting nurses, the goal is for everyone to plan *together* with a client. It is confusing for a client to hear one message from one agency and another contradictory message from another agency. Just as services within a community mental health center need to be integrated so that all staff members understand and support the same plan, multiple agencies also try to integrate services at the client level. *Regular communication that facilitates coordinated planning among all service providers promotes seamless, effective services for people.*

Understanding Benefits and Financial Planning

One of the first topics that the client and the employment specialist talk about is benefits. People are eligible for benefits based on disability status and level of income. Examples of benefits are Supplemental Security Income (SSI), Social Security Disability Insurance (SSDI), health insurance such as Medicaid and Medicare, and Section 8 housing certificates. Fear of losing benefits is the main reason that people are reluctant to consider employment. In particular, people worry about losing their health insurance if they go to work. They may have valid concerns about getting a job, losing benefits, and then perhaps losing the job and being without any income or health insurance. In many cases, however, people do not have enough information about how work income will affect their benefits. *It is critical that people are given accu-*

rate information and are helped to understand exactly what will happen to their benefits when they start working. Employment specialists, therefore, must stay up-to-date about this information. The rules are complicated and changes are not infrequent.

The Ticket to Work and Work Incentives Improvement Act was signed into law in December 1999. The law allows for people with severe mental illness on SSI or SSDI to return to work while retaining their government-sponsored health insurance. Implementation of this law varies from state to state. Employment specialists need to be knowledgeable about the rules concerning benefits, including incentives for people to return to work, in their area, to make certain that the client understands his benefit package and how different levels of income will change Social Security payments, housing assistance, health insurance, and other benefits. People need accurate information about how benefits are affected in order to make good decisions about working, weekly hours, wages, and so on.

The employment specialist becomes acquainted with the agencies that disperse benefits, and assists a client step by step through the changes, doing everything possible to help the client understand the changes. Sometimes the employment specialist and client visit the Social Security Administration office so they can speak to someone directly about individual circumstances. But even when it seems that a person understands changes in benefits due to working and accepts those changes, the employment specialist is ready to review the changes after the client receives the first benefit check with a smaller than normal figure.

The employment specialist writes out examples of how benefits are affected when working at different hourly wages for different amounts of time. A person can then determine, for a certain hourly wage, how many hours she wants to work. Computer programs are available in which information about a person's benefits and different work options are entered and calculated. The employment specialist and client keep copies of the information as a helpful reference tool during the job search. With accurate information, clients can make informed decisions.

Some mental health agencies hire benefits specialists who explain to each client how their particular package of benefits will be affected by working. There are different rules for Supplemental Security Income, Social Security Disability Insurance, Medicaid and Medicare, Section 8 housing certificates, and other state benefits. In most cases, people are able to work some amount of time and still be ahead financially and not lose their health insurance.

The Social Security Administration Redbook is a summary guide for people under SSDI and SSI, which can be viewed on line at www.ssa.gov/work. We will not attempt to describe here the different types of benefits that people have. It is the responsibility of the IPS coordinator to ensure that all the employment specialists are knowledgeable about benefits and work incentives (e.g., Impairment-Related Work Expense [IRWE], Plan for Achieving Self-Support [PASS]) and talk about them with the people on their caseloads. People need this information to make informed decisions about how much they want to work.

People who receive Social Security benefits submit work payment stubs regularly to the Social Security Administration office after they gain employment. Failure to report earnings can result in the Social Security Administration demanding repayment of overpaid benefits. People who receive Section 8 housing also are required to submit work stubs to document their earnings. The employment specialist is available to guide people through this process.

Disclosure of Disability

A second topic that the employment specialist and client discuss during the first few meetings is whether the client wants to disclose her disability status to an employer. After deciding to disclose, the employment specialist and the client decide how much information to disclose and under what circumstances. Unless the client is requesting a specific accommodation to a job (which requires disclosure of the illness to the employer in order to be covered by the Americans with Disability Act), the employment specialist and client may end up never discussing the illness with the employer. But in order to talk to employers on behalf of the client, the employment specialist needs permission from the client. To talk openly with employers, employment specialists need to be able to identify where they work and in what capacity.

Issues around disclosure are discussed between the employment specialist and the client prior to the job search. The client weighs the advantages and disadvantages of disclosing the illness. Some individuals with mental illness view the involvement of the employment specialist with employers as critical support. For example, the employment specialist can contact employers directly for job searches, advocate for accommodations if necessary, and provide information about symptoms and coping strategies if necessary. Other individuals prefer not to disclose because they fear they will be treated differently from other employees because of the stigma and lack of knowledge about mental illness among the general population.

Some individuals initially choose not to disclose but change their minds after they have been working in a job. If it becomes clear to a client who is working that a job accommodation would be helpful, she may go ahead and disclose the disability to the employer. Refer to chapter 10 for more information about job accommodations.

The employment specialist needs to educate clients that there are degrees of disclosure, that is, how much information is provided to the employer. In some cases, the employment specialist may encourage an individual not to disclose certain information. For example, some clients have become used to talking about their illness and symptoms with staff at the mental health agency where they receive services, but details about the illness may not be necessary for employers. An authorization for release of information form is used to specify what information the client releases and to whom. For vocational purposes, the release form may include employers, the Social Security Administration, and other agencies the employment specialist may relate to on behalf of the client. The form indicates what information is released and the specific purpose, for example, job search, benefits planning, job support. Typically, release of information forms are valid for up to a year unless revoked by the client. The form indicates that the client is voluntarily releasing the information.

Family Involvement

The third topic addressed with the client early in the process is the level of family involvement. Has someone at the agency had contact with the client's family? Does the client want the employment specialist to have contact with the family? How do the family members view mental illness? How do they see work fitting into the client's life? Some people do not have family members with whom they have regular contact. But, for many, family members play a significant role as to whether they support the person's work efforts. Families often provide helpful information around the family member's coping strategies, interests that may relate to jobs, and employer contacts.

Employment specialists may have had no training for working with families. The employment coordinator provides supervision to employment specialists on working with families in relation to clients' work goals. In most cases, the employment specialist works closely with the case manager and the rest of team on how to involve the family.

Timing the Employment Initiatives

Many people with severe mental illness find that working at a job provides structure and focus that can help them cope with fluctuating symptoms of the illness. If a client is experiencing increased psychiatric symptoms or a relapse in substance use and says that she does not want to work, the team may not focus on employment at that time, but instead encourages her to look forward to future vocational successes.

Mental health agency staff members have successfully engaged people with dual disorders (severe mental illness and substance use disorder) in vocational planning at times when substance abuse has caused serious problems in major life areas such as health, housing, family, and social relations. At these times, people are at a juncture and may want to make a life change. Their lives have been compromised to a point where they may welcome assistance in changing. Unfortunately, their addictions may involve such ingrained, compulsive behavior that clients are at risk of returning to substance abuse despite good intentions to change. Many people feel hopeless and unsure of their ability to change. Yet, work is a goal for people with dual disorders as well as for those with single disorders of severe mental illness. Instead of confronting the alcohol and drug abuse directly, the team encourages the client to identify goals and the barriers to achieving them. In this manner, the person may realize that his substance use is an interference in his life. Employment provides a structure that can help clients avoid old patterns and develop new ones. Once people have a positive job experience, they often start to believe in themselves and their self-image begins to improve. They realize that they can change, and work becomes a reason to be sober.

Illustration 11: Sarah, a Person with Co-Occurring Substance Use Disorder

Sarah is a 44-year-old woman with diagnoses of bipolar disorder and substance use disorder (alcohol dependence and cocaine dependence). She had 9 years of experience as a tester and quality-control worker. During the last year of her job, she started using cocaine and alcohol and missed many days of work. Eventually, she was fired for absenteeism.

Sarah looked for another job. She saw an ad in the paper for a light-assembly position. She applied for and got the job. Her case manager and psychiatrist wanted her to meet with an employment specialist but she refused. She was fearful that the employment specialist would contact the employer, and, as she had found the job on her own, she felt she could handle it by herself.

Within several months of the job, parts of Sarah's life began to unravel. Her telephone was disconnected because she did not make monthly payments. She lost her apartment for not paying the rent. She sold all her personal belongings for drugs and was fired from the job.

Sarah was referred to the community mental health center's continuous treatment team for case management services. She began meeting with the employment specialist on the treatment team. During their first couple of meetings, the employment specialist asked Sarah about her interests, experiences, skills, and so on. Sarah revealed her love for photography. Many years earlier, she had taken a course in photography. Putting ideas together, and following a personal contact, the employment specialist set up an internship for her with an independent TV station, where she edited film and photographed news.

Sarah liked her job, and her supervisor told the employment specialist that Sarah's work performance was excellent. Sarah also participated in the agency's dual diagnosis services, such as counseling with her case manager and dual diagnosis groups for support regarding her substance use. Sarah was willing to participate in dual diagnosis treatment because she loved her job and didn't want to risk losing it because of drug use.

For Sarah, focusing on employment while receiving dual diagnosis treatment was beneficial. She worked a job that she enjoyed and accepted support from the treatment team. At the same time, she learned how to live without using drugs and alcohol.

Work can be a motivator for people to accept supports in other parts of their lives. Without addressing the substance abuse problem, it was likely that Sarah would have had difficulty working continuously.

The employment specialist helps the client balance work with the other aspects of her life. Someone who is in the process of job searching but must make an unexpected housing move may decide that focusing on finding a job and a new housing situation at the same time feels too intense. She may decide to back off from the job hunt until she settles the housing dilemma. In these situations, the employment specialist spends less time with the client but remains in contact so they can resume the job search when her housing problem is resolved. Each person manages his circumstances in his own way, so what works for one person may not work for another. The employment specialist must stay flexible and focus on what the client wants to do, which may be somewhat different from what the employment specialist has in mind.

9

Comprehensive, Work-Based Assessment

The goal of the assessment phase in the employment process is to understand what the client wants to do and who that person is in terms of strengths, skills, interests, and experiences in order to support him in obtaining a job that is a good fit for him as well as the employer.

Vocational Profile

The employment specialist begins to put together a vocational profile as soon as she receives a referral. She gathers written information from different sources such as the client record and any other documentation and interviews lots of people. The employment specialist meets with the client, other team members and, with the client's permission, also talks with family members and previous employers. The goal is to gather information that formulates a picture of the person and to promote ideas for a good work situation for the individual. Traditional approaches to assessment and evaluation, such as standardized pencil-and-paper tests, vocational evaluation, or work adjustment activities prior to acquiring a job are deemphasized. Just because a person is able to type and handle phone calls in the office of the community mental health center does not mean she will be able to do the same thing in the office of the United Boxboard Co. 10 miles away.

Illustration 12 lists the main ingredients of a vocational profile.

Illustration 12: Vocational Profile

Work Goal
- client's work goal and life dream for work
- client's short-term work goal

Work Background

- education
- licenses and certifications
- work history
  previous jobs (titles, duties, dates, hours per week)
  reasons for leaving jobs
  positive experiences
  problems on jobs

Current Adjustment

- diagnosis and prodromal symptoms
- symptomatology and coping strategies
- medication management and medication side effects
- physical health
- endurance
- grooming
- interpersonal skills
- support network

Work Skills

- job-seeking skills
- specific vocational skills
- aptitude
- interests (vocational and nonvocational)
- motivation
- work habits relating to attendance, dependability, stress tolerance

Other Work-Related Factors

- transportation
- support from family and friends
- current living situation (type and with whom)
- substance use
- criminal record
- willingness to disclose mental illness
- expectations regarding personal, financial, and social benefits of working
- money management skills
- income and benefits (Social Security, medical insurance, housing assistance)
- daily activities and routines
- regular contacts
- family members' work history
- preferences for work setting, type of tasks, time of day, weekly hours, and wages
- two forms of identification (e.g., birth certificate, driver's license, state ID card)

Networking Contacts for Job Search

- family
- friends
- neighbors
- previous employers
- previous teachers
- community contacts

The client is usually the best source of information, but gathering information from other sources (e.g., providers, family, friends, previous employers) gives a more comprehensive picture of who the person is. The information helps in matching the person to an individualized job situation and revealing job networking possibilities. In appendix 2, the vocational profile form includes probes for the employment specialist to use when talking with clients around the topic areas. It usually takes several weeks to gather initial information and document it on the vocational profile form.

In IPS, vocational assessment never ends. Each job experience gives both the client and the employment specialist new information and understanding about that person as a worker, which they apply to the next experience. The assessment is a process based on regular work experiences. Work-based assessment is ongoing and sends the message to everybody involved that it is a process of growth and learning rather than establishing a one-time, make-or-break job experience. *IPS assumes that the best type of vocational assessment is quite simply to find out how well the person does in a regular job in the community.*

A community mental health center vocational coordinator said, "In IPS, the whole process becomes the assessment tool. Everything the client does gives more information about what he likes, dislikes, and is capable of doing."

Vocational assessment for each client begins with the first meeting between the client and the employment specialist and does not end until the client leaves the IPS program. The client is continuously involved in learning about herself as a worker, finding the optimal job for herself at that time, and learning how to manage her own support system. Two weeks on a part-time job may bring the person closer to getting a 3-month, half-time job. The employment specialist routinely updates the vocational profile form in the client record.

The nature of the job setting is another important part of the job match. People excel in different types of work environments depending on their preferences, skills, vulnerabilities, and coping strategies. Listed below are aspects of the job setting that people consider when conducting job searches.

Illustration 13: Job Setting Factors

Coworkers

How many coworkers are there?
How near to each other do employees work?

What are the implicit social and interpersonal requirements in this work setting?

Do employees interact with each other, have breaks together, get together after work (possible social pressures to drink or use drugs)?

Supervisor

What is the nature of supervision?
How much and how often is supervision given?
Is the gender of the supervisor a concern for the client?
What is the personality style of the supervisor?

Work schedule

What are the work hours—time of day, number of hours, days of the week?
Is there flexibility for time off?
Are sick leave, holidays, and personal time included?

Work environment

What are the characteristics of the job setting (e.g., outside/inside, artificial lighting, noisy/quiet, hot, crowded spaces, isolated, odorous)?
What types of job stress may workers experience there (e.g., pressures from the public, related to the pace, noise, dangerous equipment)?

Wages

What are the wages and payment schedule?
How will wages impact on benefits (Social Security, medical insurance, housing benefits)?

Transportation

Is transportation necessary?
What are the transportation options to reach the employment site (e.g., close proximity to a bus line, carpool, within walking distance)?
Does the work schedule coincide with the public transportation schedule?
Does the transportation plan include going through unsafe neighborhoods?

When helping people find jobs, the employment specialist and the treatment team discuss how symptoms that a person experiences may be affected by the work conditions and the work environment. Individuals cope with symptoms in different ways in different situations and environments.

Employment specialists gather as much information as possible about a job. When visiting a job site, she asks for a tour of the employment setting. She assesses the skills and abilities required for all jobs that she is investigating for clients. What are the physical demands of the job? Is the job sedentary or is the person required to lift up to 50 pounds continuously, for example? What are the cognitive requirements for completing the job? Are technical skills required? What social interactions are part of the job and work environment?

The more information that the employment specialist and client have about the job, the better able they are to determine if it is a good job fit and how to prepare for work there.

The team discusses ways to encourage someone to work and find a good job match. Information obtained from team members and others who know the client well informs the assessment process. The case manager may know that the client has experienced increased anxiety in past jobs when working around a lot of people. The psychiatrist may have learned from the client that he really wants to be a computer programmer. The goal of vocational assessment is to put together information that leads to a well-crafted job match.

Illustration 14: Joel, a Person Finding a Good Match

Joel is a 29-year-old man who has a poor work history. He briefly held a few jobs in the last 10 years. Two years ago, he worked as a dishwasher in a restaurant. He was fired for drinking the leftover alcohol from glasses when they were returned to the kitchen.

Joel was not interested in working for the next year and a half, spending most of his time isolated in his apartment and abusing alcohol. The treatment team tried to engage him in recreational activities in order to develop interests other than drinking alcohol. Periodically, different team members talked to Joel about considering work again. One day, he agreed to try another job. It was unclear why at that particular moment Joel was willing to consider work. He told his employment specialist that he figured he might give it a try, as he had been hearing for so long from the team that they thought he could do it. Joel said that he would consider a dishwashing job. He knew that he could do this kind of work as he had dishwashing jobs in the past. The employment specialist and Joel talked about the kind of work setting that he wanted to be in. They both agreed that a work environment that was alcohol-free would be best. Joel wanted a job where there were not a lot of people, because when he is around others he begins to think they are conspiring against him, a symptom of his paranoid schizophrenia.

The employment specialist arranged a job washing lunch dishes at a children's daycare facility, 5 days a week for 3 hours a day. The job was within 10 minutes' walking distance of his home. Joel stayed in this job for 1 year without missing a day of work, the longest tenure in his life. During this time, he still drank alcohol after work, but his daily intake was reduced and he looked and felt better than any other time in the previous few years.

This example depicts how a good job match is developed. Joel needed an alcohol-free work environment. He accepted a part-time dishwashing job that was close to his home. His physical stamina was limited because of years of alcohol abuse, but he was able to manage 3 hours a day. He had held dishwashing jobs in the past, so he knew he could do the work. The employer was satisfied with Joel's work performance. He cleaned the kitchen well and did not miss a day of work. He liked the setting, location, people, work tasks, and so on. Joel's case manager continued to encourage him to participate in nondrinking social activities, such as playing cards with his buddies.

New information is learned from each job experience about a person as a worker that is added to the vocational profile. As clients experience symptoms from mental illness, they may be challenged in new ways as workers. When symptoms increase, people may not be able to carry out certain parts of their job. It does not mean, however, that the person must stop working. In fact, work often helps people cope with periods of worsening symptoms. Keeping the job may be what centers a person during difficult times.

Clients draw up plans in advance with the employment specialist regarding how they want to manage periods of increased symptoms at work. The plan outlines the best ways for them to get through these periods. The person may have learned what needs to change in order to keep working. For some people, it is helpful to discuss these changes in advance with the employer. For example, one person knows that, when he experiences increased paranoia, it is best that he is around one person with whom he feels safe. As a recreational director at a nursing facility, he reduces his contact with people and concentrates on the paperwork duties of his job. The recreational aide with whom he works takes over some of his group activities and people-oriented responsibilities.

Individual Employment Plan

Getting to know a client and compiling a vocational profile provides the information needed to put together an individualized employment plan. The plan is written as part of the person's overall service plan.

Ideally, the employment plan is clear and descriptive enough to give any employment specialist who does not know the client sufficient information to start working with the client at any time in a relatively smooth manner. *The employment plan sets a course of action and includes the client's goal, the steps to accomplish the goal, who is responsible for each step, and timing for each step.*

There are many formats for employment plans, but a typical plan has four sections. Illustration 15 outlines the components of the individual employment plan.

Illustration 15: Employment Plan Components

1. A statement of the client's vocational goals (both long-term and short-term) in the client's own words.
2. A list of behavioral objectives that outline how the client will meet his goals. For example, if the client wants to find a job as a cook, but has little or no experience, the objectives describe the steps the client plans to take. He might first look for work as a kitchen helper and perhaps then enroll in a class or a training program.

3. The names of people and the services and supports that will help the client achieve the objectives. Time frames for meeting the objectives are also listed.
4. The plan is signed and dated by the client, the employment specialist, the case manager, and the psychiatrist. If there are other people involved in the treatment plan, they sign the plan as well.

The plan includes specific information about the responsibilities of the client and of the employment specialist. A client might want her employment specialist to advocate on her behalf with employers, taking a very direct and major role in developing and negotiating the job with the employer. Another client might want the employment specialist to have some contact with the employer, but only when accompanied by the client. And a third client might want the employment specialist to stay as far behind the scenes as possible and serve mainly as a source for job leads. See appendix 1 for an example of an individual employment plan.

The plan is as specific as possible to guide the employment process and is shaped from information identified in the vocational profile. An error that employment specialists sometimes make is to write plans that are generic and vague. It is not uncommon to see employment plans that simply state a goal of obtaining part-time employment over the next 6 months and an objective of meeting with the employment specialist weekly to identify job leads. It also is not uncommon to see the identical plan for every client on the employment specialist's caseload. A good plan involves specificity. What exactly is the client's employment goal? Has information from the vocational profile been used to formulate the plan? How exactly will the client achieve the goal? For example, a clear, descriptive objective is: the client and the employment specialist will visit four nursing homes in the next 2 weeks to learn about the tasks of a nurse's aide position and the requirements needed to secure this position.

The plan is drawn up within the first month of referral to IPS and is updated at least quarterly. The employment plan is a working document that identifies a person's goals and steps to achieve the goals.

Monthly Progress Note

The third paperwork item that supports the employment process is a progress note that is written in the client record. In a paragraph or two, the employment specialist summarizes the activities that occurred during the past month. The summary addresses the goals and objectives as outlined on the employment service plan. The progress note serves to document progress and enhances the planning process, as well as to communicate information to other providers who are using the client record.

Some agencies require that the employment specialist write a note following every client contact. We recommend a monthly note to deemphasize paperwork. Of course, additional paperwork may be unavoidable, because of requirements of funding sources and certification agencies. Nevertheless, in IPS programs, the goal is to limit paperwork as much as possible to provide more time for employment specialists to work with clients.

Documentation procedures are designed to support and guide the client-centered employment process. The vocational profile and employment service plan are not just paperwork requirements but also useful guides that employment specialists use regularly. If the client, the employment specialist, or the team is unsure of a direction to take, the IPS supervisor reminds people to check back with the vocational profile and employment plan.

Employment specialists and other staff members are more likely to use documents if they are readily available in the chart. Some agencies color-code forms so they attract attention and are easy to find. The vocational profile and the employment service plan may be on light blue paper, for example. This way, they are easy to find in the chart. A psychiatrist, case manager, or any other staff person is more likely to look at a form that is easily accessible.

10

Finding Jobs

Competitive Jobs

Once the vocational profile and employment plan have been written, the next step is to find a job. In IPS, the job search process is a collaboration among the client, employment specialist, VR counselor, other members of the treatment team, family members, and other support persons as identified by the client.

Over time, some people with severe mental illness let their expectations drop lower and lower. In many cases, clinicians collaborate in this gradual deflation of possibility and potential. So the employment specialist may be the first person the client has met in years who holds realistically high expectations for what she can do.

Unlike more traditional vocational programs, IPS emphasizes obtaining competitive, permanent jobs rather than participating in job readiness activities (such as sheltered work, enclaves, transitional jobs, or volunteer jobs) prior to employment. Studies show that if the client's goal is competitive employment, the most successful way to reach that goal is through a rapid job search, deemphasizing prevocational assessment and training. Many clients who participate in sheltered work settings or work adjustment programs never move on to regular jobs even when competitive employment is the goal. *Every client needs to know that the goal of the IPS program is to help her start work in a community-based, competitive job of her choice as soon as possible, without being required to participate in prevocational activities.*

Rapid job search doesn't always mean getting a job right away. Rather, it means that the client and the employment specialist make contact with employers within the first month of referral to IPS. The nature of initial contacts with employers may not be to secure a specific job, but to gather more information about different jobs. It is important to work with a client at a rate comfortable for her in the job-seeking process. She can expect, however, that in IPS she will not be delayed in obtaining an independent job by prevocational training and assessment procedures.

What about the person who says that he first wants to try a volunteer job and eventually find a competitive job? The employment specialist and the client discuss reasons why the person prefers a volunteer job. They review how the responsibilities of a volunteer job and a competitive job are similar. In both volunteer and competitive jobs, the worker is expected to follow the agreed-on schedule and carry out the assigned tasks. If the client chooses to work in a volunteer job as a step toward competitive employment, the employment specialist will help him. Some people, however, decide that they do not want to earn money, for fear of losing benefits. People who want to volunteer and do not have a goal of competitive employment are not appropriate candidates for IPS services. Case managers or other staff members can assist people in finding volunteer jobs. Employment specialists are designated to spend time with the people who have a goal of obtaining competitive employment.

What about the person who wants to go to school to advance her career options? Employment specialists help people with educational goals in the same way that they do with employment goals. They help people develop an individualized educational plan and assist in carrying out the plan. Agencies decide whether they want specific staff people or all the employment specialists to provide supported education. In the same way that case managers help some people with employment goals, they also help people with educational goals. The employment specialists are used for those people who need more intensive assistance, both in employment and education. Supported education and supported employment are quite similar, and many clients have both employment and educational goals.

Throughout this part of the book, we refer to the importance of helping people obtain regular jobs as quickly as possible. Emphasis on that simple formula has as much to do with the expectations staff members hold for all clients as it does with the way any particular client takes advantage of the IPS program. Full-time competitive employment is not a goal for all people with severe mental illness. But, by contrast, the assumption that a person's mental illness will profoundly limit her ability to work is not appropriate, either.

Expectations of providers and others probably play a large role in the goals that clients have. Clients who are surrounded by people who do not believe that they can work will probably not seek employment. If no one else thinks a client can work, why should the client think she can work? Other people's expectations can give the hope and create the energy to overcome difficulties. Without the encouragement of others' high expectations, it is far too easy to stay in the same place and forego the risks of the unknown. The employment specialist and the other team members are in positions to help clients raise their own expectations. Supporting and believing in a person can have a powerful effect.

The situation that people with mental illness find themselves in with regard to work is often far more complex than simply having low expectations for what they can do. People's vocational development has almost always been interrupted by the illness. They may have been denied the understanding of how one job leads to another, of how an adult builds a career, or a series of careers, by combining interests, abilities, opportunities, education, and even lucky breaks. People with a severe mental illness are sometimes stuck in a kind of vocational adolescence, confused by their own expectations, by a series of setbacks, by limited or nonexistent job experience, low skills, or bad work habits.

Mental health workers have tended to reinforce clients' fears about jobs in the name of protecting them from stress and failure. Too much emphasis is placed on preparation, which only delays real experiences and the subsequent rewards and learning that go with them. Much time is spent trying to find out how ready people are for work by trying them out in artificially protected environments. Another problem is that staff workers find jobs that are well below people's interests or skill levels where they fail from boredom or lack of challenge.

If people in IPS programs and mental health agencies in general—staff and clients alike—understand that the overall expectation is that each client goes to work in a job that she selects as soon as she can, even for just a few hours a week, much of the overprotective, paternalistic relationship with clients can be avoided.

Obtaining Employment

As a worker, every person has a unique set of talents, interests, inclinations, difficulties, and challenges. The employment specialist and client find the best possible match between the person and a job. The client, rather than the employment specialist or anyone else, ultimately is the person who selects and works the job. He is more likely to take pride in his work and achievements if he has chosen the job rather than someone else making the choice for him.

The employment specialist helps a client think about job possibilities that are consistent with her idiosyncratic features. This is an individualized process. If the employment specialist helps people to get jobs only as maintenance workers, she is not helping people with individualized job searches based on their preferences, strengths, and skills. Even if lots of people express an interest in maintenance work, it is probably because that is the only job that they know about or the job that has been recommended to them in the past. The employment specialist helps a person to broaden his options. The employment specialist helps people to become knowledgeable about different types of jobs. If employment specialists are really following an individualized approach, less than 10% of the people will be in the same type of job. *People are more satisfied and job tenure is twice as long when people work in jobs consistent with their preferences as compared to people with jobs that do not match their preferences* (Becker, Drake, Farabaugh, & Bond, 1996; Mueser et al., 2001).

Similarly, if the employment specialist is helping four, five, or six clients to work at the same work site, he is not conducting individualized searches. There is a temptation to direct people to jobs, regardless of their preferences, because the jobs are available. Sometimes employment specialists fall into this trap, as they establish a good relationship with an employer who has a number of openings. *The IPS coordinator always listens for the reasons why an employment specialist is helping a person obtain a particular job at a certain work site.* Is it consistent with the client's preferences, strengths, and experiences?

Employment specialists are responsible for helping people find and keep jobs. But, at the same time, they are responsible for staying attuned to how a person's illness and other aspects of her life may be affecting her work. In fact, the IPS approach recognizes that attempts to categorize and separate the different aspects of a person's life can get in the way of helping the person lead a more normal life than he may have led in the past. A diagnosis of bipolar disorder may help a psychiatrist in prescribing medication, and it may help an employment specialist understand a person's behavior, but the diagnosis usually has little bearing on that particular individual's ability to work in a specific job. In other words, people with bipolar disorder do not make better cooks than people with schizophrenia. And people without severe mental illness are not necessarily better workers and employees than people with severe mental illness.

The interaction among all the dynamic aspects of an individual's life are complex, subtle, and changeable. Work affects mood and self-perception, which in turn affects interactions with other people, which may influence mood, which could affect the way a person with mental illness experiences his symptoms, which may affect his performance on the job, which may influence decisions he makes about his life, and so on.

People who have been diagnosed with severe mental illness and have become part of the mental health system have been labeled in a way that emphasizes their differences from people who do not have mental illness, rather than their likeness with other workers. The IPS method makes every attempt to emphasize the person's individuality, just like you would with anyone looking for a job. The first questions an employment specialist asks when she interviews a new client are the same questions any employment consultant in any employment agency asks: "What skills do you have? Where have you worked? How did you do in previous jobs? What unique talents and abilities do you have that would help you stand out from the crowd? What do you want to do?"

Figuring out a good match between an individual client and a particular job is a key part of the employment specialist's job. Putting everything together takes thoughtfulness, creativity, and persistence.

Illustration 16: Antonio, a Person with a Good Job Match

Antonio is a 45-year-old man who has been a client of a mental health agency for over 10 years. He attended the rehabilitative day treatment program until it was converted to an IPS-supported employment program. His case manager encouraged him to think about the possibility of working part time. Antonio told his case manager that he couldn't work, because he has schizophrenia and because he was helping to raise his two kids. He needed to be home every day when they came home from school, at 3 pm. The case manager explained to Antonio that going to work doesn't necessarily mean a 40-hour-a-week job, and that lots of people in the agency's supported employment program worked in part-time jobs, even for only a few hours a week.

Antonio agreed to meet one of the employment specialists to discuss the possibility of work. Over the next couple of weeks, the employment specialist met with Antonio several times, read his clinical record, and talked with Antonio's case manager and psychiatrist. The employment specialist learned that Antonio loved to drive his car. He also learned that he had attendance problems in past jobs. Antonio said, "No one ever appreciated me." The employment specialist found Antonio to be a sociable and likeable person.

Antonio said that he was willing to do any job. He didn't have one specific job in mind. The employment specialist suggested a job at Meals on Wheels, as a driver for the lunch delivery. Antonio was hired and loved it right from the start. Absenteeism was never a problem, as he knew that people were counting on him to help with meal delivery. The hours were perfect (10 am to 2 pm), so he could be at home when his kids returned from school. He became good friends with the other people at his job. He told his case manager that it was wonderful to be bringing home a paycheck again. And, best of all, he said, his kids saw him going to work just like their friends' dads.

The employment specialist uses information about a person's interests, skills, symptoms, and medication side effects to think about a good job match. If a person shouts back at auditory hallucinations, the employment specialist is not going to look for a library job for him, any more than an employment consultant would try to find work in graphic design for a person who is visually impaired.

In IPS, the treatment team works around the difficulties, challenges, and style a person has, rather than trying to change the person to fit into jobs. Selecting a job and a work setting that accommodates a person well is the ideal fit. In general, most people do better in their lives if they have a job they feel good about. Even when going through an extremely stressful time, people try to keep working because the job often counteracts the difficulties they are experiencing. *Work often helps people with mental illness cope with their symptoms in the same way that it can help all people through difficult times.*

IPS is designed to offer support to individuals to help them improve their own lives. Ultimately, it is the responsibility of the individual to help make his life better, but clients in IPS are given as much help as needed to support them in achieving their work goals. It is not the responsibility of the employment specialist or other team members to control, shape, mold, and fix people according to their own perception of what a "normal" person should be. If a person has a hygiene problem, does not want to correct it, and has never shown a willingness to improve his hygiene, the treatment team works around that issue. The employment specialist looks for a job for him where good hygiene is not a requirement. People may decide to improve their hygiene as they see it helps their chances of getting employed in a broader range of jobs. In this case, the motivation is the job and not the nagging mental health worker.

IPS emphasizes that the client has a lot of things right about him, and services are available to help strengthen the positive parts of his life. As one specialist said, "We work with a person's vocational potential, and we don't see the illness as an impediment. We ask, first of all, 'What does this person have that will interest an employer?' or even, 'What's here that might at least entice an employer to talk with the person?'"

Illustration 17: Paul, a Person Using Work-Based Assessment in a Job Search

Paul dresses carelessly in badly fitting, mismatched clothes. His hair is scraggly and dirty, he is usually unshaven, and he walks with an odd, shuffling gait. He talks softly, showing no emotion and making no eye contact. He is 32 years old. Since his mother died 2 years ago, Paul has been feeling despondent, drinking more heavily, and experiencing an increase in psychotic thinking. He has schizophrenia and is taking medication for it.

He receives services from a small community mental health center that assigns each client to a treatment team that coordinates all aspects of the person's service plan. After a review of Paul's situation, the team recommended that he meet with an IPS employment specialist. When meeting with the employment specialist, Paul seemed reluctant, but expressed some interest in cooking at a restaurant, a job he had held for a year when he was 22 years old.

Paul and his employment specialist began eating lunch several times a week at a local restaurant that the employment specialist believed was a good prospect for a job. The employment specialist made a point of chatting with the owner, talking about downtown business in general and the restaurant in particular.

He introduced Paul to the owner but did not mention that Paul was a client. His purpose was to simply establish a connection with the owner and to let the owner become familiar with Paul. The employment specialist thought that Paul's appearance might put people off on first encounter. The employment specialist felt that by regularly appearing with Paul in the restaurant, he would help the owner see Paul less as a patient with mental illness and more as an individual.

After a few weeks, the employment specialist approached the owner about the possibility of paying Paul to work in the kitchen for a few hours to see if he had the necessary culinary skills and work habits because he had not worked in a restaurant for many years. The owner agreed, and after 2 weeks offered a candid evaluation of Paul, saying that he lacked the necessary speed but seemed to have an adequate knowledge of cooking skills. The owner did not believe that Paul would be a good match for his restaurant because of the fast pace.

As the weeks went by, Paul began to take more interest in the possibility of working and began to look for jobs on his own. He started taking more care with his appearance. Still, the employment specialist worried that his flat affect and disheveled appearance prevented him from finding a job. Because Paul had difficulty securing his own job, the employment specialist offered to take a more active role in finding a cooking job. A few days later, the employment specialist found a job opening as a cook at a summer camp, and Paul landed the job. Paul enjoyed the job and the employer gave him a good reference when the camp closed at summer's end.

Paul found another opening, this time for a cook at a nursing home. He gave the lead to the employment specialist, who met with someone from the human resources department and described Paul's strengths. He briefly mentioned Paul's difficulty with interpersonal skills related to his illness. The employment specialist emphasized Paul's strengths and the employment specialist's availability to meet with Paul and the employer if any assistance and support were needed.

The director of the nursing home called Paul to schedule an interview. For the first time in the 9 months he'd been working with the employment specialist, Paul showed some excitement. He got a haircut and bought a tie. The employment specialist tied the tie for him, and he took it home that way so all he'd have to do in the morning was slip it over his neck.

After the interview, the director called the employment specialist with a few questions. He was interested in Paul, but was put off by his peculiar, detached manner. The employment specialist explained briefly some of the symptoms of Paul's illness that result in poor social skills but also emphasized his dependability and cooking skills.

"To put it simply," said the employment specialist, "I told the director that Paul cooks a lot better than he interviews." Paul got the job and did well.

Paul's story illustrates the teamwork that goes on between the employment specialist and the client and the role of work-based assessment in the job search process. The employment specialist may play a more active role in the beginning, but over time the client may take over some of the job seeking tasks. The employment specialist and the client discuss their different responsibilities. In this example, the employment specialist decided it would be better to let Paul realize that how he presents himself can make a difference. The employment specialist also believed that Paul needed an experience in a real kitchen to give him a taste of working.

The client carries out as much of the job search process as possible. If a lack of good interviewing skills becomes a barrier to gaining employment, the employment specialist offers to take the lead in contacting employers. The employment specialist contacts employers only after the client decides that she is willing to disclose her disability to employers.

Sometimes the employment specialist and the treatment team feel at an impasse around the job search. This may occur because they focus more on the person's problems and deficits than on her strengths and gifts and what she wants to do. At these moments, it is helpful to return to the vocational profile and employment plan.

A client sometimes finds a job that is very different from what she and the employment specialist identified through the vocational profile and employment plan. What happens when they agree to look for certain jobs based on the vocational profile, and the client applies for and is offered a very different type of job? For example, instead of finding a part-time position working outside with plants, one client accepted a full-time position as a telemarketer. Should the employment specialist counsel the person to decline the job offer because she and the team believe the position will cause stress and end poorly? Not usually. An employment specialist avoids telling people what they should and should not do. The employment specialist may reveal her feelings of surprise and describe areas of concern, but she needs to convey to the client that she continues to support him. *The employment specialist is nonjudgmental in her role, encouraging people to weigh the pros and cons of the different options and allowing them to learn from their choices and experiences.* In this particular example, the client started the job and quit within 2 days, because he felt stressed by the job and had not made any sales. The client felt badly that the job he had chosen had not worked out. The employment specialist talked with the client about what happened in the job, what he learned about himself as a worker, and what he would do differently next time.

Job Accommodations

Individuals who have a disability may request a reasonable accommodation from the employer to complete their job requirements. When the client, and sometimes the employment specialist, are negotiating a job with an employer, they identify job accommodations that will enable the client to carry out his job despite symptoms from the mental illness. Individuals are required to provide verification of their disability to the employer in order to receive a job accommodation. The Americans with Disabilities Act (ADA) requires employers with more than 15 employees to make reasonable accommodations to employ people with disabilities who would otherwise be qualified for the job. Some examples of accommodations are listed in illustration 18.

Illustration 18: Job Accommodations

Flexible work hours

Adjusting work schedule for appointments and medical leave
Availability of time off without pay

Availability of part-time work

More frequent breaks

Modification of work space and job tasks

Minimizing distractions and noise, providing space to work alone

Access to water/liquids

Gradual introduction of tasks

Modification of job tasks

Supervisor feedback and positive reinforcement

Ways the supervisor can support the client

Using written instructions

Onsite support

Pairing a client with another coworker for support and job assistance

Temporary onsite job coaching

Crisis intervention

Procedures for emergency situations

Telephone calls to employment specialists

Private space

To date, the cost of accommodations to employers for people with severe mental illness has been small. According to Granger and colleagues (1996), 90% of accommodations for people with mental illness cost less than $100.

MacDonald-Wilson and colleagues (2002) describe the importance of identifying functional limitations of the client to help determine the types of reasonable accommodations. In their study of 191 individuals with psychiatric disabilities in supported employment programs and 204 employers, they found that participants frequently had difficulties with interpersonal relationships, such as interacting with others and understanding social cues at work. Cognitive deficits, such as being unable to concentrate and learn new skills, also were identified. The most frequent job accommodation was the involvement of a job coach for support and training.

The employment specialist's role is to educate (and not alienate) employers about the ADA and job accommodations, and the challenges of her clients. The employment specialist evaluates the work site and job duties in relation to the client's disability. Some individuals choose to negotiate job accommodations with the employer without the involvement of the employment specialist.

Approaches to Job Search

There may be as many different strategies for finding jobs as there are employment specialists. But, regardless of the style an individual develops, the essential

strategy is to meet, talk, and network with people. An employment specialist in Connecticut said, "Meeting people is the most important thing that I do. The key to job development is meeting people. Occasionally I make phone calls but afterward I quickly meet with the employers in person." He continued, "First impressions with an employer are important. I always dress professionally, convey confidence in my work, and show a positive interest in working with employers to make good job matches." Employment specialists build networks and constantly deepen and expand them. They approach their work creatively and are adept at making the connection between a job and a person's skills and interests. Over time employment specialists develop a clientele of employers who have been well served by hiring their job applicants. These are the employers who have seen what the employment specialist does to address and smooth out problems. They can serve as references to other employers as well as a resource about other job leads. Invariably, employment specialists start getting calls from employers they already know who are looking for candidates for their job openings.

Employment specialists become more skillful with experience in connecting with employers and building a network. People who have been at the job for a while develop the ability to create a strategy for each client and to make small adjustments in strategy as they get new information. Employment specialists present to employers in a business-like manner and look to provide solutions to employers' problems.

The client decides how much involvement the employment specialist has in the job search. If the client is willing to disclose to an employer that she has a mental illness, the employment specialist can be involved directly in the job-seeking process. The employment specialist describes her role to the employer and can advocate for the client. The employment specialist provides information to the employer that is pertinent to the job applicant as a worker. If the employer is aware of a person's illness, the employment specialist assesses whether the employer has accurate knowledge about mental illness. The employment specialist tries to understand the employer's perceptions of the illness and offers educational information, if necessary. Employment specialists are in a good position to mitigate stigma around mental illness through their numerous contacts with employers. Just because a client is willing to disclose does not mean automatically that the client or the employment specialist will talk to the employer about the illness. The employment specialist and the client discuss beforehand in what circumstances it would be helpful to disclose information. Employment specialists only provide information that is relevant to the person's role as a worker.

Some people are supported through the employment process without the employment specialist having direct involvement with the employer. The person may still choose to disclose to the employer about her illness or she may decide to withhold that information. Each person learns over time what works best for him in terms of disclosure and in which situations.

One simple and straightforward process for finding and negotiating jobs is when the employment specialist, with the client's résumé in hand, approaches an employer about a specific job that matches a client's interests and capabilities. If the employer has talked with the employment specialist before, or is identified through a networking connection, in all likelihood the employer will be interested. "Employers don't like the unknown," said an experienced employment specialist. "They don't like to take chances. So the more they know and trust you, the more likely they are to hire the person that you are recommending." Another employment specialist completes a generic job application with each client. The client keeps a copy to which he can refer when filling out job applications. The employment specialist carries a copy of the application with him so he is always prepared to advocate for someone when job hunting.

In IPS, the approach to finding a job begins with the individual client. Other vocational rehabilitation programs may place more emphasis on compiling lists of existing jobs in the community, on the assumption that one or more of those jobs might be appropriate for the client. But, in IPS, the employment specialist usually works in the other direction. *Rather than trying to adjust the client to fit an existing job, he takes the client more or less as the person is, and goes out to find or develop a job that is suited to that person.* Sometimes the employer does not have an advertised opening, but is willing to consider creating a job if the employment specialist has done his homework well and makes a good match between the business and the client's skills. If there is a job opening, the employment specialist negotiates the job with the employer and suggests any adjustments that may enhance the match between the person and the job.

The job search is very specific. In other words, rather then devoting a lot of time and energy to going around to all the employers in the area developing a long list of jobs, the employment specialist and the client set out to find a particular job. Although it may be helpful to know about job openings when Paul is sitting in the office, presenting with his own very particular portrait of skills, interests, problems, and inclinations, that generic list of jobs is often useless. The employment specialist often starts with a specific employer, defining responsibilities, assessing the fit among Paul, the employer, the job, the coworkers, and so on.

Another advantage to a specific job search over a more generic job search is that an employer often will consider creating a position with a specific person in mind. For example, a person who had cashiering experience and was looking for a part-time job for 2 hours in the middle of the day wanted to work in a bookstore. When talking with the employment specialist, a bookstore owner realized that a new employee could free up a salesperson to work directly with customers during the busiest time of the day.

Illustration 19 shows how an employment specialist advocates for a client with an employer.

Illustration 19: Dialogue between an Employment Specialist and an Employer

> *Employment Specialist:* Hello. My name is Sammy Ramirez. I am a job developer for Work Opportunities Consultants. I was given your name by Michael Johnson at the Riverside Grille, where I have helped a couple of people get employed. I am working with a woman who is interested in finding a job as a cook. Marie Johnson has substantial work experience as a cook, as you can see on her résumé.
>
> *Employer:* Oh, yes. I know Michael. I told him that I need another cook. I see on her résumé that Marie has not worked for a while. Will she have problems if I hire her as a cook?
>
> *Employment Specialist:* Marie has been out of work for the past couple of years but is ready to work now. She is somewhat nervous about starting a job, but I am confident that you will find that she has good culinary skills. When you meet her, she may seem quiet, but that doesn't mean she is disinterested. Part of my job is to be sure that the employer is satisfied when hiring someone that I recommend. I will be available if you have any concerns.
>
> Marie would very much like the opportunity to talk with you about working in your restaurant. She has good cooking skills and works well with different types of people. She also is a flexible person so you will find that she always is willing to help out. I believe you will find her to be an asset to your business. Is there a time that is convenient that I could introduce Marie to you?

The employment specialist stresses positive aspects of the applicant, and includes information about her that may be relevant to her employment.

Sometimes the employment specialist makes an initial contact with a business without mentioning the candidate that she has in mind. The task is to find out more about the business and the specific jobs there. What is the employer looking for in job applicants? Will this be a good match between the employer and the job applicant? The employment specialist asks for a tour of the business to note the working conditions. During these visits it is important that the employment specialist presents professionally, in a friendly manner, and demonstrates a real interest in the business.

The employment specialist makes a point of being friendly to everyone at the business. In particular, she is friendly with the receptionist who often is in a critical position of determining who gets a chance to see the owner or the supervisor.

The employment specialist uses good listening skills and asks the employer his opinion about what will improve his business. She emphasizes to the potential employer that she is here to learn about his hiring needs so she can recommend qualified candidates. The employment specialist avoids asking at the beginning of the conversation if there are any job openings, as she will find out soon enough. She learns as much as possible to figure out what the employer needs in a job candidate. The goal is to keep the employer talking, get a foot in the door, and set up a follow-up visit. At the end of each employer contact, the employment specialist states the next step. When a client and/or an employment specialist meet with an employer about a job opportunity, it is courteous to send a brief thank you letter. Sample letters from employment specialists and clients are in appendix 4. These simple gestures often stand out in the minds of employers and may be what makes the difference when an employer chooses a work candidate.

Illustration 20 shows an employment specialist who is trying to find out more information about positions from an employer. The employment specialist may have someone in mind for the work site but is unsure until she obtains more information. She may decide not to describe a specific job candidate to the employer but opt instead to gather information about the business and develop a relationship with the employer.

Illustration 20: An Employment Specialist Engaging with an Employer

> *Employment Specialist:* Hello. My name is Marcia Gooding. I am an employment specialist and am gathering information about different businesses in this part of the city in order to be as knowledgeable as possible when recommending job applicants to employers. I have not visited your business before and would like to ask you a couple of questions about the types of positions you have here and the qualifications you look for in people to fill the positions. I have helped to fill positions with other employers in the same line of business but have not worked with you. I hope to correct that one day.

The employment specialist stays alert to how the employer is responding to her. Is he showing interest and encouraging her to continue talking? Some employers may brusquely turn the employment specialist away saying that there are no openings. And still others may show some doubt but allow room for the employment specialist to continue. Employers may have incorrect assumptions about people with special challenges, such as mental illness. The employment specialist does not want to argue his position with an employer, but instead present information that will educate the employer and hopefully modify her original belief.

Effective job development is a critical skill. *We recommend that IPS supervisors initially accompany employment specialists on visits to employers to model how to engage employers. The supervisor teaches the employment specialist the skills for effectively negotiating work opportunities for clients and then in turn observes the employment specialist talking to employers.* Asking the employment specialist to describe to the supervisor an interaction that has occurred between the employment specialist and an employer often does not reflect accurately what transpired. The supervisor needs to observe the employment specialist contacting employers directly to assess whether the employment specialist is using good communication and job development skills.

Employment specialists build their own strategies for finding and developing jobs based on clients' preferences and profiles, the local community and its economy, and creative solutions to specific challenges. Good strategies tend to have one element in common: understanding and sensitivity to the individual client. The employment specialist constantly reviews whether she is listening to what the client is saying and helping her to pursue the client's goal. The next section describes some of the strategies that IPS employment specialists use to successfully locate jobs.

Strategies for Locating Jobs

Newspaper Employment Ads

Newspaper ads can be a productive source of job leads. Because the ads are available to lots of job seekers, however, there are usually lots of applicants for each position. The want ads are just one source for job leads, as many job opportunities are never advertised in local papers. Employment specialists usually read the ads daily, just to stay in touch with the types of jobs that are floating to the surface of the market through the ads.

Employment specialists typically scan the rest of the newspaper looking for other job possibilities. The sports page, for example, includes the game schedule for the city's professional baseball team, which reminds an employment specialist of all the jobs at the ballpark. Headline stories of new stores coming to town, the opening of a nursing home, and other such business news indicate upcoming job openings.

Contacting Employers Directly

Many employment specialists visit an employment site during a slow time of the day. Whether the employment specialist is prospecting for a job possibility, carrying a client's résumé, or inquiring about an actual job opening, he uses his best judgment about how to get to talk directly with the employer or hiring supervisor. Face-to-face is best. It is too easy for busy employers to say no to an unknown voice on the telephone. Taking the time to figure out who is doing the hiring and how to access that person often pays off. Getting by the receptionist can be the biggest hurdle of all. He is stationed in part to protect managers and supervisors from time-consuming interruptions such as job seekers. The employment specialist is friendly with everybody she meets, trying to build relationships and alliances.

The employment specialist needs to be prepared for what she wants to say to an employer. Time is valuable. Job developers know that if they can keep an employer from saying no in the first minute, the job developer will get a much better hearing and the employer will be more open to what he has to say. The employment specialist identifies why she is contacting the employer, what she has to offer the employer (i.e., a qualified job applicant), what the next step will be (i.e., to arrange a job interview with the applicant). Basically, the employment specialist is there to help the employer find good employees.

Proposing a Job Possibility

An employment specialist who visited the Program for Assertive Community Treatment in Madison, Wisconsin, learned how they developed a job by proposing that an employer create a position of distributing coupons. The IPS employment specialist used this idea when she learned of a new restaurant opening. The owner was not interested in coupons but, after talking with the employment specialist, decided that he could hire two people to distribute menus in the neighborhood, door-to-door, for his new restaurant.

Business owners are sometimes too busy to come up with all the ideas about their business that they would like. But many are receptive to ideas that will make their life easier and business better. The employment specialist who thinks like a businessperson and comes up with job possibilities suited both to her clients and to area businesses will never be at a loss for job opportunities. An idea can come from simply noticing that a restaurant parking lot is always littered with debris and the shrubbery is in need of trimming.

The employment specialist watches for businesses under new management, newly built stores, or businesses that recently opened. The employment specialist's own creativity is usually the key to finding job opportunities.

Personal Networks

One of the most effective ways to find job opportunities is by networking. The employment specialist contacts colleagues, former employers, neighbors, local family members, friends, friends of friends, former classmates, teachers, church friends, community acquaintances—anybody she can think of. And it is not only the employment specialist who thinks of her contacts but also the rest of the treatment team. Who do they know who may have a connection with a pet store, pet hospital, or veterinarian to assist Jon with his interest in working with animals? These contacts often provide great leads for jobs, even if they have no specific openings. *The employment specialist and treatment team members are constantly thinking about job leads even in their everyday life outside of work.* This process becomes such a habit that people come across job leads outside of their regular work schedule, in the evenings and on weekends. For example, a psychiatrist was having difficulty picking up his laundry at the end of the day from his dry cleaner. During his next visit to the dry cleaner, he mentioned to the clerk that the store was often closed during late afternoon store hours. She explained that they were having difficulty keeping dependable workers. He told the clerk that he worked with a job developer who might be able to help them out. The psychiatrist went to the office the next day and relayed this information to the employment specialists. One of the employment specialists visited the dry cleaner business that same day to begin investigating the job lead. Job development is a 24-hour-a-day activity.

Employment specialists help clients think about their own networks for job leads. Who do they know? Do they belong to a church? What are the connections of the church members? Who do they spend time with? The possibilities expand as the network broadens.

Agency Boards and NAMI

Employment specialists make presentations to the mental health agency's board of directors, and inquire about their networks and contacts. They craft a clear, precise presentation of IPS. In the same way as a job search is conducted for a particular client, the employment specialist describes briefly the kind of work a person is trying to secure and the person's qualifications and strengths. Presenting a description of the individual personalizes the job lead request for board members. In some agencies, board members are expected to provide job leads.

Meeting with the local chapter of NAMI taps into the networks of family members. Employment specialists follow up on all leads. Some of the leads may identify job openings for which no clients are interested and qualified at the time. But the employment specialist stays in contact with the employer, laying the groundwork and developing the good relations for when there is a client who is interested in the position.

Chamber of Commerce and Other Business Networks

Employment specialists belong to the Chamber of Commerce, Rotary Club, and other business and community service groups. These organizations provide lots of good opportunities to meet employers and exchange leads and ideas. We recommend that employment specialists join one or two of these groups, attend the regular meetings, and volunteer for committee work. Employment specialists join different groups to expand networking opportunities. Employment specialists always look for chances to give presentations or information sessions. Many employers are interested in learning about the Americans with Disabilities Act and how to make accommodations for people with disabilities.

The Department of Employment Security— sometimes called Department of Employment and Training—is another resource for job opportunities. The employment office has listings of available jobs in the community.

Job Fairs

Attending job fairs is a good way to meet employers. In general, employers at job fairs are interested in talking to people who will help them find qualified candidates for their job openings. People who are interested in part-time work can be valuable to an employer. One employment specialist met a manager from a pharmacy chain who explained that once a week, on "truck day" (when deliveries to the store are made), people are needed to unload the trucks, stock the shelves, and do "facing" (face the product toward the aisle for the customer).

Hospital and City Hall Human Resources Listings

Job openings are posted publicly on bulletin boards. Employment specialists get to know the human resource directors. Openings often are posted before they appear in newspapers, and the employment specialist tries to get on a mailing list. Employment specialists visit the human resources department regularly.

The Internet

Career-related Web sites provide information about many job opportunities. Job listings from the Department of Employment Security are listed on the Internet. Examples of Internet job search sites include: www.careershop.com, www.wetfeet.com, www.monster.com, www.hotjobs.com, www.ajb.dni.us.

Local Colleges and Independent Schools

Educational institutions are another source of job opportunities. Employment specialists find out where job openings are listed and check the listings routinely. The number of jobs that are available increases when work-study students are not at school during vacations.

Incentives for Employers

The work opportunities tax credit is an incentive for an employer if the client is hired on a permanent basis. This credit allows the employer to write off the first $2,400 of employee wages if the employee has a disability and is permanently hired. The Department of Employment Security has information about the tax credit, including application forms.

Employment specialists offer prescreening information on job applicants, which saves time for the employer. Employers usually do not have a reference person like an IPS worker who visits the work site to advocate for a job applicant. Employment specialists offer consultation to the employer as needed after the person has been hired. Many employers view this back up and support as a real advantage over hiring candidates without this assistance. Employment specialists tell employers that they want to be sure employers are satisfied with the worker's job performance.

Sometimes all an employer needs in order to make a decision on hiring a client is the knowledge that an employment specialist will be there with guidance and backup support if there are any difficulties. The employment specialist describes to employers the specific ways that they can provide support. The employment specialist gives examples of how he has helped other employers. For references about supported employment and the work of employment specialists, they give the names of other businesses where IPS employment specialists have facilitated a job hire. One employer said, "This is great. Usually when a new worker doesn't show up, I can't find him and don't know what happened."

Job Shadowing

Employment specialists arrange for clients to observe workers at job sites, which can give clients greater understanding of the tasks and responsibilities of specific jobs and can serve as a way of establishing a relationship with an employer. The client literally follows a regular employee for a few hours, observing, asking questions, and generally getting a feeling for the job without actually doing the work. There are no strings attached, so the employer does not feel as though he may be pushed to hire the client. But, of course, the employment specialist who sets up a job shadowing situation can talk with the employer about other jobs, and perhaps other clients, preparing the opening for a future hire.

Volunteer Work

Some clients decide that they do not have the confidence to try a regular competitive job but are willing to start with a volunteer job. Although the goal of IPS is always competitive community-based employment, it is important to listen to what people are saying. If the person is unwilling to go directly into a regular job, even with encouragement and support, the treatment team reviews what the person wants to do. For some, volunteer work feels less frightening. Many volunteer jobs are in nonprofit agencies, such as hospitals or museums. Occasionally, volunteer jobs shift into paying jobs when people demonstrate good work skills.

Illustration 21: Gloria, a Person with an Individualized Job Search

Gloria is a 50-year-old woman with eccentric ideas and speech patterns. She carries a diagnosis of schizotypal personality disorder. She has been unemployed for about 10 years. She last worked at a college where she assisted a psychology professor, taking care of the animal colony. Gloria worked for the professor on a part-time basis for over 5 years. When the professor retired, Gloria lost her job.

When Gloria met with the IPS employment specialist, she assured him that she could get a job again with the college, as she was an educated woman and came from a highly educated family. The employment specialist realized that Gloria valued academia and wanted to be in that environment, even though she had dropped out of college many years ago because of mental illness and had never completed her degree.

Gloria made many attempts at securing further employment at the college, but to no avail. The employment specialist also tried to negotiate job opportunities for her but was unsuccessful. Because Gloria was eager to work, the employment specialist believed that finding a job as soon as possible was important. Gloria, however, was adamant about working at the college. Knowing that academia was important to Gloria, the employment specialist thought about other related job settings. She proposed working at one of the city's libraries. Gloria agreed to explore this possibility.

The employment specialist scheduled an appointment with a library director. During their meeting, the employment specialist identified himself as an employee of Westgate Behavioral Health. He said, "I am an employment specialist and I assist people in finding good work situations that match their skills and interests with the needs of the employer." He went on to explain Gloria's strengths. "She is a dedicated worker as demonstrated by her employment at the college." He continued, "I believe the gap in work history has mostly been because she doesn't interview well. She has good organizational skills and is very deliberate in everything that she does. I believe she would do an excellent job shelving and straightening books, and other clerical duties. She wants to work in a setting where education and learning are valued, which led us to a library setting. She loves to read. If you would consider Gloria for a position, I would be available to meet with you and Gloria together to review her work performance." He concluded by saying, "Can we schedule a time for you to meet Gloria?"

The library director explained that she did not have a paid position available now but she could consider Gloria for volunteer work. Gloria started volunteering 1 day a week for 3 hours a day. After a couple of months, this was increased to 2 days a week, 4 hours a day. Gloria expressed pride in her job and began to refocus her job goal to a paid position in the library. At the end of her first year, the library director offered her a 12-hour-a-week permanent, paid position as a library aide. Gloria is now in her third year working at the library.

In this example, the employment specialist was creative in finding a work situation that reflected Gloria's attraction to books and learning. Most volunteer jobs do not turn into paying jobs as Gloria's did. But, for some people, volunteer work can boost their confidence as a worker as well as provide recent work experience that is added to the résumé.

The IPS coordinator monitors the number of people working in volunteer jobs. If an employment specialist has a lot of people on her caseload volunteering, it is likely that she has not embraced the idea that people with severe mental illness can work in regular paying jobs. Expectations play a big role in what people do. The supervisor works closely with the employment specialist to keep the focus on competitive employment. But for that individual who is sure she should try a volunteer job before a competitive job, the employment specialist assists in her efforts.

Introducing a Person

A client should not be seen as a person with mental illness for whom an employment specialist is trying to find some work. Instead, he is a worker—with unique skills, talents, and potentials—who happens to have a disability. Depending on the client and the job, the person's disability may be almost invisible. So, when talking with an employer about a client, the employment specialist always talks in terms of job strengths and the person's suitability for the job. The employment specialist mentions symptoms of mental illness only to the extent that they have some direct bearing on the person's ability to do the job.

If a client's disabilities are not likely to interfere with job performance, why discuss them? If the client proves to be a capable employee, issues relating to the client's mental illness can be brought to the attention of the employer on a need-to-know basis. Balancing this information with a good work record can help to take away the stigma associated with mental illness.

Many employers are interested in hiring a person with a mental illness because they have a family member or a neighbor with a mental illness. They understand the difficulties that the person is facing and want to provide an opportunity. The employer may have her own mental illness or substance use problem and be willing to give a qualified candidate a chance. Disclosing a mental illness to an employer who is knowledgeable about mental illness through a personal experience or someone they are close to often gives the job applicant an advantage. Some employers will hire the qualified candidate with a disability over the qualified candidate without a disability. Disclosing the mental illness to employers who are interested in hiring people with disabilities increases the possibility of clients getting hired.

The bottom line for the employment specialist is finding a good job match for the client and the employer. Employment specialists who are persistent and creative in their job seeking efforts are able to help clients find good job matches. It is not uncommon to hear employment specialists who are not helping clients obtain competitive jobs blame a bad economy or blame clients for not being "work ready" or "motivated." Supervisors need to address these issues and help employment specialists build the skills and attitudes that support successful job searches.

Not all employers will be friendly and receptive to hiring a candidate whom the employment specialist recommends. Employment specialists must not be discouraged by rejections. Employment specialists who are assertive in the job search are usually successful. A benefit of having employment specialists work together as a unit is that they can provide the support and encouragement to each other as they encounter frustrating experiences with some employers.

A final word to employment specialists: be persistent. Never give up on people who express some interest in working. The circumstances around a person's life may appear insurmountable in terms of achieving a competitive job. But people often rise to the occasion when they feel that others believe in them.

Denise Bissonnette's book, *Beyond Traditional Job Development: The Art of Creating Opportunity* (1994), provides many excellent strategies for seeking employment. We highly recommend this book and believe that it is a must for employment supervisors.

11

Maintaining Jobs

Follow-Along Support

Studies of different vocational programs for people with severe mental illness show that without ongoing help with the problems and challenges of working, many people have difficulty maintaining employment. *In IPS, follow-along supports are individualized and provided on an ongoing and as needed basis.* The kind and amount of supports vary over time. Even though supports are long-term, the employment specialist and the treatment team hold true to the goal of helping people become as independent as possible. Through work experiences, people develop confidence and skills, and as that happens the level of supports is decreased. Most important, the employment specialist asks the client what will help her keep the job. Some people are better than others in articulating their needs, and it is the responsibility of the entire team to find out what supports the client needs.

In IPS, support is always offered by the treatment team. All members of the treatment team help a client with his goal of working. In many situations, people have natural supports such as family members, friends, employer, coworkers, and other community members.

The client's individual employment plan outlines the supports to help her work. Examples of supports include: negotiating accommodations with employers; providing education and guidance to employers; social skills training; adjusting medications; counseling to address work-related problems; dual diagnosis treatment; money management; family support; benefits counseling; transportation; and leisure time activities.

A person's religion or spirituality generally has been ignored in mental health treatment. For many people, spirituality is an important aspect of support. Asking the person how spirituality helps her through difficult times can reveal information about coping strategies. How does she gain strength from her religion or spirituality? Are there people to whom she relates who can provide support?

Supports are provided by the whole treatment team and are never on the shoulders of just the employment specialist. A case manager, for example, may not be used to working with people who are employed and therefore may not know how to help them through the accompanying stress and anxiety. She may believe that the stress created by a new job is somehow the responsibility of the employment specialist. The case manager may see the solution to the client's stress as reducing the number of work hours or even quitting the job. But this attitude defeats the overall approach of integrating supports for the client so that she can lead a richer and more independent life. A tenet of IPS is that the employment specialist and case manager are part of the same team supporting the client in a job. They talk frequently and avoid working at cross-purposes.

All follow-along supports in IPS are designed to complement, rather than work against, the client's increasing involvement with some form of work, whether it is a full-time job or a 2-hour-per-week job. Clinical services such as individual therapy, group treatment, medication checks, and 24-hour emergency services are adjusted, if necessary, to take into account changes in the client's needs as a result of working.

There are specific categories of support that relate directly to finding, staying in, and transitioning out of jobs.

Specific Categories

Emotional Support

How a person feels about himself and his ability to work in a competitive job impacts on his work performance. Support at this level is crucial and is dependent on the uniqueness of each individual. Treatment team members, family members, and friends can provide emotional support for a client's work efforts. In general, the employment specialist's role is to do whatever he can to "be there" for the client. The "being there" may literally mean that the employment specialist goes to the client rather than waiting for the client to come to him. Whenever possible, they meet outside of the mental health center, in a location that is comfortable for the client, to reinforce living and working in the community.

A client who is upset or has missed work may benefit from some immediate support. The employment specialist may call and simply say, "I understand things aren't going too well. Would you like me to come over so we can talk a bit?" The client may be able to get things in perspective before a small problem begins to look like an overwhelming failure. Timing is the key to emotional support. If possible, the employment specialist sits down with the client the same day he hears that the client is having difficulties.

Regular visits with the client around work, meetings for lunch or breakfast, or coffee at the client's home, even while things are going well, can help for those times when things are not going well. A client may want to talk about what is happening at work, both the positive and the negative aspects. If she thinks her boss has been singling her out for criticism, the employment specialist helps her recognize the difference between constructive feedback and vengeful criticism. The employment specialist helps the client think about how to resolve the issue. It is easier to spot subtle changes in a client's attitude or behavior, which may suggest the onset of troubling symptoms or problems with medication, if the employment specialist knows the individual well and sees her regularly. At the same time, supervisors caution employment specialists not to attribute all odd or negative behaviors to symptoms of mental illness. A client is first and foremost an individual person and is more similar to mental health providers than dissimilar.

Some people have never worked a competitive job and others have not held a job recently. Some are unfamiliar with standard work procedures, such as notifying an employer when she is going to be absent from work because of illness. It is the responsibility of the employment specialist to educate clients about these procedures. Role-playing and rehearsing how to handle different situations enhance a person's work skills and job performance.

The employment specialist often is the member of the treatment team with whom the client spends the most amount of time, particularly during transitional periods such as beginning or ending a job. The client may develop a close and active relationship with the employment specialist, and will tend to take greater risks with job situations if he feels the security of that relationship.

Emotional support includes outreach to clients who may have drifted away from the IPS program. If a client is missing appointments, the employment specialist and treatment team need to understand why the person is not engaging. The employment specialist attempts to make contact with a client through telephone calls, letters, or visits to his home or hangout spot. Another team member may connect with the client and know why the person is not engaging with the employment specialist. The person may be fearful about working or discouraged from a bad experience. There will be people who decide not to work or participate in the IPS program. An employment specialist may keep a person on her caseload for as long as 4 to 6 months to allow the client time to resolve some of her ambivalence. *If the person decides that she does not want a competitive job, the employment specialists will discontinue working with her, and the case manager assumes the responsibility of periodically checking in with the person about working.* In all situations, the employment specialist meets the client where he is, both literally and figuratively, to help him move forward with his plans.

The rest of the team, family members, and friends also offer emotional support. They ask the client about work and listen to what he says and how he is feeling. People speak words of encouragement during difficult times and provide hope for future work experiences. Oftentimes, just listening to someone is a great support.

Support in the Workplace

A professional employment consultant who has a candidate to fill a position will negotiate with the employer on behalf of the employee, troubleshoot difficulties and misunderstandings before the job begins, and periodically follow up on how the job is going during the first month or two. If wrinkles develop, the consultant is the one who is in the position to iron them out. In IPS, the employment specialist serves in that same way. The difference is that the employment specialist's involvement may be much more intensive than the consultant's, and the employment specialist's involvement with the client around work is long-term.

The nature of supports varies over time according to the challenges and wishes of the client. The goal is always to enable a person to be as independent as possible. *The employment specialist finds the balance between offering enough support but allowing room for the person to grow and be as independent as possible.* The employment specialist always asks herself, "Is this helping the client with his vocational efforts?"

Illustration 22: Ruth, a Worker Using an Employment Specialist's Support

Ruth, a woman in her mid-30s, was hired as a seasonal salesperson in a department store before the Christmas rush. When hired, she was told the position could become permanent depending on her work performance. She was told that she'd work in all the departments and would need to know all aspects of making sales and running the cash register. The store put her through a 2-day training seminar, but because of the level of stress that Ruth felt, she learned very little and showed up at the job unable to open the cash drawer or ring up a sale.

Ruth's employment specialist, VR counselor, and work supervisor discussed the problem with Ruth and decided that the employment specialist would go through the training session with Ruth. The two women spent 2 days learning the job, and it seemed as though Ruth was ready to solo on the sales floor. The employment specialist, at Ruth's request and with the consent of the manager, hovered nearby while Ruth tried to do the job. She still lacked the necessary knowledge, and had to ask the employment specialist for help, but by the end of her shift she had developed some confidence.

The employment specialist felt that one additional training session would give Ruth the tools she needed to do the job. The employer was unwilling to pay Ruth for time in another training session, and Ruth felt discouraged about doing a third session, this time without pay. Ruth's VR counselor authorized training funds to pay her for the 2 days.

Ruth attended the session alone, and this time, because she'd had hands-on experience, she believed she was able to learn from the training. The employment specialist sat in a coffee shop in the mall across from the store the first morning Ruth worked, just to be there if Ruth needed her, but, as it turned out, she didn't. The employment specialist asked Ruth what could she do to support her. They decided to meet for lunch later in the week to stay in touch.

Each step of the way the employment specialist and the client evaluate what kind of support will help her in her work efforts. Illustration 23 provides another example of how support is provided in the workplace.

Illustration 23: Donald, a Worker Benefiting from Individualized Job Support

Donald had been working as a part-time night janitor in a restaurant. He let his employment specialist know that the owner complained about his work. The employment specialist called the owner and was told that Donald couldn't seem to get the floors clean. So the employment specialist rearranged her schedule and went to work with Donald at 11 pm. What she found was that Donald had been using a mop bucket that had not been emptied and refilled by employees during the day, so he'd been trying to clean with the day's dirty water. The employment specialist showed him how to fill it with clean water. The employer was appreciative and impressed by how dedicated the employment specialist was in solving the problem.

The employment specialist honors her word to the employer that she is available to address problems around a worker's job performance. She responds to the employers concerns as soon as possible.

The employment specialist sometimes finds that she needs to give the employer some help and support in working with an employee. For example, she can interpret seemingly peculiar ways that a person is behaving, can help the employer understand the nature of mental illness and its effects on people, and can give the employer help with talking to the person if there are difficulties.

If a client's symptoms become troublesome to the point that his work is affected, and he wants to continue working, the employment specialist may need to negotiate some time off or reduced work hours for the client. The employment specialist may suggest that the client complete the parts of his job with which he has less difficulty.

If the employment specialist has contact with the employer, it is often helpful for the client, employment specialist, and the employer to meet occasionally to review progress. Particularly during the first few weeks on the job, it is critical that the employment specialist assess whether the client is receiving direct feedback from the employer. Is the client hearing the feedback accurately? The employment specialist can model good communication skills to help solve problems.

In all dealings with employers, the employment specialist must be careful about the position she takes in terms of specific clients. She always respects how clients want to be represented and what level of involvement the client wishes her to have. Some clients do not want employers to know about the mental illness. In these situations, clients have sole contact with the employers and the employment specialist supports people outside of the job setting.

In general, most of the support that the employment specialist provides is away from the job site. Many clients find it stigmatizing to have their employment specialist visit them on the job. And, in most cases, the client does not need support in completing her work tasks. Some clients want the employment specialist to help them get started at a new job. This is true for people who have not worked for a long time or are just plain nervous about starting a job.

Right from the beginning, the employment specialist should have a plan for phasing out her onsite support. The employer needs to assume supervision of the new employee, and the new employee needs to be able to complete his job without the employment specialist there. If the person requires ongoing onsite support to complete the job, then the job is probably not a good fit for her.

The most common reason that people with severe mental illness end jobs badly (fired or quit) is interpersonal difficulties, specifically miscommunication with supervisors and coworkers. Sorting out these issues with the client can usually be accomplished away from the job site.

Family Support

Families have an important role in relation to a client's work efforts. As part of the vocational profile, the employment specialist finds out about the client's family relationships. The employment specialist inquires if anyone on the treatment team has contact with the family. The employment specialist asks the client about her family and how she wants to have the family involved. If possible and appropriate, a client's family—parents, spouse, children, or other close relatives—are encouraged to offer support. A client who is worried about starting a job can be helped greatly if he feels that family members are supporting him. The support can be as specific as a spouse who makes sure that the worker gets up in time to make it to the job, or as general as a parent who shows interest in a family member's job. As clients begin to work, family support may become stronger, giving the client even more confidence. Families sometimes feel discouraged when their expectations about family members and work are unmet. Drawing attention to the small successes a client is making is helpful. The employment specialist talks with families about their expectations and how progress may seem slow, but each step is a success and should be acknowledged. If the case manager is the person who already has a good working relationship with the family, the team may decide that she is the best person to address employment issues with them.

The family's expectations around the family member and work are often what determine whether the person works. Some families are hesitant about having the family member start working. One reason involves finances. The monthly SSI check or SSDI check may help to support the household. Risking the loss of the monthly check may threaten financial stability for the household. Work expectations also are influenced by the role the family member plays at home, for example, watching small children or an ill relative. Previous bad work experiences are a third reason families may not want the family member to work. They remember difficulties the family member experienced when she worked in the past and want to protect her from stress or failure.

Families sometimes have expectations that are too high. For example, an ex-wife believed that since her ex-husband had been working successfully for 10 hours a week, he should be able to work 20 or 30 hours a week and contribute more to child support. He accepted more work hours because he wanted to do all that he could for his children, but he soon became overwhelmed and quit the job. Employment specialists and case managers help educate families about supported employment and the ways they can help their family member in their work efforts.

Families are a helpful source of information about a client's interests, talents, and skills when thinking about individualized job searches. The employment specialist asks the family about the family member's talents and gifts. What did he excel in at school? Families also can provide the employment specialist with a network of contacts for job leads. Families may provide helpful suggestions for supporting the family member.

Supervisors work closely with employment specialists to encourage them to contact families and to develop the skills for talking with families. Employment specialists who are inexperienced in working with families benefit from seeing how case managers and other clinicians connect with families. Group meetings with the family, case manager, and employment specialist are helpful to engage the family around supported employment.

Peer Support

People often feel that they get the most support from their peers. This may occur in structured situations such as in self-help and peer-run programs or through informal social relationships. Clients benefit from hearing about the work experiences of their peers to know that others have encountered similar situations. Peers motivate and encourage each other and become role models.

IPS programs host awards banquets to recognize the work efforts of all clients of the mental health agency. All staff members, including the executive director, the medical director, clients, and families are encouraged to attend and celebrate people's work success. The banquet offers an opportunity to reinforce people's efforts, as well as to stimulate interest in others for considering employment. These events show clinicians, case managers, and other agency workers what clients can accomplish. One way agency leaders show their support is by attending the banquet. Their presence is appreciated by the staff and clients alike. And, for many agency leaders, it becomes an eye-opening experience to learn what people are achieving. Highlighting successes helps to raise people's expectations. Supportive employers are recognized and honored at the banquets as well.

Skills Training and Problem Solving

Some vocational programs have provided skills training as a preparatory step to becoming employed. During the training, individuals are taught the skills to maintain work. One of the disadvantages of providing the training prior to gaining employment is that the material does not have a specific context. That is, the client does not have a job to make the material meaningful, and the skills learned may in fact be irrelevant for the job the client gets. More recently, vocational providers have begun to conduct skills training after people have gained employment. The specific problems that a client encounters on a specific job can be addressed. Skills training, both in group and individual formats, is a valuable tool to help people stay employed.

One example of skills training is the Workplace Fundamentals Module developed by Charles Wallace and colleagues at University of California at Los Angeles (UCLA). This module is part of the UCLA social and independent living skills series. The module is a self-contained curriculum that covers nine skill areas. Two examples of the skill areas are: (1) using problem solving to manage symptoms and medications at the workplace; and (2) using problem solving to recruit social support on and off the job. The groups are conducted with a trainer and typically four to eight participants. The groups usually meet biweekly for 90-minute sessions for 8 to 12 weeks.

The most common difficulties that people have on the job involve interpersonal relations. Social skills training, in either an individual or group format, offers clients a way to learn new social skills through techniques of role modeling, rehearsing and positive reinforcement, and practicing new skills on the job. For example, before a client abruptly leaves a job because she feels that her supervisor is being too critical, she can learn new ways to handle her frustration. As another example, a client who complains of not knowing what to say to coworkers during breaks can learn conversational skills.

In IPS, employment specialists review with clients the skills and information they need to have as they prepare for starting a specific job. For example, how is the person going to get to work? Does the person know how to take the bus? Does she have a bus pass? Does she have the bus schedule and know where to get off the bus? Does he have clothes to wear to the job and know what to wear? Are the clothes clean? Does he have access to laundry facilities? Does he know where to report for his first day of work? Does he know what procedures to follow when he cannot go to work due to illness? Discussions around work culture and work rules are helpful to review with people, particularly those who are not used to working. Once the job has started, the reviews, discussions, and practice can be more extensive.

Transitions

Like most people, people with severe mental illness move along to better jobs, quit jobs they do not like, get laid off during cutbacks, or get fired from jobs when things do not work out. *In IPS, job endings are always framed in positive terms. Something new is learned with each job experience.* The employment specialist and the treatment team examine with the client what was learned about the person as a worker. What did he like about the job? What does he want to do differently in his next job? Although the employment specialist helps to frame the job experience in positive terms, the end of a job, for whatever reason, can be a time of stress and difficulty. The employment specialist and the treatment team help the client through the transition. Preparing a client for leaving a job, and knowing how to use what he learned from the experience, begins early in the client's IPS experience. The treatment team helps him evaluate the work experience and identify what he wants in the next job situation.

Illustration 24: Linda, a Worker Using Support to Transition Out of a Job

Linda was hired by a nursing home as a maintenance worker to clean the kitchen. Over the course of the first few months, she began to show carelessness about her work. Her supervisor talked with her several times, but her job performance continued to decline, so the supervisor called Linda's employment specialist. The supervisor was frustrated and concerned that if Linda couldn't do a better job, he might get into trouble with the health department. He told the employment specialist that if Linda's work didn't improve dramatically over the next few days, he'd have to let her go.

The employment specialist arranged to have coffee with Linda to talk about the job performance problem. They discussed what she could do differently to improve her work performance. Linda, appearing irritated, said she wasn't sure she wanted to stay in the job.

The employment specialist asked Linda to write down the pros and the cons of working the job and include all the reasons that she thought this was a good job for her and all the reasons why she should leave the job. Linda and the employment specialist discussed the pros and cons that she identified and decided that the job was not going to work for her. Now that she had made the decision, Linda wanted to quit immediately. However, the employment specialist explained that if she left abruptly, her nursing home supervisor wouldn't be able to give her a good reference. Having a job reference would help her in the next job search.

The employment specialist talked with Linda about her accomplishments on the job—her punctuality and her ability to work independently. He suggested that Linda give at least a week's notice when quitting the job and ask the employer to mention these positive qualities in a letter of reference.

Linda understood the employment specialist's logic, gave her notice, worked fairly well for the last week, and then began to look for another job. The employment specialist was relieved by the way things worked out, because Linda took responsibility for leaving a job that wasn't working out, because she got a reasonable letter of reference, and because the employer would still be interested in talking with the employment specialist about other applicants or job leads.

Helping a person leave a job is an important part of the employment process. The employment specialist talks with the client about appropriate ways to leave jobs and how that benefits the client. Securing a reference is helpful toward getting the next job. Encouraging the person to process what happened in the previous work experience and applying it to the next experience promotes growth and better work functioning.

Part III

Special Issues

The third part of this book provides illustrations of special issues that employment specialists encounter. Chapter 12 deals with employment and dual diagnosis (severe mental illness and co-occurring substance use disorder). Traditionally, people with dual disorders have been screened out of receiving employment support. Chapter 13 focuses on the challenges for people with severe mental illness who have been highly trained and/or have had advanced work careers. Chapter 14 addresses supported education. Many people are interested in developing careers by advancing their knowledge and skills through education. Chapter 15 examines the need for employment specialists and treatment team members to incorporate cultural sensitivity throughout the employment process. Each chapter provides a vignette highlighting these special issues, followed by a discussion that includes recommendations for practitioners.

12

Dual Diagnosis and Work

People with severe mental illness and a co-occurring substance use disorder often have difficulties accessing vocational services to help them obtain employment. Some practitioners believe that people need to be abstinent from alcohol and drugs to utilize services successfully and become employed. Yet, work often motivates people to manage their alcohol and drug use. In this way, work is therapeutic and plays a role in the process of recovery from substance abuse. Research shows that people with dual diagnosis do well in supported employment programs. The following illustration highlights some of the issues related to employment for people with dual diagnosis.

Illustration 25: Josephine, a Worker with Dual Disorders

Josephine is a 33-year-old African-American woman who has been diagnosed with paranoid schizophrenia and substance use disorder (alcohol abuse and cocaine abuse). She has received services from Wayne County Community Mental Health Center for the past 3.5 years. The center, located in a large, depressed, urban setting, serves primarily African-American and Hispanic clients.

The consequences of Josephine's substance abuse have included beatings by drug dealers, and her leg and arm have been broken on one occasion. She often has been without money and has engaged in prostitution frequently. For the last few years, Josephine has been homeless, living in shelters or in the city parks. Three years ago, she lost custody of her daughter, who now is being cared for by Josephine's mother.

Wayne County Community Mental Health Center has operated the IPS employment program for about 6 months. A senior case manager has referred a few clients on his caseload to IPS but has not considered Josephine as a candidate. She has a poor work history, has dual diagnosis, and has never expressed an interest in working.

During the yearly service plan review, Josephine's psychiatrist asked her if she wanted to have a job. Josephine laughed. "How can I? Look at my life. I use (drugs) and haven't worked in years. I have no clothes."

Josephine's psychiatrist has been the champion of IPS at the center. Seeing the positive impact that work has on clients and especially for those people for whom no one ever imagined work a possibility has convinced him of the value of supported employment. Whenever possible, he asks clients about work, and the answers sometimes surprise case managers who have been slower to embrace this new approach. Many of the staff members still believe that clients need to prepare for work gradually by attending day program groups, prevocational work activities at the center, sheltered work, and volunteer jobs.

Josephine's psychiatrist said, "It may not seem doable to you, but we believe that you can hold a job. We can help you find a part-time job. It can be a few hours a week if you want. There is an employment program here at the center that helps people who want to work. Some people in the program have never held a job before. The only requirement is that you want to give it a try. If you are interested, we will introduce you to an employment specialist who will help you figure out what job you might like to do and then help you find it. We (the team) will support you in your efforts. And if the first try doesn't work well for you, we will help you find a different work situation."

Josephine thought about this offer for a moment. She said, "I have nothing to do. Everyone I know uses drugs. If I'm going to have a prayer of cleaning up and having a life, I'm going to need something to do." She continued, "I'd like money to buy my baby girl some things. And to buy some clothes for me, too. But if I start making money, we all know what I am going to do with it." Her case manager responded, "We can come up with a plan on how to manage the money you earn from working so you're not tempted to buy drugs. Sometimes people who are working want someone from the mental health center to be with them when paychecks are handed out. Let's talk about it more and figure out a plan that will work for you."

Josephine explained to the team that she had once tried to get help from a vocational program but she was turned down because of her drug use. The case manager explained, "That is fairly common. Lots of programs have a rule that people can't be using drugs or even have a recent history of use in order to be eligible for services. But IPS is different. It is based on the idea that work often helps people feel better and motivates them to manage their alcohol and drug use. While work is not altogether stress-free, people find there is a lot to be gained by having a job."

Josephine's case manager reflected on not talking about work with all of his clients, including Josephine. By simply introducing the idea of a job and offering team support, the psychiatrist opened a door for Josephine.

Josephine agreed to give IPS a try. Her case manager filled out the brief referral form and gave it to the IPS coordinator. Josephine was assigned to work with one of the two IPS employment specialists on the case management team. The employment specialist contacted her case manager to set up a time when the three of them could get together in the next week.

Two days later, Josephine was introduced to the employment specialist. Josephine and the case manager provided some background information. Josephine had recently been arrested for minor assault and robbery for snatching an elderly woman's purse. The case manager was helping her with the legal matters. They discussed how alcohol and drug use could be problematic with regard to employment. Josephine had recently been court-ordered to a halfway house for women, and was told that she needed to stay clean or else she would end up in jail.

At the meeting, the case manager reminded Josephine that he and the employment specialist were part of a team working together to provide services. He explained that they shared information in order to help Josephine with her goals. So, if the case manager learned that Josephine was using crack, he would let the rest of the team, including the employment specialist, know this. Having current information helps everybody in planning and providing good services.

The employment specialist met with Josephine the next day to start talking about her job preferences, skills, work history, challenges to work, and so on. He could see that her drug use had really left its mark. She hadn't been taking care of herself. She obviously needed to bathe and have different clothing before she could interview for a job.

Josephine at first couldn't tell the employment specialist what she wanted to do for work. Like many people who have had their work careers interrupted by mental illness and substance abuse, Josephine did not know a lot about the world of work. She told the employment specialist that her job preference was data entry. About 6 years earlier, she had worked briefly for the local community college as a data entry worker. She thought that she could do data entry again.

At their next appointment, the employment specialist put together a small data entry exercise at the center to observe her skills. She typed slowly and made quite a few errors. The employment specialist told her that her skills might not be good enough, but Josephine insisted that she could do the work and that in a real job she would be all right.

The employment specialist told Josephine that he would help her try to find a data entry job. He explained that he would take her to interviews as long as she didn't use alcohol and drugs before the interviews. She agreed, and he set up an interview at a temporary job agency. The employment specialist figured that this was a way to find out about her data entry skills and allow her to receive feedback from a real employer, which would probably be more meaningful to Josephine than advice he could give her.

Because Josephine had no clothes to wear for an interview, the case manager requested money from a client fund at the center. The employment specialist and Josephine went to a secondhand clothing store, where Josephine picked out a pair of slacks, a blouse, and a blazer. When she tried on the outfit, she looked in the mirror and said, "Maybe I can work after all."

The employment specialist transported Josephine on the shopping trip because he feared that she might spend the money on drugs. He also was concerned that she might barter the clothes for drugs. He suggested that she leave the clothes at the center to be sure that they were ready for the interview. She agreed, also thinking it was wise to remove the opportunity of selling them.

The employment specialist accompanied Josephine to the interview. She interviewed well and expressed her interest in the job. She was asked to take a test to demonstrate her data entry skills. She started the test but did not know how to use the computer. She kept asking the interviewer questions about what she was supposed to do. About 20 minutes into the testing period, the interviewer ended the interview and told Josephine that her skills were not sufficient to get the job that she wanted. The interviewer suggested that Josephine take a course to improve her data entry skills. Josephine wanted a job right away, so decided to explore other options.

Josephine told the employment specialist that cleaning or stock work positions were also job possibilities. They both agreed that Josephine should start working a few hours a day, a couple of days a week, as a way of getting used to being a worker again. The employment specialist suspected that her stamina was probably poor from the years of substance abuse. He recommended that she work morning hours so she wouldn't have a lot of time before work to use drugs. He also suggested that they look for a work environment in which other workers were not using alcohol or drugs (either on the job or after work).

During a weekly IPS group supervision meeting, Josephine's employment specialist learned about a job lead at a local health food store. The owner was looking for someone to stock shelves and clean the store. The employment specialist told Josephine about the job and she expressed interest in the position. The employment specialist accompanied Josephine to the job interview 2 days later. During the interview, Josephine had trouble explaining why she had been out of work for the past few years. The employment specialist explained to the employer that Josephine had been dealing with personal difficulties and was now wanting to work. He went on to explain that in his position as employment specialist he helped people find jobs that match their interests and skills as well as the needs of the employer. He said that he provided support to help the person stay employed and would be available to meet with the employer as needed to ensure that she was satisfied with Josephine's work performance. The employer offered Josephine a position for 2 hours a day, Monday, Wednesday, and Friday, from 9 am to 11 am at an hourly wage of $6.75.

When Josephine was hired, the employment specialist scheduled a meeting with her and her case manager to discuss how to manage her paycheck. The agency was Josephine's representative payee for her SSI check. At the meeting, Josephine stated that she didn't want to work unless she got her entire paycheck. The employment specialist and the case manager felt that if she got her check, Josephine would go out and buy drugs. She wasn't used to having extra money and she had poor impulse control.

The employment specialist helped Josephine identify items that she could buy with her earnings. She needed several items related to working. For example, an alarm clock would help her get up on time for work. She needed an adequate supply of toiletries such as toothpaste and deodorant. She was going to need laundry money so she would have clean clothes for work. After much discussion, Josephine agreed to a plan that if she stayed clean for a month, she would receive $20 a month from her paychecks for extra spending money, in addition to the $40 a month that she receives from her SSI check. The rest of the SSI check covered housing and meal expenses and the remainder of her paychecks would go into her savings account. After each month of clean time, the amount would increase by $10. Josephine made it through the first month and got her extra spending money. She immediately spent the money on drugs, which dropped her back to the base amount of $40.

At the team meeting the next day, the employment specialist and the case manager gave an update about Josephine's relapse. The psychiatrist reminded the team that part of Josephine's substance abuse treatment plan was to attend the dual diagnosis groups at the center. He said, "Even though Josephine has rarely attended the group, she may find it more helpful now that she is trying to work. I think we should all encourage her to attend one meeting a week. She is going to need a lot of support to learn new ways of managing money, finding friends who don't use, spending her leisure time substance-free, and coping with cravings. These changes don't happen overnight. She will need a lot of support and she probably will continue to have relapses. But over time, she may decrease her drug use and at the same time increase her job tenure."

During the first month of employment, Josephine had attended work faithfully as scheduled. The employment specialist had called the employer weekly and had received a good report about how Josephine was doing on the job. At the beginning of the second month (when she received extra money from the paycheck), the employer called the employment specialist several times to say that Josephine was starting to show up early for work and leave early, or show up late and leave early, or go in and say that she had something going on and couldn't work at all that day.

The employment specialist immediately checked in with the case manager to see if this might be a sign that Josephine was using drugs again. The case manager said that when Josephine uses, she loses sense of time and doesn't maintain her schedule. She also has increased paranoia when she uses, which leads to her isolation from others. The employment specialist met with Josephine that day to talk about her attendance. When asked if she had been using, Josephine said that she had used two times but that it wasn't interfering with her job. She explained, firmly, that how she spent her time outside of work was her business. The employment specialist discussed the ways alcohol and crack use can interfere with work, including poor attendance and poor work performance. He asked her what she thought was causing the poor attendance. Josephine was silent. The employment specialist returned to the center and left a voice mail message to the case manager about his conversation with Josephine.

The employment specialist met with the employer the next day. He encouraged the employer to use the normal disciplinary procedures that she uses with other employees. The employment specialist wanted Josephine to experience the natural consequences for poor work performance which helps to cut through the denial some people have about drug use not interfering with their lives.

Josephine continued to have poor attendance over the next month, and she insisted that she wasn't using alcohol or drugs. She received a verbal warning, a written warning, and a 3-day work suspension. The employer terminated Josephine's employment following continued work absences. Josephine was employed at this job for only 2 months.

At the next treatment team meeting, the case manager reported that he believed that Josephine's erratic work attendance was related to her anxiety about going back to court. The court was to decide if she could move from the halfway house. For Josephine, the halfway house had been a savior. It was the first time she was able to stay clean for a substantial amount of time. Realizing that she might be discharged from the halfway house and moving somewhere else, Josephine felt overwhelmed by the responsibility this signified for her. She told her case manager that she was worried about living in a neighborhood with other drug users and feared that her life would fall apart again. The team discussed the importance of finding housing in an area where drug use was not prevalent.

Shortly after she lost her job, Josephine relapsed again and ended up hospitalized for treatment of psychosis and drug detoxification. When she was discharged 1 week later, she said she was ready to resume a job hunt. Josephine said she wanted to work and also wanted to stay away from her drug-using friends. She agreed to go to a dual diagnosis group at the center at least one time a week and contact her case manager when she had cravings to use.

The employment specialist continued to update the team on Josephine's progress. The case manager pointed out that Josephine had really made some progress. He said, "In her first attempt at returning to work, she had been clean for 1 month and held a job for 2 months."

The employment specialist asked the team to help him think of other work ideas for Josephine based on what they knew about her. The psychiatrist mentioned that Josephine always talked about her daughter and wondered if she might like to work with children. The team nurse said that her sister-in-law worked for a daycare center. She would find out whether the employment specialist could talk to someone there, but she was curious about how an employment specialist could help someone get a job who was probably going to abuse drugs. Wasn't he worried about his relationship with the employer and even his own professional reputation? The employment specialist explained that creating a good job match for the client and the employer, in a work setting where alcohol and drugs are not available, is essential. He said, "We want to identify stressors for Josephine and avoid them in a job setting. Stress is often a trigger for substance use. Even if a client is willing to disclose his disability to the employer, I usually don't describe the substance use. For many people, including employers, there is a perception that substance abuse is associated with irresponsible people who just need to shape up. Instead, I identify that I work for the mental health center and that I help people find and keep jobs. I tell the employer about a person's strengths and why this person might be a good fit for the job. If I think that someone will behave in a certain way that may seem odd or suspicious on the job, I discuss these behaviors directly with the employer. For example, if someone has auditory hallucinations and copes with the voices by using headphones, I might request an accommodation with the employer and explain how people manage these symptoms while they work."

He continued, "On occasion, I have worked with employers who have learned about someone's substance abuse problem and have supported their work effort. One employer said, 'I know what it is like to be at the bottom of the barrel. I was there once, too. I am willing to give anyone a chance if they want to work.' Many employers are interested in hiring people who have a disability, particularly if I am available to support the client and the employer. The client may not work out at a job but many employers are willing to keep working with us and give someone else a try if they meet the requirements for the position. I really stress that people should be treated like other employees. If someone comes to work smelling of alcohol, the employer should respond as she would with any of her other employees."

The nurse continued with her questioning, "What about employers who are doing urine screens to find out if employees are using drugs? I understand that this may occur as part of the hiring process and is becoming a routine practice within many employment sites for its employees." The employment specialist explained, "This is really not a problem. The testing helps cut through the denial when a client says that he is not using or that it does not interfere with his life. I always educate clients about these practices as we are looking for work." He continued, "In fact, the team and I first learned of one client's drug use through an employment urine screen. Knowing that he was using helped to explain a lot of his behavior."

The employment specialist talked over the daycare center idea with Josephine, who said she was interested. He followed up on the lead at the daycare center and learned at his meeting with the director that daycare centers sometimes have a door monitor position. The door monitor greets the parents and children in the morning when they come to the center. The director said that she didn't have any openings but recommended two other centers. She gave him the names of the directors.

The employment specialist set up meetings with both directors. One of the daycare centers did not have a door monitor position, so James proposed developing the position. He told the employer that Josephine had not worked recently and was looking for a part-time job. She liked children and was generally a sociable person. The employment specialist offered to accompany her on the job for the first couple of mornings as she was learning the routine. The employer decided to give Josephine a chance and took the employment specialist up on his offer to help Josephine get started.

On the first morning, Josephine told James that she was scared and didn't know what to say to the parents and the kids when they arrived. The employment specialist modeled for her how to greet them. Josephine was soon at ease greeting people. The employment specialist met with Josephine every day after work for the first week to talk about how she did. They set a goal for her to complete 1 month of work and not use alcohol or drugs during that time. If she succeeded, they would go out to lunch to celebrate.

As the next court date neared, with the possibility of moving from the halfway house, the team talked to Josephine about different housing options and her fears of making a move. They reviewed with her strategies that helped her remain alcohol- and drug-free, such as going to the dual diagnosis group and contacting a support person when she has cravings. The case manager agreed to help Josephine find housing in a different neighborhood.

The employment specialist said to the team, "I think she is starting to believe that she can have a more satisfying life. She wants to be successful holding a job and is thinking of possibly going back to school. She says that in order to be clean she has to stay away from her drug-using friends and make a new life for herself." The team agreed that Josephine had made a great start.

This illustration shows the possibilities of work for people with dual diagnosis. Many programs don't admit people who are using alcohol and drugs or who have used recently. Yet, for many people, work is therapeutic and normalizing. Work structures time and provides opportunities for healthy, substance-free activities and relationships. For many people like Josephine, work is a motivator to manage and reduce their use.

Using motivational interviewing, case managers and other practitioners work with clients on the goals that they want to achieve. When someone with dual diagnosis wants to work, the team provides encouragement and assistance. The clinician does not pass judgment on the client or dictate the barriers that he sees to the client's goal. Instead, the clinician facilitates the client's understanding of the barriers by asking questions.

Through different job experiences, people usually begin to realize that their substance use interferes with successful employment. In general, people are interested in their own goals and figuring out for themselves what the obstacles are and removing them. In the illustration, Josephine was realizing that her drug use had been a barrier to successful employment. In the past, the team had had little success with helping Josephine reduce her alcohol and drug use. By working with her on *her* goal of employment, in combination with a substance-free housing environment, Josephine was beginning to deal with her substance abuse. For some people with dual diagnosis, supported employment is the key to engaging them in services.

It is important to have someone at the mental health agency champion the idea that people with dual diagnosis can work. In this example, the psychiatrist helped to bring the team along and encourage all clients to think about work. The case manager had not considered Josephine for employment services, yet was able to quickly reconsider her potential as the psychiatrist demonstrated his belief and support.

Some people with dual diagnosis don't believe that life can be any different. They have spent years with nonworking peer groups. They may view their life role as a drug user. They have tremendous difficulty even imagining the possibility of assuming the role of a worker. But sometimes simple acts such as buying an outfit for work or getting one's hair done are enough to spark the idea that change is possible.

The team plays a role in building hope, helping people see that they can have a different life. By providing individualized, long-term support, through integrated services, the team works closely with people, building on their strengths and providing support and encouragement when they falter.

People with dual diagnosis have relapses, and may lose their jobs. Through these experiences, they learn that they must manage their difficulties with alcohol and drugs in order to work. Many programs require a period of abstinence before helping someone find another job. But in IPS, the team stays with the client, helping that person figure out what she can do differently. She is not terminated from services because of problematic behaviors such as drug use, insolence, or absenteeism. The employment specialist and the team develop plans that address these problems. How the employment specialist supports the client is determined, in part, by the pattern of abuse. For example, an employment specialist decided to stop contacting employers directly about job opportunities for someone who had been terminated from a series of jobs, which the employment specialist had developed, due to using alcohol or drugs on the job. The employment specialist recommended that the client contact employers about jobs himself. The employment specialist would provide supports away from the job settings. Many people with dual diagnosis stop using alcohol and drugs gradually in response to negative events relating to substance abuse (i.e., loss of jobs).

On receiving a referral for IPS services, the employment specialist begins meeting with the client right away to develop a plan for work. The employment specialist gathers information about the person, including specific information related to substance use. What is the pattern of alcohol and drug use? How often does she use? What drugs does she use? What are the triggers for her use? Does she use when she is in specific social settings? What stage of recovery is she in? What coping strategies have been successful for her? All of this is done with a straightforward, nonjudgmental, problem-solving approach.

The goal is to identify a good job match for the person in which the job and work environment support her sobriety. The employment specialist and team help to identify work settings that are not likely to trigger substance abuse. They try to avoid work sites where alcohol and drugs are found, such as in bars and restaurants, or where it may be part of the work culture, such as in some construction sites. Stress is often a trigger for substance use. What is stressful for the client and how will that relate to a job and work setting? For people with long histories of substance abuse, their physical stamina is likely to be poor. As with Josephine, people start working a few hours a day, a few days a week. All job searches are based on client preferences as well as information related to the substance use disorder.

Money is often a cue for people with dual diagnosis to buy alcohol and drugs. The employment specialist and the case manager work together with the client to develop a plan for managing paychecks. Some clients say that they want someone to help them manage their money so they won't buy drugs. Earnings from work can go into a savings account for items they want to purchase, for example, a car, clothes, and so on, or go toward the expenses of everyday living. Employment specialists can meet clients on payday to accompany them to a bank where the money is deposited. People assume greater responsibility for managing their money independently as they transition into recovery from substance abuse.

Throughout the employment process, the team provides services that support a person's work efforts. Substance abuse treatment, mental health treatment, and rehabilitation are integrated through the team approach. Team members are constantly communicating with each other about clients' progress. For example, an employment specialist observed changes in a client's behavior at work and suspected substance use. The employment specialist contacted the case manager to convey this information. The case manager was able to increase her contact with the client and learn that she was spending time with her drug-abusing ex-boyfriend. The case manager encouraged the client to attend the dual diagnosis group and talk about the situation. The employment specialist met with the client after work three times a week to review her job progress and contacted the employer to be sure that she was satisfied with the client's work performance.

The team helps people deal with conflicts that occur on the job. The employment specialist or case manager can role play with clients different ways to respond to coworkers who suggest going out for a drink after work. The team helps clients develop strategies for managing impulses and cravings. The team increases the level of support during periods of increased stress when a client may be at a higher risk of using. The team helps clients address issues around housing. For Josephine, living in a substance-free halfway house helped her stay away from many of her drug-using friends. The team encourages people to identify whether their housing situations and social networks contribute to their pattern of alcohol and drug abuse. Overall, the team helps people change old patterns and develop new routines, new friends, and successful coping styles.

People do not change overnight from being an unemployed drug user to a worker who is abstinent. People with dual disorders usually have multiple job starts. Some clients have found that urine toxicology screens help them remain substance free. Although there may be relapses, over time many people develop the skills to manage the symptoms of dual diagnosis and learn to be good workers. Many clients say that what is most important is having the unconditional support of the team to help them get through difficult times and achieve their goals.

In summary, IPS services for people with dual diagnosis are essentially the same as for people with a single diagnosis of severe mental illness. The same principles and practices are followed. When working with people with dual diagnosis, the team highlights the following areas:

- All people are encouraged to think about the possibility of work in their lives. People who have a substance-use disorder are not excluded from supported employment.
- Information about the person's substance-use disorder is incorporated in the vocational profile.
- The employment specialist and the team develop with the client a good job match that supports recovery.
- The client and the team identify a plan that helps the person manage her earnings from work.
- The treatment team provides assistance around substance abuse treatment, in finding safe and substance-free housing, in developing friends and a social network that engages in substance-free activities.

The team helps clients to change old patterns that contributed to substance abuse and to develop new ways of living without alcohol and drug use. People often use out of idleness and boredom. Work provides a healthy alternative. For many people, the structure of work and the opportunity to meet new people and develop new roles facilitates the recovery from dual diagnosis.

13

Highly Trained Individuals and Work

People who develop severe mental illness later in life, after they have been educated and have developed successful careers, can have difficulty returning to work at the same level as prior to the onset of the illness. One of the roles of the employment specialist and the team is to provide hope that people can achieve their goals. They do this by breaking down goals into smaller steps and helping people to achieve each step. The challenges in returning to work are somewhat different for highly trained individuals who develop mental illness than for people who are beginning entry-level jobs that are consistent with their experiences and training.

Illustration 26: Bartolo, a Person with Advanced Training Returning to Work

Bartolo is a 48-year-old former professor who has recently moved to a large, urban city in the Southwest to be closer to his two sons. Bartolo has been in and out of psychiatric hospitals for the past 8 years, during which time he lost his job at the university. He has received different diagnoses, including major depression, schizoaffective disorder, paranoid schizophrenia, and substance use disorder (alcohol abuse). His pattern includes taking antipsychotic medication after a psychotic episode and then rapidly discontinuing the medication. He has attended day treatment programs, which he found boring and in which he had difficulty in relating to the people. He has attended several vocational programs but dropped out when he did not find employment.

Bartolo was referred to Counseling Services of Clark County. He was assigned to a multidisciplinary team that serves approximately 60 people. At the intake interview, he expressed interest in the supported employment program, because he wanted to resume his career as a sociology professor.

Bartolo was introduced to an employment specialist who said that he would try to help Bartolo get back to work. The employment specialist began collecting background information from previous service agencies where Bartolo had received help. The employment specialist asked him if they could meet with his sons, because family members are often helpful in making suggestions around work. Bartolo agreed to a meeting but said that he already knew what he wanted to do for work—to find a job as a sociology professor.

The employment specialist found a consistent theme after talking with Bartolo, reviewing clinical records, and meeting with the family. Since his illness, Bartolo had put in numerous applications for jobs as a professor. He had not been offered any positions. The sons thought that it was a folly for their father to be pursuing teaching jobs. During the past 8 years, Bartolo had written about a theory that he had been developing. It was unclear to the sons, to the employment specialist, and to previous vocational workers whether the theory was scientifically valid.

The employment specialist decided that he needed to find out if Bartolo's writings were of academic quality that could be used to resume his sociology career. As he had a neighbor who worked at a community college, he contacted her and asked for advice regarding how he should go about approaching someone in the sociology department. The neighbor got back to him a few days later with the name of a sociology professor who would be a good person to contact. With Bartolo's permission, the employment specialist left a copy with the professor. The professor said that it was an interesting paper that included some sophisticated ideas but also included material that was contradictory and nonsensical.

After discussing the professor's feedback, the employment specialist and Bartolo began meeting weekly, trying to help him to broaden the range of work that he would consider. Would he like to work in an academic setting? Would he like to write? Bartolo always returned to his goal of obtaining a job as a sociology professor.

The employment specialist presented Bartolo's situation at one of the weekly case management meetings. He was feeling frustrated by the lack of progress he had made with Bartolo. The team leader said, "Our job is not to try to make people change in ways that we think are good for them. One role we have is to provide hope and respect for people. Bartolo is having difficulty accepting the loss of his professional status as a result of the illness. He appears to feel the shame of having a mental illness as well as shame for losing his successful career. At some level, he must sense the disappointment in his sons. I doubt there is a way that we can know when Bartolo might be willing to consider another job. But we need to keep thinking together creatively about work for Bartolo. In addition, I suggest that his counselor do some grief work with him."

The counselor began talking with Bartolo about what it meant for him to work again. During these sessions, Bartolo started expressing the sense of loss and despair that he felt following the onset of his illness. He believed that only if he could get back to working as a sociology professor would he be well again. He wanted his sons to see him as the dad he had always been before the illness. The counselor arranged a family meeting where the sons clarified their love for their dad.

About a month later, the employment specialist heard about a position that was available for a grant writer at a peer support center. The position was part-time, 20 hours a week for 6 months. Depending on funding, the position might be extended. The employment specialist brought up the position at a team meeting with a client in mind who had been active in the consumer movement in the county. One of the case managers asked whether this might be a position that Bartolo would consider. The employment specialist said he would ask Bartolo.

To the surprise of the employment specialist and the team, Bartolo decided to pursue the position. He said that he still wanted to work as a professor but figured he could do this work in the meantime. Bartolo was hired for the position.

Bartolo worked at the job for 6 months. He donated extra time by working more than 20 hours a week. The team commented that he looked much happier. He was giving greater attention to his appearance, buying new clothes and getting a haircut. During this period, Bartolo devoted his energy to his job and did not talk about pursuing sociology.

Bartolo's job ended after 6 months. There was hope that at the beginning of the new fiscal year the agency could reinstate the grant writer position. The employment specialist and Bartolo resumed talking about his job search, and this time Bartolo was interested in considering other positions with human service organizations.

This illustration shows some of the difficulties that highly educated people encounter when they decide to return to work. Many people in this situation want to return to the type of work that they had been doing prior to the illness but find that they are unable to do so. Some people who have become ill while working at high-level positions are fearful about whether symptoms will return if they go back to the same line of work. For example, a man in his 40s became ill with severe depression while he was working as a physical therapist. He was treated for his depression and wanted to return to work but was terrified that he would have another depressive episode. He had been working in a large physical therapy practice where he felt stressed by the number of patients he was required to treat. After much agony in planning to return to work, he decided to take a part-time physical therapist position in a clinic that was known for being low-key. He disclosed his illness to the employer, who provided flexibility in his work schedule based on how he was feeling. Over the course of several years, he was able to carry a full caseload and work full time. The employment specialist provided ongoing supportive counseling. On many occasions, he expressed his doubt about being able to work successfully.

The employment specialist and the team encouraged him around his work efforts. The case manager helped him with cognitive restructuring to avoid negative thoughts.

Other people have difficulty incorporating new information about how they function in relation to a job. For example, some people who develop schizophrenia experience cognitive deficits that make it difficult to perform complex tasks. Difficulties with social interactions also may limit some of the tasks they had previously performed well. In all of these situations, it can be hard for people to realize and accept that their skill levels have changed.

The employment specialist and the team do not tell clients what they believe they are capable of doing or not doing. Many people can remember when they were told by a caregiver, such as a psychiatrist, psychologist, or social worker, that they would never work again. Later, they found someone who believed in them. And, of course, those people have gone on to work. Having hope and providing high expectations help people in their recovery process and in finding what is right for them.

The employment specialist needs to listen to the client and hear what she is saying. What does she want to do? All too often, employment specialists will suggest low-paying, low-skilled positions that feel demeaning and demoralizing. The challenge for the team is to think creatively with the client to find a job match that will work for her. For a long time, Bartolo appeared rigid in what job he wanted. But he was able to move from that position, possibly because of the grief work.

The employment specialist and the team may become frustrated that people are not making faster progress toward gaining satisfying employment, but the goal of the team is to support people in reaching for their goals and not to give advice on what the team believes they should be doing.

Supervisors and team leaders address with employment specialists issues of frustration, impatience, and irritation about their work with clients. Team members can support each other and remind the team of the progress that people have made toward their goals.

The team helps people mourn their losses when they are ready. Bartolo was able to begin processing his losses resulting from mental illness after many years. He had lost his wife to divorce, had become unemployed after losing his academic job, had lost a sense of identity, and had lost the role that he had played in his sons' lives.

Many people have recounted the pain involved in accepting these losses and moving on with their lives. All too often, people are forced to live on vastly reduced incomes and in mediocre or poor housing conditions. Not uncommonly, people say that being treated with respect and dignity and being valued as a human being is an important part of the healing process.

In summary, when working with people who have developed a mental illness after becoming highly trained and having advanced careers, the team incorporates the following guidelines in their practice:

- The team provides hope and encouragement to people for achieving their goals. The team does not give up hope when progress toward the goals is slow.
- The team listens to what the person wants to do, and helps the person identify specific steps toward reaching the goal.
- The team thinks creatively about jobs that relate to what the person wants to do. As long as the client is interested in pursuing employment, the team provides suggestions on an ongoing basis without knowing when one of the ideas will work for the person.
- People in these situations have suffered severe losses, including falls in economic and social status, and deserve to be treated with respect and dignity.
- The team helps people mourn their losses when they are ready to do so.

People who have had successful careers often have difficulty reentering the work world. Symptoms of the illness can interfere with the ability to return to the same level of functioning. The goal for the employment specialist and the team is to provide hope and support that will encourage people to achieve their own goals.

14

Supported Education

Improving skills and increasing employability through education is a goal of many people with severe mental illness. The principles and practices of supported education are similar to those of supported employment. Services are individualized and are based on client preferences. Supported education is integrated with mental health treatment. Services are primarily community-based and are continued as needed. The goal is to help people with severe mental illness access postsecondary education in integrated settings with other people without disabilities and to provide support for the person to use the educational opportunities as fully as possible. Employment specialists can provide supported education within an IPS program.

Illustration 27: Mark, a Person Utilizing Supported Education

Mark is a 26-year-old man who lives in a large midwestern city. He has a diagnosis of schizoaffective disorder. He first experienced symptoms of mental illness during the fall of his freshman year in college. He failed four courses that semester and dropped out of school. Over the last 8 years, he worked a few brief jobs. He worked for a landscaping company, mostly mowing lawns. He was fired from the job after going to work late too many days. A few months later, he was hired as a delivery person for a pizza parlor. He was fired from that job after receiving a couple of tickets for speeding and reckless driving.

Mark lived at home and was treated by a private psychiatrist for 7 years. When the psychiatrist moved out of state, he referred Mark to a local community mental health center for medication monitoring and support services. At the intake interview, Mark was asked what services he wanted. He said that he had decided to go back to school but was apprehensive and would like someone to give him advice.

Mark was referred to the IPS program and assigned to work with an employment specialist. The employment specialist told Mark that she helped people to find work and also helped people to go to school. She could help him secure funding for schooling, help him go through the application process, assist him in registering with disability services at a school, go over class schedules, request accommodations if needed, and discuss issues related to being a student, such as study habits, and interacting with other students and teachers.

Mark received SSI and was going to need financial assistance to return to school. The employment specialist recommended that as a first step they talk with a vocational counselor at the office of Vocational Rehabilitation. Mark was worried that working with VR might slow the process down. The employment specialist explained that she worked very closely with several of the VR counselors and was sure that they could get in to see one of them quickly. The following week, Mark met with the employment specialist and a VR counselor at the mental health center. Mark described his interest in biology and how he had excelled in math and sciences in high school. He wanted to have more of a life than what he had now; he believed that going back to school would help him get somewhere. He said that most of his friends from high school had gone to college, and some to graduate school, and were in good jobs.

The counselor suggested that Mark take a class at the state university as a way of getting started. VR would pay for the class. At the same time, Mark could apply for a Pell grant—a grant that does not have to be repaid, for people in undergraduate or professional programs who demonstrate they cannot afford the tuition—and look into other financial aid options. The employment specialist and VR counselor would help him complete the applications for schools that he wanted to attend. Mark thought that this was a reasonable plan. He decided to take the introductory biology course. Mark didn't want anyone at the school to know that he received mental health services, so the employment specialist helped him through the process at a distance.

Mark attended the classes as scheduled. The first exam was scheduled 3 weeks into the class. As the exam date got closer, Mark became more and more anxious. The employment specialist asked him what they could do to help him get through this exam. He told her that he felt paralyzed every time he thought about taking the exam. He had been reading the assignments and doing the homework, but didn't know how to study for the test.

The test was now 1 week away. The employment specialist suggested that they write down on a calendar how he was going to spend his time over the next week. They wrote in the times that he went to class, they marked in time each day to study, and time for shopping, his appointment to see his case manager, and meetings with the employment specialist. The employment specialist suggested that they talk on the phone every morning to review his plan for the day. The employment specialist also suggested that he make an appointment with his professor to review what he had been studying for the exam. Mark said he would think about talking to the professor, but he didn't want to look stupid.

The employment specialist met Mark after the test at a restaurant across from the campus. Mark did not want to meet her on the campus in case anyone knew that she worked for a mental health agency. Mark told her that he didn't finish the test. He had a hard time concentrating. But he thought that he probably answered correctly the questions he did answer.

The employment specialist explained that because he has symptoms from mental illness that interfere with his ability to demonstrate his knowledge on the test, he would qualify to receive an accommodation. She explained, "The symptoms interfere with your ability to concentrate. If you were given additional time to complete the test and to take the test in a separate room without distractions, you would probably score higher. Most schools have a disability services office that helps to arrange these accommodations. But in order to request an accommodation, you would need to send documentation from the mental health agency that you have a disability. Your professors would not be told the nature of your disability, only that you have a disability and are entitled to accommodations. I can assist you in contacting the disability services office if you like."

The employment specialist told Mark that it was up to him whether he wanted to disclose the disability. She wanted to be sure that he understood his rights. If he didn't want to disclose it now, he could always change his mind at a later time. Mark told her that he didn't want to be treated differently from any of the other students. And he didn't want anyone to know that he received services at the mental health center.

Mark completed his course and received a passing grade. He was disappointed in his performance, as he found the work easy. He was determined to get a B.S. in biology, and hoped to go on for advanced training as well. He knew that he was going to have to change something if he was going to achieve these goals.

Mark applied to the state university and was accepted for the fall semester. He struggled with the decision about disclosing his disability to receive the assistance of the disability services office, but he finally decided that he would do it. He wanted to take advantage of all the resources that he could so that he would be able to make it in school this time.

Supported education is a way that people with severe mental illness can access assistance in returning to school. Like work, school is a vehicle for getting on with one's life. It is against the law for people to be asked during the admission process about having a disability. Academic institutions cannot deny admission to people with disabilities if they are otherwise qualified. The Americans with Disabilities Act of 1990 and Section 504 of the Rehabilitation Act of 1973 protect people with disabilities from discrimination.

The issues related to going back to school are similar to the issues of going back to work. In both situations, people need to decide whether they are going to disclose their disability status. The stigma surrounding a mental illness causes many people to decide not to disclose their status. People don't want to be treated differently, and they fear discrimination. Over time, some people change their minds and decide to disclose so that they can take advantage of extra services and supports, including accommodations.

Mark eventually realized that for him the advantages of disclosure outweighed the disadvantages. The employment specialist can accompany students to the disabilities office to access services and make recommendations about what accommodations might be helpful to the student. The goal of the disabilities office is to ensure nondiscriminating policies and procedures for students with disabilities. Students must present documentation of their diagnosis to verify their disability status. When working directly with teachers, the disability office staff does not reveal the nature of the disability. People are usually assigned one counselor from the office whom they meet with as needed during their time at the school. The counselor can help negotiate accommodations, help with selecting courses and academic planning, and provide supportive counseling. The counselor becomes a part of the team of people supporting the client. As in all team approaches, it is important that the team members work together, sharing information and giving the client the same message.

Accommodations are modifications in academic procedures that eliminate discrimination against people with disabilities because of the disability. Examples of accommodations for people with severe mental illness in school are:

> tape-recording classroom sessions
> extending time for test taking
> arranging individual or private space for test taking
> extending due dates for assignments and tests
> permitting more breaks during class time
> waiving required classes that are not essential for course of study
> assigning an incomplete grade instead of a failing grade because of a
>   medical leave

As in supported employment, the whole team provides supports to help people with their educational goals. The employment specialist is often most aware of how the person is functioning at school. The employment specialist reports to the psychiatrist if the client appears to be experiencing side effects from medication such as drowsiness, difficulty concentrating, or memory problems. The psychiatrist might decide to change the dosage or the time when the client takes the medication, or might consider a different medication to help improve his academic performance.

Case managers and other clinicians help people with interpersonal relationships at school. How to interact with the professor is a common area of concern. If the person has disclosed, she may agree to the employment specialist talking directly with the professor to negotiate accommodations. Some employment specialists find it helpful to talk directly with a counselor at the disabilities office as well as the professors. They can help the school understand how they can best work with a student. Helping students manage their time is an important role of the employment specialist. Many people find that taking care of the details of everyday living is time-consuming, and adding student responsibilities can be overwhelming. The employment specialist works closely with the student to help her pace her life and organize her time so that she can be successful in her academic pursuits.

Supported education programs have not been widely implemented for people with mental illness. Yet, higher education and training are an important part of being able to develop careers. The team needs to encourage people to consider going back to school if they want. Consistent with the principles and practices of supported employment, the employment specialist and the team follow similar guidelines for supported education.

- The team talks about schooling and advanced training with all clients.
- The employment specialist helps the client throughout all phases of the educational process, including completing financial aid applications, admissions applications, course selections, and ongoing supports.
- The employment specialist discusses the advantages and disadvantages of disclosing the disability status to the academic institution.
- The employment specialist helps access services at the disabilities services office if desired by the client.
- The employment specialist recommends accommodations at school based on the experiences and wishes of the client.

Supported education services are individualized based on the preferences, skills, and challenges of the student. The goal is to provide people access to further education so they can build opportunities just as others who have not had to experience the trials of mental illness.

15

Work and Cultural Competence

Cultural competence refers to services that are sensitive to and tailored for the cultural context of the person receiving services. To provide effective services, the employment specialist and the rest of the team must be able to see the world through the eyes of the client. The cultural values, beliefs, customs, communication, and behavior of people from different ethnic, racial, and socioeconomic backgrounds influence how a person perceives mental illness, what strategies are used to manage it, and what role work plays in peoples' lives. Supervisors and team leaders ensure that employment specialists and other team members provide culturally competent services.

Illustration 28: Kwan, a Person Receiving Culturally Competent Services

Kwan is a 29-year-old man who lives in a large city on the West Coast. He moved with his mother and father to the United States from Vietnam about 10 years ago. Kwan's father died 5 years ago, and Kwan now lives with his mother in a small one-bedroom apartment.

Soon after Kwan moved to the United States, he took a class to learn English. He later enrolled in a night class in computer programming at a community college. He dropped out of the class because of concentration problems. He found it difficult to sit quietly through the lectures and was distracted by other people in the class whom he believed were staring at him.

Three years ago, Kwan was hospitalized for 1 week. At the time, he was convinced that people who lived near him were plotting to kill him because they had found out that he was going to be the next world leader. Kwan was convinced that he had to find these people and turn them in to the authorities. He started warning his neighbors about these dangerous people. He told a cashier at a local market. He became argumentative when the cashier told him that it was not true. The police were called and he was taken to the hospital.

On discharge from the hospital, Kwan was referred to a mental health center for follow-up services. He was assigned to meet with a female case manager. Kwan attended appointments with the case manager but communicated very little to her. The team leader suggested that Kwan work with a male case manager who could speak Vietnamese. Kwan appeared to like this switch and started talking about what he wanted to do. He told the case manager that he would eventually like to return to school so that he could obtain a degree in computer programming. But, in the meantime, he needed to take care of his mother. She had difficulty with mobility, so he was responsible for doing the food shopping, washing the clothes, and cleaning the apartment. The case manager talked with him about the importance of taking care of family but also taking care of one's self. The case manager suggested that they could develop a plan of taking care of his mother and obtaining a job or going to school.

Kwan agreed to meet with the case manager two times a month but did not believe that it was necessary to meet more frequently. Kwan met with the psychiatrist one time a month. He did not like taking the medication that the psychiatrist prescribed and did not believe that it was necessary.

The case manager periodically asked Kwan about whether he wanted to return to school or look for a job. He usually responded that he would do this eventually but needed to take care of his mother now. The case manager asked about the possibility of meeting Kwan's mother. Kwan said that she was not well and he did not want the case manager to contact her.

At Kwan's yearly service plan review, the team asked Kwan about whether he wanted to pursue work or school. He said that he would like to further his education and be able to earn money to help support his mother.

The psychiatrist suggested that Kwan and his mother meet with his case manager and the team's employment specialist to talk about this plan. Kwan's mother was monolingual but the employment specialist and the case manager spoke Vietnamese, so there was no language barrier. Kwan did not understand why mental health workers needed to speak with his mother, but as he wanted to get a job and make money and also begin taking classes, he decided to go along with the team's suggestion.

The employment specialist and case manager met with Kwan and his mother. The mother appeared supportive of Kwan finding a job and going to school. The four of them came up with a plan that the employment specialist would help Kwan find a part-time job. They also would help him find a computer class after he had been working for a few months. The employment specialist suggested that Kwan not take on too much at once, as he needed to balance his responsibilities at home with work and possibly school.

The employment specialist began meeting more frequently with Kwan to discuss what type of job that he wanted. When the employment specialist suggested jobs that were in his neighborhood, Kwan rejected them. He said he could not work in his neighborhood. Kwan said that he would like to work around computers if possible.

The following week, the employment specialist visited a computer store at one of the universities downtown. He chose this location because it was far enough away from Kwan's neighborhood and also might be a school where Kwan would take classes at a later time. He spoke with the store manager and told him that he was looking for job opportunities for a very bright individual who would be going back to school part-time within the next year in computer programming but needed part-time work now. He explained that Kwan was an introverted, hard-working person who works well independently. The manager said that he would be willing to meet with him.

The employment specialist contacted Kwan about the job lead. Kwan agreed to go to the interview and saw no need for the employment specialist to accompany him. The employment specialist agreed and wished him good luck. Kwan telephoned the employment specialist the next day to say that he was hired for the position and was starting the job the following week.

This illustration shows how the team tried to respond to the cultural values and norms of a young man who had immigrated to the United States from Vietnam. For Kwan, family responsibilities took priority in how he spent his time. On the death of his father, he became the head of the household and needed to care for his mother, whose health was failing. The role of parents and adult children vary across cultures. For example, in some cultures, women are expected to stay home and take care of the family, while men seek employment and earn money. Understanding these roles improves the employment specialist's ability to work effectively with people.

Kwan benefited from receiving services from a male case manager who spoke his primary language, Vietnamese. Services cannot be effective if they are not provided in the language the client is most comfortable speaking. Bilingual staff members improve an agency's ability to outreach and engage people from different cultures who may be reluctant to seek mental health services.

The employment specialist and case manager wanted to visit Kwan's mother to learn what she thought about Kwan going to work or school. The team also wanted to understand the health needs of Kwan's mother to see if she would benefit from services from a home health care agency. The employment specialist and the team members reach out to the families who may play a role in determining if the family member will seek employment.

Like many Asian people, Kwan and his family felt stigma from the symptoms of mental illness. In fact, Kwan's understanding of the illness was different from the Western medical model of disease and treatment. Kwan did not see the mental health center as central to helping him manage his situation. He reluctantly took medication. He did not want agency staff meeting with his mother. Furthermore, he did not want to work in the Vietnamese community.

He felt shame about his situation and did not want others from his community to know about it. He had heard from another Vietnamese client at the mental health center that no Vietnamese employers would hire her after they found out that she went to the mental health center, because they thought it would be bad luck. Employment specialists need to take advantage of their contacts with employers and families to dispel myths about mental illness and provide accurate information. Finding business leaders within communities to advocate hiring people with disabilities is helpful.

Language is a barrier to employment for some immigrants or refugees. For people who are monolingual, the employment specialist helps them access training to learn the essential language for the job that they prefer. The employment specialist tries to find interested employers who speak the same language of the clients he is working with.

Understanding a person within her cultural context enhances the employment specialist's ability to engage her and provide services that are helpful to her. Simple gestures such as how to greet or address a person vary across cultures. What may be a casual gesture of acquaintance for one person may be an insult to someone else.

Agency staff workers outreach to clients, families, and employers of different cultural backgrounds to provide education about mental illness, the benefits of medication, and the possibilities for hiring good employees from their own communities.

How people view work also varies across cultures. When working with refugees and immigrants, employment specialists need to look at the work practices of the countries that people come from. A primary goal for many Asian refugees and immigrants who live in the United States is to take advantage of economic opportunities derived from work. The employment specialist is more likely to help clients if he understands the meaning of work for people from different backgrounds. For some people, the primary interest in work is to make money. For others, the meaning of work involves defining who they are and assuming a normative role in society. Some people want to make money so they can stop receiving the benefit check. Other people believe that they are entitled to a benefit check. Why should they try to get by on low-paying, entry-level jobs? Understanding these values is critical in providing supported employment services to people from different backgrounds.

Cultural sensitivity does not mean making gross generalizations about groups of people that can lead to stereotypes and inaccurate information. Within a group of people with similar backgrounds and ethnicity, different values, beliefs, and perceptions exist. Furthermore, within the United States people have different cultural backgrounds. For example, growing up in urban poverty, in the rural South, or in a Greek neighborhood of Chicago can confer strong values that might be considered a culture. Similarly, being part of a gay community or some other minority group can confer strong cultural values. The point is that the employment specialist and the team must try to understand each client for who she is, where she comes from, and what she believes.

Incorporating this information into the planning process enhances the effectiveness of services and improves communication between clients and clinicians. The employment specialist and the team follow basic guidelines of cultural competence.

- The agency should have a cultural competency advisory board that includes community representatives from local minority groups and that reviews policies, programs, and personnel issues related to cultural competency.
- The agency hires employment specialists and other clinicians who are bilingual/bicultural to provide services to people with similar backgrounds.
- The agency arranges for translators for less commonly used languages as needed.
- The agency provides education and training to all staff members to sensitize them to their own cultural beliefs and biases and to introduce them to the customs, values, belief systems, social networks, and communication and behavior of clients from different cultures and backgrounds.
- Clinicians incorporate strategies that are effective and sensitive to the cultural context of clients they are serving.
- The employment specialist and team members reach out to family members to understand their values and worldview and how it impacts on the family member returning to work or school.
- Employment specialists and clinicians educate clients, families, and employers from different cultural backgrounds whenever possible about how people with severe mental illness can benefit from competitive employment.

People from different cultural and ethnic backgrounds have the right to receive services that are culturally competent. Mental health agencies are charged with ensuring that staff members are given the information, training, and supervision to provide services that are culturally competent to the people who receive them. Communicating with clients and families in their language and incorporating information about their cultural values and norms improves outreach efforts and the effectiveness of ongoing services.

16

Conclusions

In the last 10 years, enormous developments in the field of supported employment for people with psychiatric disabilities have been observed. Since we wrote *A Working Life* in 1993, the knowledge base has expanded in many ways. IPS and similar supported employment programs have developed techniques for practitioners, procedures for administrators, and a strong evidence base regarding effectiveness. These programs have spread rapidly across the United States, and similar programs have emerged in Canada and in several European and Asian countries. Accompanying this growth in supported employment services has been a new optimism regarding employment, community inclusion, and recovery.

We have been privileged to be a part of this movement and doubly privileged to document in this book the role that IPS has played in creating change and improving outcomes. The techniques for practitioners contained herein have been developed and refined by hundreds of IPS employment specialists across the country and have been empirically demonstrated to help people get jobs, achieve vocational success, and move on with their lives.

At the same time, we anticipate continued and rapid developments on many fronts. Among the most important of these is removing administrative barriers so that people who want employment are not constrained artificially. The major impediment to employment continues to be the structure of benefits and incentives rather than disability. Like other Americans, people with disabilities should be able to improve their lot through hard work and should not have to risk their health insurance, health care, housing, and financial security by working hard. Efforts are underway at many levels to eliminate barriers of this type so that the environment facilitates rather than impedes functioning, inclusion, and recovery. We look forward to witnessing and studying these changes.

The organizational rigidity between mental health and vocational agencies presents another artificial barrier. Service integration is a critical concept for people with multiple needs, especially those with cognitive deficits. Current efforts underway to create integration unfortunately are threatened by ubiquitous forces that tend to fragment services. Nevertheless, we expect further efforts to overcome these rigidities, hopefully at the federal and state levels as well as in local programs.

Science advances inexorably, and current research underway will undoubtedly improve our understanding of cognition, illness heterogeneity, rehabilitation, and treatment in ways that will enhance the effectiveness of supported employment. So far, these efforts do not translate directly into matching different vocational approaches with different types of clients, but considerable progress is likely in the next 10 years.

Already within our reach is the possibility of understanding better the long-term course of rehabilitation, employment, education, and career development, and of clarifying how these outcomes are related to the concept of recovery. The short-term window of current research needs to be expanded so that we can better enable people to recover as fully as possible.

It perhaps goes without saying that all of these efforts will be enhanced by efforts to overcome stigma, to make services more culturally competent, to include consumers and families in service development and testing, to develop a coherent service system in the United States, and to eliminate disparities between mental health and general medical funding. We all have important roles to play in these efforts.

Appendix 1

Individual Employment Plan

The employment plan is part of a client's overall service plan. It is developed by the employment specialist and the client and is based on information from the vocational profile. The plan is updated regularly. Below is an example of a completed employment plan.

Overall Vocational Goal: To work in a part-time competitive job (about 10 hours a week) using my typing skills and interest in computers.
Date: 1/4/05

Objective 1: To find a job that will use my clerical skills and will have opportunities for computer work.
Intervention: I will meet with J. Conway at least weekly to identify job leads, update my résumé, and attend job interviews as scheduled. J. Conway and I will identify networking contacts for possible job leads related to data entry and other computer-related jobs.
People Responsible: Sarah Williams, consumer; Jill Conway, employment specialist
Target Date: 4/4/05
Date Objective Achieved: 3/1/05 Employed at Miller and Associates for data entry. 10 hrs./wk. at $7.50/hr.

Objective 2: I will take my medication in order to help me keep a job.
Intervention: I will attend the medication group (led by T. Williams) and work group (led by J. Conway) at least 2x/mo. for 2 months to discuss how medication affects my ability to work. I will meet with my case manager and psychiatrist at least 1x/mo. I will use a daily planner for medication.
People Responsible: Sarah Williams, consumer; Helen Howard, psychiatrist; Tom Williams, case manager; Jill Conway, employment specialist
Target Date: 7/4/05
Date Objective Achieved:
Signatures:

Appendix 2

Vocational Profile

Vocational Profile

This form is completed by the employment specialist within the first few weeks after the client is referred. Sources of information include: the client, the treatment team, the clinical record, and with the client's permission, family members, friends of the client, and previous employers. Suggested probes for eliciting information when interviewing the client are provided in parentheses. The probes are meant to begin a discussion around the topic area. Update the form as new information becomes available over time.

Work Goal

• client's work goal and life dream for work (What would you say is your dream job? What kind of work have you always wanted to do?)

• client's short-term work goal (What job would you like to have now?)

Work Background

• education (What school did you attend last? What was the highest grade you completed?)

- licenses and certifications (Have you completed any training program for which you received a certificate?)

- work history
  1. most recent job (What job did you do most recently [job title]? What were the job duties? About when did you start and end the job? How many hours a week did you work?)

     reason for leaving job (Why did the job end?)

     positive experiences (What did you like best about the job?)

     problems on job (What did you not like about the job?)

  2. next most recent job (What job did you do before the most recent job? What were the job duties? About when did you start and end the job? How many hours a week did you work?)

     reason for leaving job (Why did the job end?)

     positive experiences (What did you like best about the job?)

     problems on job (What did you not like about the job?)

- Use Back of Sheet for Additional Jobs

Current Adjustment

- diagnoses

- prodromal symptoms (What are the first signs that you may be experiencing a symptom flare-up?) (At times when you are not feeling well or having a bad day, how would I be able to tell?)

- symptomatology and coping strategies (How can you tell that you are not feeling well and what do you do to feel better?)

- medication management and medication side effects (What medication do you take and when do you take it? Do you encounter any problems from the medication?)

- physical health (How would you rate your physical health?

  Poor __ , Fair __ , Good __ , Excellent __ ; Do you have difficulties sitting, standing, walking, or lifting for periods of time? Do you wear eyeglasses or a hearing aid?)

- (Do you have any physical limitations that might influence your work needs? What are they? How are you taking care of your physical problems?)

- endurance (What are the most number of days you could work per week? What are the most hours you can work in a day?)

- grooming

- interpersonal skills (How well do you get along with people?)

- support network (Who do you spend time with? How often do you see or talk to them?)

Work Skills

- job-seeking skills (How have you looked for work in the past?)

- specific vocational skills (What skills have you learned either on the job or in school?)

- aptitude (What have others told you that you are good at?)

- interests—vocational and nonvocational (What have you always been good at? What kinds of things do you like to do?)

- motivation (What will you get out of working?)

- work habits relating to attendance, dependability, stress tolerance (How was your attendance in previous jobs? What kinds of situations and tasks cause you to feel stress?)

Other Work-Related Factors

- transportation (How would you get to work? Do you have a driver's license?)

- family and friend relationships and type of support (Do you have family and/or close friends that you have contact with? Do these people support you? If so, how do they support you?)

- current living situation—type and with whom (Where do you live and with whom do you live?)

- substance use (Have you ever used street drugs or alcohol? Have other people in your life been concerned about your substance use? Do you smoke cigarettes? About how many cigarettes do you smoke a day?)

- criminal record (Have you ever been arrested?)

- disclosure of mental illness (Are you willing to tell employers about your illness?)

- expectations regarding personal, financial, and social benefits of working (What do you think work will do for you personally, financially, and socially?)

- money management skills (Do you handle your own money? Pay your own bills?)

- income and benefits—social security, medical insurance, housing assistance, VA benefits

- daily activities and routines (Describe what a typical day is for you from the time you wake up until the time you go to bed.)

- regular contacts (Who do you spend time with? What do you do with them?)

- family members' work history (What jobs have different members of your family had?)

- preferences for work setting, work tasks, time of day, weekly hours, wages (What type of work setting would you like, for example, outside/inside, work close to other people, work mostly alone? What kinds of work tasks do you like to do?)

- two forms of identification (Do you have a birth certificate, a driver's license, a state ID card, or a Social Security card?)

Networking Contacts for Job Search

- family

- friends

- neighbors

- previous employers

- previous teachers

- community contacts

Completed by: _____ Date:_____

Updates: (Include new information, signature, and date in the space provided below)

Appendix 3

Job Descriptions

Employment Specialist

Overall Function:

Carries out the services of the IPS-supported employment program by assisting consumers obtain and maintain employment that is consistent with their vocational goals.

Responsibilities:

Engages consumers and establishes trusting, collaborative relationships directed toward the goal of competitive employment in community job settings with other workers without psychiatric disabilities.

Assists consumers in obtaining information about their benefits (e.g., SSI, Medicaid, etc.) and how they will be affected by employment in order for consumers to make good decisions about employment opportunities.

Assesses consumers' vocational functioning on an ongoing basis utilizing background information and work experiences. With the consumer's permission, provides education and support to family members. Discusses consumer's preference for disclosure of psychiatric status to employers.

Conducts job development and job search activities directed toward positions that are individualized to the interests and uniqueness of the people on his/her caseload, following the principles and procedures of IPS.

Provides individualized follow-along supports to assist consumers in maintaining employment.

Provides education and support to employers as agreed on by consumers that may include negotiating job accommodations and follow-along contact with the employer.

Provides outreach services as necessary to consumers when they appear to disengage from the service. Maintains some contact with consumers even without a vocational focus if necessary to sustain engagement.

Meets regularly with treatment team members to coordinate and integrate vocational services into mental health treatment.

Develops an individual employment plan with the consumer, case manager, other treatment team providers, and updates it quarterly.

Conducts at least 65% of direct service time in the community.

Provides supported education, using principles similar to IPS, for consumers who express interest in education to advance their employment goals.

Qualifications:

Education and experience equivalent to undergraduate degree in mental health, social services, or business. Experience working with people with severe mental illness, experience providing employment services, and knowledge of the work world are preferred. Ability to work as an effective team player is essential.

Employment Coordinator

Overall Function:

Oversees the IPS-supported employment program by supervising employment specialists and providing administrative liaison to other coordinators within the mental health agency.

Responsibilities:

Accepts referrals for IPS services and assigns consumers to work one-on-one with employment specialists.

Hires, trains, and evaluates employment specialists.

Conducts weekly employment supervision to the IPS employment specialist team using individual examples and following principles and procedures of IPS. Oversees weekly job development meetings to explore job leads.

Provides individual supervision to employment specialists and ensures that employment specialists learn the skills necessary to complete their jobs.

Monitors the employment specialist's role and participation on the case management treatment teams to enhance integrated, seamless services at the delivery level.

Acts as liaison to other department coordinators in the mental health agency.

Arranges regular in-service training to all staff about principles and practices of IPS and evidence-based supported employment.

Tracks employment outcomes, on a monthly basis and by employment specialist, including job dates, hours worked, wages earned, and quality of job match.

Provides IPS services to small caseload of individuals.

Qualifications:

Master's degree in rehabilitation counseling or related field. Previous experience as an employment specialist assisting clients with severe mental illness in obtaining and maintaining competitive employment is desired. Previous supervisory experience is desired.

Appendix 4

Sample Letters to Employers

Sample Employment Specialist Thank You Letter

January 1, 2005

Mr. Juan Castillo
Stop N Shop Grocery
4141 Parkway
Chesterfield, IL 33210

Dear Mr. Castillo,

Thank you very much for taking the time to meet with me today in regards to Maria Franco's application for a cashier position at Stop N Shop. While you stated that there are no openings at this time, I encourage you to consider Ms. Franco for future cashier positions. She is interested in working at Stop N Shop Grocery in particular because she lives in the neighborhood. I believe you will find her to be a reliable and responsible employee.

I will contact you again about future openings for her. Thank you for your time and consideration.

Sincerely,

Julia Perez
Employment Specialist

Sample Employment Specialist Thank You Letter

June 1, 2005

Mr. John Smith
Hopkins Nursing Home
1122 Main Street
River, CA 11234

Dear Mr. Smith,

Thank you for meeting with me this afternoon to discuss the possibility of hiring Stan Johnson for a part-time kitchen helper position at Hopkins Nursing Home. Stan is looking forward to meeting you to learn more about the nursing home and the kitchen helper position.

As I mentioned to you during our meeting, Stan has experience in the food service industry. In the past, he has held positions including dishwasher, food prep worker, and chef. He is interested in returning to work in a part-time position as soon as possible. I believe that two of his strengths are that he is both reliable and responsible. As we discussed, I will continue working with Stan to support him as he returns to work. Also, I will stay in touch with you regarding his work performance if he is hired. I believe that this is a terrific opportunity for Stan and that he will prove to be a valuable employee.

Again, thank you for your time and consideration of Stan Johnson.

Sincerely,

Amy Snyder
Employment Specialist

Sample Client Thank You Letter

June 1, 2005

Mr. John Smith
Hopkins Nursing Home
1122 Main Street
River, CA 11234

Dear Mr. Smith,

Thank you for taking the time to meet with me this afternoon to discuss the possibility of a part-time kitchen helper position at Hopkins Nursing Home. As we discussed, I have experience working in the food service industry. I would welcome the opportunity to work at Hopkins Nursing Home. Please let me know if you need any further information regarding my job application.

I look forward to hearing from you. Thank you for your time and consideration.

Sincerely,

Stan Johnson

Sample Employment Specialist Thank You Letter After 1 Month

August 1, 2005

Mr. John Smith
Hopkins Nursing Home
1122 Main Street
River, CA 11234

Dear Mr. Smith,

I want to thank you for the support that you and others at Hopkins Nursing Home have given to Stan Johnson to help him work in the part-time kitchen helper position. While he had a few difficulties getting started in the job, the staff at Hopkins Nursing Home has been very kind to him and supportive of his efforts. In particular, his supervisor, Sherry Arnold, has been helpful in making sure that Stan understands his job duties. Because of Stan's memory difficulties, she listed his job tasks on a poster that he is able to check each workday to be sure that he has completed the tasks. Sometimes a small accommodation can make a world of difference for someone in completing his job!

Stan sometimes has difficulty expressing his thoughts and emotions. I can assure you that he is very grateful for this position. He is proud of his work and glad to be an employee of Hopkins Nursing Home.

I look forward to our continued collaboration.

Sincerely,

Amy Snyder
Employment Specialist

Appendix 5

Supported Employment Fidelity Scale

Implementation Questions

To complete the supported employment fidelity scale, the rater obtains objective information from a variety of sources, including agency records, employment specialists, other practitioners and supervisors, program managers, and consumers. Individual meetings are recommended. Listed below are suggested questions that can be used to elicit information. The rater tries to obtain accurate information and not lead respondents to the desired answers that may not reflect the actual practice at the site. The format for interviewing is conversational and the questions listed here are not meant to be used as a structured interview. Information to make the ratings is not necessarily obtained in the order that the items are listed on the scale.

STAFFING

1. Caseload size:

   • Does each vocational staff person have a discreet caseload?
   • How many clients does each vocational staff person (full-time equivalent) have on his/her caseload?
   • How often does the vocational staff person meet with each person on the caseload? Approximately how long do clients stay on the caseload? When is a client removed from the caseload?

2. Vocational services staff:

   • Do any of the vocational staff provide other services besides vocational, such as case management, day programming, or residential services?
   • How much of their time do they provide nonvocational services?

3. Vocational generalists:

   • Do different vocational staff persons provide different aspects of the vocational service? For example, one person only does job development or one person only does job support. What different aspects of the vocational process does each provide?

ORGANIZATION

1. Integration of rehabilitation treatment with mental health treatment:

   • Do vocational workers interact with case managers about their mutual clients?
   • In what situations do they interact and how regularly (meetings, telephone, etc.)?
   • Are vocational workers assigned to work with specific case managers or case management teams?
   • Do they participate in shared decision making about client services? Who (staff) makes the final decision?
   • Where are the offices located for case managers and for vocational workers?

2. Vocational unit:

   • Do the vocational workers have the same supervisor?
   • Do the vocational workers meet as a group for supervision? How often?
   • Do the vocational workers provide services for each others' clients?

3. Zero exclusion criteria:

   • What are the criteria to be eligible to receive vocational services? (Who is not eligible?)
   • Who makes referrals?
   • Who conducts the screening?
   • Are there provisions made for being sure no one is excluded?
   • What is the rate of referral?

SERVICES

1. Ongoing, work-based vocational assessment:

   • Does the program include vocational evaluation procedures?
   • What type of assessment procedures do you use and in which settings?
   • Are their certain assessment procedures that must be completed prior to obtaining a competitive job, for example, testing, prevocational work adjustment?
   • How much preplacement assessment do you do?
   • How much time is spent on vocational assessment?

2. Rapid search for competitive job:

   • What is the average length of time between when a person begins the program and the first contact with a competitive employer? What is the range of time?
   • What is the philosophy of the program about when to start the job search?
   • Are there steps in the program that people take before starting to look for a job?

3. Individualized job search:

   • How is it decided which jobs are identified in the job search? Who makes these decisions? What information is it based on?
   • How has the nature of the job market affected the type of jobs clients obtained?

4. Diversity of jobs developed:

   • Does the vocational worker ever suggest to clients that they work at the same job setting as other clients? What percentage of clients work in the same job settings?
   • Does the vocational worker ever suggest to clients that they obtain the same type of job as other clients? What percentage of clients have the same type of work?

5. Permanence of jobs developed:

   • What percentage of the jobs that the vocational worker suggests to clients are permanent, competitive jobs?
   • Does the vocational worker ever suggest jobs that are temporary, time-limited, or volunteer? How often?

6. Jobs as transitions:

   • Do vocational workers help clients to find another job when one ends?
   • What percentage of the vocational worker's clients who have ended jobs have been provided assistance in finding another job?
   • What are reasons a vocational worker would not help a client find another job when one has ended? (e.g., client was fired because of poor attendance, problems with substance abuse?)

7. Follow-along supports:

   • Does the vocational worker provide follow-along supports to the client and the employer? What kind of supports?
   • What percentage of working clients has follow-along supports provided?
   • Is there a time limit for providing supports?

8. Community-based services:

   • Where do the vocational workers spend most of their time?

• What percentage of their time is spent outside the mental health facility? (Ask the employment specialist to review how she spent her time over the last couple of days to determine location of services.)

9. Assertive engagement and outreach:

• Does the vocational worker provide any outreach if a client does not engage or drops out of services?
• What kinds of outreach are provided? How often are outreach attempts made? Is there a time limit to providing outreach if a client stops attending? What is the time limit?

Supported Employment Fidelty Scale (formerly the IPS Model Fidelity Scale)

Rater: _____   Site: _____   Date: _____   Total Score: _____

Directions: Circle one anchor number for each criterion.

Criterion	Data Source*	Anchor
Staffing		
1. Caseload size: Employment specialists manage vocational caseloads of up to 25 clients.	VL, MIS, DOC, INT	1 = Ratio of 81 or more clients/employment specialist. *Or* Cannot rate due to no fit. 2 = Ratio of 61-80 clients/employment specialist. 3 = Ratio of 41-60 clients/employment specialist. 4 = Ratio of 26-40 clients/employment specialist. 5 = Ratio of 25 or less clients/employment specialist.
2. Vocational services staff: Employment specialists provide only vocational services.	MIS, DOC, INT	1 = Employment specialists provide nonvocational services such as case management 80% of the time or more. *Or* Cannot rate due to no fit. 2 = Employment specialists provide nonvocational services such as case management about 60% time. 3 = Employment specialists provide nonvocational services such as case management about 40% time. 4 = Employment specialists provide nonvocational services such as case management about 20% time. 5 = Employment specialists provide only vocational services.

3. Vocational generalists: Each employment specialist carries out all phases of vocational service, including engagement, assessment, job placement, and follow-along supports.

VL, MIS, DOC, INT

1 = Employment specialist only provides vocational referral service to vendors and other programs. *Or* Cannot rate due to no fit.

2 = Employment specialist maintains caseload but refers clients to other programs for vocational service.

3 = Employment specialist provides one aspect of the vocational service (e.g., engagement, assessment, job development, job placement, job coaching, and follow-along supports).

4 = Employment specialist provides two or more phases of vocational service but not the entire service.

5 = Employment specialist carries out all phases of vocational service (e.g., engagement, assessment, job development, job placement, job coaching, and follow-along supports).

ORGANIZATION

1. Integration of rehabilitation with mental health treatment: Employment specialists are part of the mental health treatment teams with shared decision making. They attend regular treatment team meetings (not replaced by administrative meetings) and have frequent contact with treatment team members.

VL, MIS, DOC, INT

1 = Employment specialists are part of a vocational program, separate from the mental health treatment. No regular direct contact with mental health staff, only telephone or one face to face contact per month. *Or* Cannot rate due to no fit.

2 = Employment specialists attend treatment team meetings once per month.

3 = Employment specialists have several contacts with treatment team members each month and attend one treatment team meeting per month.

4 = Employment specialists are attached to one or more case management treatment teams with shared decision making. Attend weekly treatment team meetings.

5 = Employment specialists are attached to one or more case management treatment teams with shared decision making. Attend one or more treatment team meetings per week and have at least three client-related case manager contacts per week.

2. Vocational unit: Employment specialists function as a unit rather than a group of practitioners. They have group supervision, share information, and help each other with cases.

MIS, INT

1 = Employment specialists are not part of a vocational unit. Or Cannot rate due to no fit.
2 = Employment specialists have the same supervisor but do not meet as a group.
3 = Employment specialists have the same supervisor and discuss cases between each other. They do not provide services for each other's cases.
4 = Employment specialists form a vocational unit and discuss cases between each other. They provide services for each other's cases.
5 = Employment specialists form a vocational unit with group supervision at least weekly. Provide services for each other's cases and backup and support for each other.

3. Zero exclusion criteria: No eligibility requirements such as job readiness, lack of substance abuse, no history of violent behavior, minimal intellectual functioning, and mild symptoms.

DOC, INT

1 = Clients are screened out on the basis of job readiness, substance use, history of violence, low level of functioning, and so on. Referrals first screened by case managers. Or Cannot rate due to no fit.
2 = Some eligibility criteria. Screened by vocational staff who make client referrals to other vocational programs.
3 = Some eligibility criteria. Screened by vocational staff of the program that will provide the vocational service.
4 = All adult clients with severe mental disorders are eligible,

including dual disorders of substance abuse and mental illness. Services are voluntary.

5 = All clients are encouraged to participate. Referrals solicited by several sources (self-referral, family members, self-help groups, etc.).

SERVICES

1. Ongoing, work-based vocational assessment: Vocational assessment is an ongoing process based on work experiences in competitive jobs.

DOC, INT

1 = Vocational evaluation is conducted prior to job placement with emphasis on office-based assessments, standardized tests, intelligence tests, work samples. Or Cannot rate due to no fit.

2 = Client participates in a prevocational assessment at the program site (e.g., work units in a day program).

3 = Assessment occurs in a sheltered setting in which clients carry out work for pay.

4 = Most of the assessment is based on brief, temporary job experiences in the community that are set up with the employer.

5 = Vocational assessment is ongoing. Occurs in community jobs rather than through a battery of tests. Minimal testing may occur but not as a prerequisite to the job search. Aims at problem solving using environmental assessments and consideration of reasonable accommodations.

2. Rapid search for competitive job: The search for competitive jobs occurs rapidly after program entry.

DOC, INT, ISP

1 = First contact with an employer about a competitive job is typically more than 1 year after program entry. Or Cannot rate due to no fit.

2 = First contact with an employer about a competitive job is typically at more than 9 months and within 1 year after program entry.

3 = First contact with an employer about a competitive job is typically at more than 6 months and within 9 months after program entry.

4 = First contact with an employer about a competitive job is typically at more than 1 month and within 6 months after program entry.

5 = First contact with an employer about a competitive job is typically within 1 month after program entry.

3. Individualized job search: Employer contacts are based on clients' job preferences (relating to what they enjoy and their personal goals) and needs (including experience, ability, symptomotology, and health, etc., and how they affect a good job and setting match) rather than the job market (i.e., what jobs are readily available).	DOC, INT, ISP	1 = Employer contacts are based on decisions made unilaterally by the employment specialist. These decisions are usually driven by the nature of the job market. Or Cannot rate due to no fit. 2 = About 25% employer contacts are based on job choices that reflect client's preferences, strengths, symptoms, and so on, rather than the job market. 3 = About 50% employer contacts are based on job choices that reflect client's preferences, strengths, symptoms, and so on, rather than the job market. 4 = About 75% employer contacts are based on job choices that reflect client's preferences, strengths, symptoms, and so on, rather than the job market. 5 = Most employer contacts are based on job choices that reflect client's preferences, strengths, symptoms, and so on, rather than the job market.
4. Diversity of jobs developed: Employment specialists provide job options that are diverse and are in different settings	DOC, INT, ISP	1 = Employment specialists provide options for either the same types of jobs for most clients, for example, janitorial, or jobs at the same work settings most of the time. Or Cannot rate due to no fit.

2 = Employment specialists provide options for either the same types of jobs, for example, janitorial, or jobs at the same work settings about 75% of the time.

3 = Employment specialists provide options for either the same types of jobs, for example, janitorial, or jobs at the same work settings about 50% of the time.

4 = Employment specialists provide options for either the same types of jobs, for example, janitorial, or jobs at the same work settings about 25% of the time.

5 = Employment specialists provide options for either the same types of jobs, for example, janitorial, or jobs at the same work settings less than 10% time.

5. Permanence of jobs developed: Employment specialists provide competitive job options that have permanent status rather than temporary or time-limited status, e.g, TEPs.

DOC, INT, ISP

1 = Employment specialists usually do not provide options for permanent, competitive jobs. Or Cannot rate due to no fit.

2 = Employment specialists provide options for permanent, competitive jobs about 25% of the time.

3 = Employment specialists provide options for permanent, competitive jobs about 50% of the time.

4 = Employment specialists provide options for permanent, competitive jobs about 75% of the time.

5 = Virtually all of the competitive jobs offered by employment specialists are permanent.

6. Jobs as transitions: All jobs are viewed as positive experiences on the path of vocational growth and development. Employment specialists help clients

VL, DOC, INT, ISP

1 = Employment specialists prepare clients for a single lasting job, and if it ends, will not necessarily help them find another one. Or Cannot rate due to no fit.

2 = Employment specialists help clients find another job 25% of the time.

end jobs when appropriate and then find new jobs.

3 = Employment specialists help clients find another job 50% of the time.
4 = Employment specialists help clients find another job 75% of the time.
5 = Employment specialists help clients end jobs when appropriate and offer to help them all find another job.

---

7. Follow-along supports: Individualized follow-along supports are provided to employer and client on a time-unlimited basis. Employer supports may include education and guidance. Client supports may include crisis intervention, job coaching, job support groups, transportation, treatment changes (medication), networked supports (friends/family).

VL, DOC, INT

1 = Follow-along supports are nonexistent. Or Cannot rate due to no fit.
2 = Follow-along supports are time-limited and provided to less than half of the working clients.
3 = Follow-along supports are time-limited and provided to most working clients.
4 = Follow-along supports are ongoing and provided to less than half the working clients.
5 = Most working clients are provided flexible follow-along supports that are individualized and ongoing. Employer supports may include education and guidance. Client supports may include crisis intervention, job coaching, job support groups, transportation, treatment changes (medication), networked supports (friends/family).

---

8. Community-based services: Vocational services such as engagement, job finding and follow-along supports are provided in natural community settings.

VL, MIS, DOC, INT

1 = Employment specialist spends 10% time or less in the community. Or Cannot rate due to no fit.
2 = Employment specialist spends 11-39% time in community.
3 = Employment specialist spends 40-59% time in community.
4 = Employment specialist spends 60-69% time in community.
5 = Employment specialist spends 70% or more time in community.

9. Assertive engagement and outreach: assertive engagement and outreach (telephone, mail, community visit) are conducted as needed.

VL, MIS, DOC, INT

1 = Employment specialists do not provide outreach to clients as part of initial engagement or to those who stop attending the vocational service. Or Cannot rate due to no fit.

2 = Employment specialists make one telephone or mail contact to clients as part of initial engagement or to those who stop attending the vocational service.

3 = Employment specialist makes one or two outreach attempts (telephone, mail, community visit) as part of initial engagement and also within 1 month that client stops attending the vocational service.

4 = Employment specialist makes outreach attempts (telephone, mail, community visit) as part of initial engagement and at least every 2 months on a time-limited basis when client stops attending.

5 = Employment specialists provide outreach (telephone, mail, community visit) as part of initial engagement and at least monthly on a time-unlimited basis when clients stop attending the vocational service. Staff demonstrate tolerance of different levels of readiness using gentle encouragement.

*Data sources:
VL   Vocational Logs
MIS   Management Information System
DOC   Document review: clinical records; agency policy and procedures
INT   Interviews with clients, employment specialists, mental health staff
ISP   Individualized Service Plan

2/14/96
6/20/01, Updated

Fidelity Scale Score Sheet

Rater: _____   Site: _____   Date: _____

Staffing

1. Caseload ___
2. Vocational services staff ___
3. Vocational generalists ___

Organization

1. Integration of rehabilitation with MH treatment ___
2. Vocational unit ___
3. Zero exclusion criteria ___

Services

1. Ongoing, work-based assessment ___
2. Rapid search for competitive job ___
3. Individualized job search ___
4. Diversity of jobs developed ___
5. Permanence of jobs developed ___
6. Jobs as transitions ___
7. Follow-along supports ___
8. Community-based services ___
9. Assertive engagement and outreach ___

Total: ___

66-75 = Good Supported Employment Implementation
56-65 = Fair Supported Employment Implementation
55 and below = Not Supported Employment

Program Descriptors

Agency name: _____

Location: _____ urban _____ rural

Targeted population: specify _____

Parent organization type:

_____ mental health center
_____ rehabilitation agency (SMI only)
_____ rehabilitation agency (other)
_____ N/A - free-standing agency

VR contact:

_____ none
_____ minimal
_____ regular

Agency's vocational emphasis:

_____ minimal
_____ moderate
_____ major

Number of vocational staff: _____

Number of clients served last year: _____

Recency of program:

_____ less than 1 year
_____ more than 1 year

References

Abrams, K., & Teplin, L. (1991). Co-occurring disorders among mentally ill jail detainees: Implications for public policy. *American Psychologist, 46*(10), 1036–1044.

Allness, D. J., & Knoedler, W. H. (1998). *The PACT model of community-based treatment for persons with severe and persistent mental illness: A manual for PACT start-up.* Arlington, VA: National Alliance for the Mentally Ill.

Alverson, M., Becker, D. R., & Drake, R. E. (1995). An ethnographic study of coping strategies used by people with severe mental illness participating in supported employment. *Psychosocial Rehabilitation Journal, 18*(4), 115–128.

American Psychiatric Association. (1987). *Diagnostic and statistical manual of mental disorders, fourth edition.* Washington, DC: Author.

American Psychiatric Association. (1994). *Diagnostic and statistical manual of mental disorders, third edition-revised.* Washington, DC: Author.

Andreasen, N. (1985). *The broken brain: The biological revolution in psychiatry.* New York: Harper & Row.

Anthony, W. A. (1993). Recovery from mental illness: The guiding vision of the mental health service system in the 1990s. *Psychosocial Rehabilitation Journal, 16*(4), 11–23.

Anthony, W. A., & Blanch, A. (1987). Supported employment for persons who are psychiatrically disabled: An historical and conceptual perspective. *Psychosocial Rehabilitation Journal, 2,* 4–23.

Anthony, W., Cohen, M., & Farkas, M. (1990). *Psychiatric rehabilitation.* Boston: Center for Psychiatric Rehabilitation.

Anthony, W., Cohen, M., Farkas, M., & Gagne, C. (2002). *Psychiatric rehabilitation.* Boston: Center for Psychiatric Rehabilitation.

Bailey, E. L., Ricketts, S. K., Becker, D. R., Xie, H., & Drake, R. E. (1998). Do long-term day treatment clients benefit from supported employment? *Psychiatric Rehabilitation Journal, 22*(1), 24–29.

Bailey, J. (1998). I'm just an ordinary person. *Psychiatric Rehabilitation Journal, 22*(1), 8–10.

Beard, J. H., Propst, R. N., & Malamud, T. J. (1982). The Fountain House model of psychiatric rehabilitation. *Psychosocial Rehabilitation Journal, 5,* 47–53.

Becker, D. R., Bebout, R. R., & Drake, R. E. (1998). Job preferences of people with severe mental illness: A replication. *Psychiatric Rehabilitation Journal, 22*(1), 46–50.

Becker, D. R., Bond, G. R., McCarthy, D., Thompson, D., Xie, H., McHugo, G. J., et al. (2001). Converting day treatment centers to supported employment programs in Rhode Island. *Psychiatric Services, 52*(3), 351–357.

Becker, D. R., & Drake, R. E. (1993). *A working life: The Individual Placement and Support (IPS) Program.* Concord, NH: New Hampshire-Dartmouth Psychiatric Research Center.

Becker, D. R., & Drake, R. E. (1994). Individual Placement and Support: A community mental health center approach to vocational rehabilitation. *Community Mental Health Journal, 30,* 193–205.

Becker, D. R., Drake, R. E., Bond, G. R., Xie, H., Dain, B. J., & Harrison, K. (1998). Job terminations among persons with severe mental illness participating in supported employment. *Community Mental Health Journal, 34*(1), 71–82.

Becker, D. R., Drake, R. E., Farabaugh, A., & Bond, G. R. (1996). Job preferences of clients with severe psychiatric disorders participating in supported employment programs. *Psychiatric Services, 47*(11), 1223–1226.

Becker, D. R., Smith, J., Tanzman, B., Drake, R. E., & Tremblay, T. (2001). Fidelity of supported employment programs and employment outcomes. *Psychiatric Services 52*(6), 834–836.

Becker, D. R., Torrey, W. C., Toscano, R., Wyzik, P. F., & Fox, T. S. (1998). Building recovery-oriented services: Lessons from implementing IPS in community mental health centers. *Psychiatric Rehabilitation Journal, 22*(1), 51–54.

Bell, M. D., Milstein, R. M., & Lysaker, P. H. (1993). Pay as an incentive in work participation by patients with severe mental illness. *Hospital and Community Psychiatry, 44,* 684–686.

Bernheim, K. F., & Lehman, A. F. (1985). *Working with families of the mentally ill.* New York, W.W. Norton.

Bissonnette, D. (1994). *Beyond traditional job development: The art of creating opportunity.* Chatsworth, CA: Milt Wright & Associates.

Bleuler, E. (1911). *Dementia praecox or the group of schizophrenias.* New York: International Universities Press.

Bond, G. R. (1992). Vocational rehabilitation. In R. P. Liberman (Ed.), *Handbook of psychiatric rehabilitation* (pp. 244–275). New York: Macmillan.

Bond, G. R. (1998). Principles of the Individual Placement and Support Model: Empirical support. *Psychiatric Rehabilitation Journal, 22*(1), 11–23.

Bond, G. R., Becker, D. R., Drake, R. E., Rapp, C. A., Meisler, N., Lehman, A.F., et al. (2001). Implementing supported employment as an evidence-based practice. *Psychiatric Services, 52*(3), 313–322.

Bond, G. R., Becker, D. R., Drake, R. E., & Vogler, K. M. (1997). A fidelity scale for the individual placement and support model of supported employment. *Rehabilitation Counseling Bulletin, 40*(4), 265–284.

Bond, G. R., Dietzen, L., McGrew, J., & Miller, L. (1995). Accelerating entry into supported employment for persons with severe psychiatric disabilities. *Rehabilitation Psychology, 40,* 91–111.

Bond, G. R., & Dincin, J. (1986). Accelerating entry into transitional employment in a psychosocial rehabilitation agency. *Rehabilitation Psychology, 31*, 143–155.

Bond, G. R., Drake, R. E., Mueser, K. T., & Becker, D. R. (1997). An update on supported employment for people with severe mental illness. *Psychiatric Services, 48*(3), 335–346.

Bond, G. R., & Resnick, S. G. (2000). Psychiatric rehabilitation. In R. G. Frank & T. Elliott (Eds.), *Handbook of rehabilitation psychology* (pp. 235–258). Washington, DC: American Psychological Association.

Bond, G. R., Resnick, S. G., Drake, R. E., Xie, H., McHugo, G. J., & Bebout, R. R. (2001). Does competitive employment improve nonvocational outcomes for people with severe mental illness? *Journal of Consulting and Clinical Psychology, 69*, 489–501.

Brekke, J. S., Levin, S., Wolkon, G. H., Sobel, E. & Slade, E. (1993). Psychosocial functioning and subjective experience in schizophrenia. *Schizophrenia Bulletin, 19*, 599–608.

Campbell, J. (1997). How consumers/survivors are evaluating the quality of psychiatric care. *Evaluation Review, 21*, 375–363.

Capponi, P. (1992). *Upstairs in the crazy house: The life of a psychiatric survivor.* Toronto: Viking.

Carling, P. J. (1995). *Return to community: Building support systems for people with psychiatric disabilities.* New York: Guilford Press.

Chamberlin, J. (1978). *On our own: Patient-controlled alternatives to the mental health system.* New York: McGraw-Hill.

Chamberlin, J., & Rogers, J. A. (1990). Planning a community-based mental health system: Perspective of service recipients. *American Psychologist, 45*(11), 1241–1244.

Chandler, D., Meisel, J., Hu, T., McGowen, M., & Madison, K. (1997). A capitated model for a cross-section of severely mentally ill clients: Employment outcomes. *Community Mental Health Journal, 33*, 501–516.

Clark, R. E. (1998). Supported employment and managed care: Can they coexist? *Psychiatric Rehabilitation Journal, 22*(1), 62–68.

Clark, R. E., Bush, P. W., Becker, D. R., & Drake, R. E. (1996). A cost-effectiveness comparison of supported employment and rehabilitative day treatment. *Administration and Policy in Mental Health, 24*(1), 63–77.

Clark, R. E., Xie, H., Becker, D. R., & Drake, R. E. (1998). Benefits and costs of supported employment from three perspectives. *Journal of Behavioral Health Services and Research, 25*(1), 22–34.

Cnaan, R. A., Blankertz, L. M., Messinger, K. W., & Gardner, J. R. (1990). Expert assessment of psychosocial rehabilitation principles. *Psychosocial Rehabilitation Journal, 13*(3), 59–73.

Cook, J., & Razzano, L. (2000). Vocational rehabilitation for persons with schizophrenia: Recent research and implications for practice. *Schizophrenia Bulletin, 26*, 87–103.

Copeland, M. E. (1997). *Wellness recovery action plan.* Brattleboro, VT, Peach Press.

Covell, N. H., Jackson, C. T., Evans, A. C., & Essock, S. M. (2002). Antipsychotic prescribing practices in Connecticut's public mental health system: Rates of changing medications and prescribing styles. *Schizophrenia Bulletin, 28*, 17–29.

Deegan, P. E. (1988). Recovery: The lived experience of rehabilitation. *Psychosocial Rehabilitation Journal, 11*(4), 11–19.

DeSisto, M. J., Harding, C. M., McCormick, R. J., Ashikaga, T., & Brooks, G. W. (1995) The Vermont-Maine three decade studies of serious mental illness: Longitudinal course comparisons. *British Journal of Psychiatry, 167*, 420–426.

Dickey, B., & Sederer, L. I. (Eds.). (2001). *Improving mental health care: Commitment to quality*. Washington, DC: American Psychiatric Press.

Dincin, J. (1975). Psychiatric rehabilitation. *Schizophrenia Bulletin, 13*, 131–147.

Dixon, L., McFarlane, W. R., Lefley, H., Lucksted, A., Cohen, M., Falloon, I., et al. (2001). Evidence-based practices for services to families of people with psychiatric disabilities. *Psychiatric Services, 52*(7), 903–910.

Draguns, J. G. (1980). Psychological disorders of clinical severity. In H. C. Triandis and J. G. Draguns (Eds.), *Handbook of cross-cultural psychology: Psychopathology* (Vol. 6, pp. 99–174). Boston: Allyn and Bacon.

Drake, R. E., & Becker, D. R. (1996). The individual placement and support model of supported employment. *Psychiatric Services, 47*(5), 473–475.

Drake, R. E., Becker, D. R., Biesanz, J. C., Torrey, W. C., McHugo, G. J., & Wyzik, P. F. (1994). Rehabilitative day treatment vs. supported employment: I. Vocational outcomes. *Community Mental Health Journal, 30*, 519–532.

Drake, R. E., Becker, D. R., Biesanz, J. C., Wyzik, P. F., & Torrey, W. C. (1996). Day treatment versus supported employment for persons with severe mental illness: A replication study. *Psychiatric Services, 47*(10), 1125–1127.

Drake, R. E., Becker, D. R., Bond, G. R., & Mueser, K. T. (in press). A process analysis of integrated and nonintegrated approaches to supported employment. *Journal of Rehabilitation*.

Drake, R. E., Becker, D. R., Clark, R. E., & Mueser, K. T. (1999). Research on the Individual Placement and Support model of supported employment. *Psychiatric Quarterly, 70*, 289–301.

Drake, R. E., Becker, D. R., Xie, H., & Anthony, W. A. (1995). Barriers in the brokered model of supported employment for persons with psychiatric disabilities. *Journal of Vocational Rehabilitation, 5*, 141–149.

Drake, R. E., Fox, T. S., Leather, P. K., Becker, D. R., Musumeci, J. S., Ingram, W. F., et al. (1998). Regional variation in competitive employment for persons with severe mental illness. *Administration and Policy in Mental Health, 25*(5), 493–504.

Drake, R. E., McHugo, G. J., Bebout, R. R., Becker, D. R., Harris, M., Bond, G. R., et al. (1999). A randomized clinical trial of supported employment for inner-city patients with severe mental illness. *Archives of General Psychiatry, 56*, 627–633.

Drake, R. E., McHugo, G. J., Becker, D. R., Anthony, W. A., & Clark, R. E. (1996). The New Hampshire study of supported employment for people with severe mental illness. *Journal of Consulting and Clinical Psychology, 64*(2), 391–399.

Egan, G. (1986). *The skilled helper*. (3rd ed.). Monterey: Brooks/Cole.

Essock, S. M. (2002). Editor's introduction: Antipsychotic prescribing practices. *Schizophrenia Bulletin, 28*(1), 1–4.

Estroff, S. (1981). *Making it crazy: An ethnography of psychiatric clients in an American community*. Berkeley: University of California Press.

Fabian, E. S., Edelman, A., & Leedy, M. (1993). Linking workers with severe disabilities to social supports in the workplace: Strategies for addressing barriers. *Journal of Rehabilitation, 59*, 29–34.

Fabian, E. S., & Wiedman, M. (1989). Supported employment for severely psychiatrically disabled persons: A descriptive study. *Psychosocial Rehabilitation Journal, 2*, 53–60.

Fergeson, D. (1992). In the company of heroes. *The Journal, 3*(2), 29.

Fisher, D. B. (1994). Health care reform based on an empowerment model of recovery by people with psychiatric disabilities. *Hospital and Community Psychiatry, 45*, 913–915.

Foucault, M. (1965). *Madness and civilization: a history of insanity in the age of reason.* New York: Vintage Books.

Glater, S. I. (1992). The journey home. *The Journal, 3*(2), 21–22.

Goddard, K., Burns, T., & Catty, J. (in press). The impact of day hospital closeure on social netwroks, clinical status and service use: A naturalistic experiment. *Community Mental Health Journal.*

Goffman, E. (1961). *Asylums.* Garden City, NY: Doubleday.

Goldman, H. H., Ganju, V., Drake, R. E., Gorman, P. G., Hogan, M., Hyde, P. S., & Morgan, O. (2001). Policy implications for implementing evidence-based practices. *Psychiatric Services, 52*(12), 1591–1597.

Gowdy, E. A. (2002). *Work is the best medicine I can have: Identifying best practices in supported employment for people with psychiatric disabilities.* Unpublished doctoral dissertation, University of Kansas, Lawrence.

Granger, B., Baron, R. C., & Robinson, S. (1996). *A national study on job accommodations for people with psychiatric disabilities: Final report.* Philadelphia, PA: Matrix Research Institute, MRI/Penn Research and Training Center on Vocational Rehabilitation and Mental Illness.

Harding, C., Brooks, G., Ashikaga, T., Strauss, J. S., & Breier, A. (1987). The Vermont longitudinal study: II. Long-term outcome of subjects who retrospectively met DSM-III criteria for schizophrenia. *American Journal of Psychiatry, 144*, 727–735.

Harding, C., Strauss, J., Hafez, H., & Liberman, P. (1987). Work and mental illness: I. Toward an integration of the rehabilitation process. *Journal of Nervous and Mental Disease, 175*, 317–326.

Harris, M., & Bergman, H. C. (Eds.). (1993). *Case management: Theory and practice.* New York: Harwood Academic.

Hopper, K., & Wanderling, J. (2000). Revisiting the developed versus developing country distinction in course and outcome in schizophrenia: Results from Iso9S, the WHO Collaborative Followup Project. *Schizophrenia Bulletin, 26*, 835–846.

Huston, P. E., & Pepernick, M. C. (1958). Prognosis in schizophrenia. In L. Bellak (Ed.), *Schizophrenia: A review of the syndrome* (pp. 531–546). New York: Logos Press.

Johnson & Johnson Community Mental Health Program. (2002). New Brunswick, NJ: Author.

Kiesler, C. A. (1992). U.S. mental health policy: Doomed to fail. *American Psychologist, 47*, 1077–1082.

Kraepelin, E. (1971). *Dementia praecox and paraphrenia.* Huntington, NY: Robert E. Krieger.

Lamb, H. R., & Bachrach, L. L. (2001). Some perspectives on deinstitutionalization. *Psychiatric Services, 52*, 1039–1045.

Latimer, E. A. (2001). Economic impacts of supported employment for persons with severe mental illness. *Canadian Journal of Psychiatry, 46*(6), 496–505.

Leete, E. (1993). The interpersonal environment: A consumer's personal recollection. In A. B. Hatfield & H. P. Lefley (Eds.), *Surviving mental illness* (pp. 114–128). New York: Guilford Press.

Lefley, H. P. (1996). *Family caregiving in mental illness.* Thousand Oaks, CA: Sage.

Lehman, A. F., Goldberg, R. W., Dixon, L. B., McNary, S., Postrado, L., Hackman, A., et al. (2002). Improving employment outcomes for persons with severe mental illness. *Archives of General Psychiatry, 59*(1), 165–172.

Liberman, R. (1992). *Handbook of psychiatric rehabilitation.* Boston, MA: Allyn and Bacon.

Liberman, R. P., Hilty, D. M., Drake, R. E., & Tsang, H. W. H. (2001). Requirements for multidisciplinary teamwork in psychiatric rehabilitation. *Psychiatric Services, 52*(10), 1331–1342.

MacDonald-Wilson, K. L., Rogers, E. S., Massaro, J. M., Lyass, A., & Crean, T. (2002). An investigation of reasonable workplace accommodations for people with psychiatric disabilities: Quantitative findings from a multisite study. *Community Mental Health Journal, 38*(1), 35–50.

McCarthy, D., Thompson, D., & Olson, S. (1998). Planning a statewide project to convert day treatment to supported employment. *Psychiatric Rehabilitation Journal, 22*, 30–33.

McFarlane, W. R., Stastny, P., & Deakins, S. (1995, October). *Employment outcomes in Family-Aided Assertive Community Treatment (FACT).* Paper presented at the Institute on Psychiatric Services, Boston, MA.

McHugo, G. J., Drake, R. E., & Becker, D. R. (1998). The durability of supported employment effects. *Psychiatric Rehabilitation Journal, 22*(1), 55–61.

Mead, S., & Copeland, M. E. (2000). What recovery means to us: Consumers' perspectives. *Community Mental Health Journal, 36*(3), 315–328.

Meisler, N., Williams, O., & Kelleher, J. (2000, October). *Rural-based supported employment approaches: Results from South Carolina site of the Employment Intervention Demonstration Project.* Paper presented at the Fourth Biennial Research Seminar on Work, Matrix Research Institute, Philadelphia.

Mellen, V., & Danley, K. (1987). Special issue: Supported employment for persons with severe mental illness. *Psychosocial Rehabilitation Journal, 9*(2), 1–102.

Mellman, T. A., Miller, A. L., Weissman, E. M., Crismon, M. L., Essock, S. M., & Marder, S. R. (2001). Evidence-based pharmacologic treatment for people with severe mental illness: A focus on guidelines and algorithms. *Psychiatric Services, 52*(5), 619–625.

Miller, W., & Rollnick, S. (1991). *Motivational interviewing: Preparing people to change addictive behavior.* New York: Guilford Press.

Mueser, K. T., Becker, D. R., Torrey, W. C., Xie, H., Bond, G. R., Drake, R. E., et al. (1997). Work and nonvocational domains of functioning in persons with severe mental illness: A longitudinal analysis. *Journal of Nervous and Mental Disease, 185*(7), 419–426.

Mueser, K. T., Becker, D. R., & Wolfe, R. (2001). Supported employment, job preferences, and job tenure and satisfaction. *Journal of Mental Health, 10*(4), 411–417.

Mueser, K. T., Bond, G. R., Drake, R. E., & Resnick, S. G.(1998). Models of community care for severe mental illness: A review of research on case management. *Schizophrenia Bulletin, 24*(1), 37–74.

Mueser, K. T., Clark, R. E., Haines, M., Drake, R. E., McHugo, G. J., Bond, G. R., et al. (2002, May). The Hartford study of supported employment for severe mental illness: Employment and non-vocational outcomes. Paper presented at the 155th Annual Meeting of the American Psychiatric Association, Philadelphia, PA.

Mueser, K. T., Drake, R. E., & Bond, G. R. (1997). Recent advances in psychiatric rehabilitation for patients with severe mental illness. *Harvard Review of Psychiatry, 5*(3), 123–137.

Nelson, G., Lord, J., & Ochocka, J. (2001). *Shifting the paradigm in community mental health.* Toronto: University of Toronto Press.

Noble, J., Honberg, R., Hall, L. L., & Flynn, L. M. (1997). *A legacy of failure: The inability of the federal-state vocational rehabilitation system to serve people with severe mental illness.* Washington, DC: National Alliance for the Mentally Ill.

Noordsy, D., O'Keefe, C., Mueser, K., & Xie, H. (2001). Six month outcomes for patients who switched to olanzapine treatment. *Psychiatric Services, 52*(4), 501–507.

Phillips, S. D., Burns, B. J., Edgar, E. R., Mueser, K. T., Linkins, K. W., Rosenheck, R. A., et al. (2001). Moving assertive community treatment into standard practice. *Psychiatric Services, 52*(6), 771–779.

Quimby, E., Drake, R. E., & Becker, D. R. (2001). Ethnographic findings from the Washington, DC. Vocational Services Study. *Psychiatric Rehabilitation Journal, 24*(4), 368–374.

Ralph, R. O. (2000). *Review of recovery literature: A synthesis of a sample of recovery literature 2000.* Arlington, VA, NASMHPD/National Technical Assistance Center for State Mental Health Planning.

Rapp, C. A. (1998). *The strengths model: Case management with people suffering from severe and persistent mental illness.* New York: Oxford University Press.

Rapp, C. A., & Poertner, J. (1992). *Social administration: A client-centered approach.* White Plains, NY: Longman.

Rappaport, J. (1987). Terms of empowerment/exemplars of prevention: Toward a theory for community psychology. *American Journal of Community Psychology, 15,* 121–144.

Report of the Surgeon General on Mental Health. (1999). Washington, DC: Department of Health and Human Services, U.S. Public Health Service.

Rogers, E. S., Walsh, D., Masotta, L., & Danley, K. (1991). *Massachusetts survey of client preferences for community support services (final report).* Boston: Center for Psychiatric Rehabilitation.

Rosenheck, R., Cramer, J., Xu, W., Thomas, J., Henderson, W., Frisman, L., et al. (1997). A comparison of clozapine and haloperidol in hospitalized patients with refractory schizophrenia: Department of Veterans Affairs Cooperative Study on Clozapine in Refractory Schizophrenia. *New England Journal of Medicine, 337,* 809–815.

Russert, M. G., & Frey, J. L. (1991). The PACT vocational model: A step into the future. *Psychosocial Rehabilitation Journal, 14,* 7–18.

Rutman, I. D. (1993). How psychiatric disability expresses itself as a barrier to employment. *Psychosocial Rehabilitation Journal, 17*(3), 15–35.

Salyers, M. P., Becker, D. R., Drake, R. E., Torrey, W. C., & Wyzik, P. (submitted). Ten-year follow-up of clients in a supported employment program.

Scheff, T. J. (Ed.). (1967). *Mental illness and social processes.* New York: Harper & Row.

Scheid, T. L., & Anderson, C. (1995). Living with chronic mental illness: Understanding the role of work. *Community Mental Health Journal, 31,* 163–176.

Schorske, C. E. (1981). *Fin-de-siècle Vienna.* (1981). New York: Vintage.

Shafer, M. S., & Huang, H. W. (1995). The utilization of survival analysis to evaluate supported employment services. *Journal of Vocational Rehabilitation, 5,* 103–113.

Stanton, A. H., & Schwartz, M. S. (1954). *The mental hospital.* New York: Basic Books.

Steadman, H. J., Mulvey, E. P., Monahan, J., Robbins, P. C., Appelbaum, P. S., Grisso, T., et al. (1998). Violence by people discharged from acute psychiatric inpatient facilities and by others in the same neighborhoods. *Archives of General Psychiatry, 55*(5), 393–401.

Steele, K., & Berman, C. (2001). *The day the voices stopped: Memoir of madness and hope.* New York: Basic Books.

Stein, L. I., & Santos, A. B. (1998). *Assertive community treatment of persons with severe mental illness.* New York: Norton.

Stein, L. I., & Test, M. A. (1980). Alternatives to mental hospital treatment: Conceptual model, treatment program and clinical evaluation. *Archives of General Psychiatry, 37*, 392–397.

Steinwachs, D. M., Kasper, J. D., & Skinner, E. A. (1992). *family perspectives on meeting the needs for care of severely mentally ill relatives: A national survey.* Baltimore: Johns Hopkins University, Center on the Organization and Financing of Care for the Severely Mentally Ill.

Test, M. A., Allness, D. J., & Knoedler, W. H. (1995, October). *Impact of seven years of assertive community treatment.* Paper presented at the Institute on Psychiatric Services, Boston, MA.

Torrey, W. C., Bebout, R. R., Kline, J., Becker, D. R., Alverson, M., & Drake, R. E. (1998). Practice guidelines for clinicians working in programs providing integrated vocational services for persons with severe mental disorders. *Psychiatric Rehabilitation Journal, 21*(4), 388–393.

Torrey, W. C., Becker, D. R., & Drake, R. E. (1995). Rehabilitative day treatment vs. supported employment: II. Consumer, family and staff reactions to a program change. *Psychosocial Rehabilitation Journal, 18*(3), 67–75.

Torrey, W. C., Drake, R. E., Dixon, L., Burns, B. J., Rush, A. J., Clark, R. E., et al. (2001). Implementing evidence-based practices for persons with severe mental illnesses. *Psychiatric Services, 52*(1), 45–50.

Torrey, W. C., Mead, S., & Ross, G. (1998). Addressing the social needs of mental health consumers when day treatment programs convert to supported employment: Can consumer-run services play a role? *Psychiatric Rehabilitation Journal, 22*(1), 73–75.

Torrey, W. C., & Wyzik, P. (2000). The recovery vision as a service improvement guide for community mental health center providers. *Community Mental Health Journal, 36*(2), 209–216.

Trotter, S., Minkoff, K., Harrison, K., & Hoops, J. (1988). Supported work: An innovative approach to the vocational rehabilitation of persons who are psychiatrically disabled. *Rehabilitation Psychology, 33*, 27–36.

Tsuang, M., Woolson, R. F., & Fleming, J. (1979). Long-term outcome of major psychoses, I. Schizophrenia and affective disorders compared with psychiatrically symptom-free surgical controls. *Archives of General Psychiatry, 36*, 1295–1301.

Wehman, P., & Moon, M. S. (1988). *Vocational rehabilitation and supported employment.* Baltimore: Paul Brookes.

Wennberg, J. (1991). Outcomes research, patient preference, and the primary care physician. *Journal of the American Board of Family Practice, 4*, 365–367.

Wing, J. K. (1978). The social context of schizophrenia. *American Journal of Psychiatry, 135*(11), 1333–1339.

Suggested Readings

Ahrens, C. S., Frey, J. L., & Burke, S. C. (1999). An individualized job engagement approach for persons with severe mental illness. *Journal of Rehabilitation, 65*(4), 17–24.

Alverson, H., & Vincente, E. (1998). An ethnographic study of vocational rehabilitation for Puerto Rican Americans with severe mental illness. *Psychiatric Rehabilitation Journal, 22*(1), 69–72.

Anthony, W. A., & Blanch, A. (1987). Supported employment for persons who are psychiatrically disabled: An historical and conceptual perspective. *Psychosocial Rehabilitation Journal, 11*(2), 5–23.

Bailey, J. (1998). I'm just an ordinary person. *Psychiatric Rehabilitation Journal, 22*(1), 8–10.

Baron, R., & Salzer, M. S. (2000). The career patterns of persons with serious mental illness: Generating a new vision of lifetime careers for those in recovery. *Psychiatric Rehabilitation Skills, 4,* 136–156.

Becker, D. R., & Bond, G. R. (Eds.). (2002). *Supported employment implementation resource kit.* Rockville, MD: Center for Mental Health Services, Substance Abuse and Mental Health Services Administration.

Becker, D. R., & Drake, R. E. (1993). *A Working Life: The Individual Placement and Support (IPS) Program.* Concord, NH: New Hampshire-Dartmouth Psychiatric Research Center.

Becker, D. R., Smith, J., Tanzman, B., Drake, R. E., & Tremblay, T. (2001). Fidelity of supported employment programs and employment outcomes. *Psychiatric Services, 52* (6), 834–836.

Becker, D. R., Torrey, W. C., Toscano, R., Wyzik, P. F., & Fox, T. S. (1998). Building recovery-oriented services: Lessons from implementing IPS in community mental health centers. *Psychiatric Rehabilitation Journal, 22*(1), 51–54.

Bedell, J. R., Draving, D., Parrish, A., Gervey, R., & Guastadisegni, P. (1998). A description and comparison of experiences of people with mental disorders in supported employment and paid prevocational training. *Psychiatric Rehabilitation Journal, 21*(3), 279–283.

Berven, N. L., & Driscoll, J. H. (1981). The effects of past psychiatric disability on employer evaluation of a job applicant. *Journal of Applied Rehabilitation Counseling, 12,* 50–55.

Bissonnette, D. (1994). *Beyond traditional job development: The art of creating opportunity.* Chatsworth, CA: Milt Wright & Associates.

Bond, G. R. (1992). Vocational rehabilitation. In R. P. Liberman (Ed.), *Handbook of psychiatric rehabilitation* (pp. 244–275). New York: Macmillan.

Bond, G. R., Becker, D. R., Drake, R. E., Rapp, C. A., Meisler, N., Lehman, A. F., & Bell, M. D. (2001). Implementing supported employment as an evidence-based practice. *Psychiatric Services, 52*(3), 313–322.

Bond, G. R., Dietzen, L. L., McGrew, J. H., & Miller, L. D. (1995). Accelerating entry into supported employment for persons with severe psychiatric disabilities. *Rehabilitation Psychology, 40,* 91–111.

Bond, G. R., Drake, R. E., Mueser, K. T., & Becker, D. R. (1997). An update on supported employment for people with severe mental illness. *Psychiatric Services, 48*(3), 335–346.

Bond, G. R., & McDonel, E. C. (1991). Vocational rehabilitation outcomes for persons with psychiatric disabilities: An update. *Journal of Vocational Rehabilitation, 1,* 9–20.

Bond, G. R., Resnick, S. G., Drake, R. E., Xie, H., McHugo, G. J., & Bebout, R. R. (2001). Does competitive employment improve nonvocational outcomes for people with severe mental illness? *Journal of Consulting and Clinical Psychology, 69,* 489–501.

Braitman, A., Counts, P., Davenport, R., Zurlinden, B., Rogers, M., Clauss, J., Kulkarni, A., Kymla, J., & Montgomery, L. (1995). Comparison of barriers to employment for unemployed and employed clients in a case management program: An exploratory study. *Psychiatric Rehabilitation Journal, 19*(1), 3–18.

Caswell, J. S. (2001). Employment: A consumer's perspective. In D. R. Becker & M. Barcus (Eds.), *Connections—State Partnership Initiative* (Vol. Spring/Summer, p. 5). Fairfax, VA: Virginia Commonwealth University.

Clark, R. E. (1998). Supported employment and managed care: Can they coexist? *Psychiatric Rehabilitation Journal, 22*(1), 62–68.

Cook, J. A. (1992). Job ending among youth and adults with severe mental illness. *Journal of Mental Health Administration, 19*(2), 158–169.

Cook, J. A., & Pickett, S. A. (1994). Recent trends in vocational rehabilitation for people with psychiatric disability. *American Rehabilitation, 20*(4), 2–12.

Cook, J. A., Pickett, S. A., Grey, D., Banghart, M., Rosenheck, R. A., & Randolph, F. (2001). Vocational outcomes among formerly homeless persons with severe mental illness in the ACCESS program. *Psychiatric Services, 52,* 1075–1080.

Cook, J., & Razzano, L. (2000). Vocational rehabilitation for persons with schizophrenia: Recent research and implications for practice. *Schizophrenia Bulletin, 26,* 87–103.

Drake, R. E., & Becker, D. R. (1996). The Individual Placement and Support model of supported employment. *Psychiatric Services, 47*(5), 473–475.

Drake, R. E., Becker, D. R., Clark, R. E., & Mueser, K. T. (1999). Research on the Individual Placement and Support model of Supported Employment. *Psychiatric Quarterly, 70,* 289–301.

Employment Intervention Demonstration Program. (2000). *Principles for employment services and support* (Brochure, UICC R&T Center).

Ford, L. H. (1995). *Providing employment support for people with long-term mental illness.* Baltimore: Paul H. Brookes.

Frey, J. L., & Godfrey, M. (1991). A comprehensive clinical vocational assessment: The PACT Approach. *Journal of Applied Rehabilitation Counseling, 22*(2), 25–28.

Gervey, R., & Kowal, R. (1995). Job development strategies for placing persons with psychiatric disabilities into supported employment jobs in a large city. *Psychosocial Rehabilitation Journal, 18*(4), 95–113.

Goering, P., Cochrane, J., Potasznik, H., Wasylenki, D., & Lancee, W. (1988). Women and work: After psychiatric hospitalization. In L. L. Bachrach & C. Nadelson (Eds.), *Treating chronically mentally ill women* (pp. 45–61). Washington, DC: American Psychiatric Press.

Goldberg, R. W., Lucksted, A., McNary, S., Gold, J. M., Dixon, L., & Lehman, A. (2001). Correlates of long-term unemployment among inner-city adults with serious and persistent mental illness. *Psychiatric Services, 52*, 101–103.

Harding, C. M., Strauss, J. S., Hafez, H., & Liberman, P. B. (1987). Work and mental illness. I. Toward an integration of the rehabilitation process. *Journal of Nervous and Mental Disease, 175*, 317–326.

Harris, M., Bebout, R. R., Freeman, D. W., & Hobbs, M. D. (1997). Work stories: Psychological responses to work in a population of dually diagnosed adults. *Psychiatric Quarterly, 68*, 131–153.

Hogan, M. F. (1999). *Supported employment: How can mental health leaders make a difference?* Columbus, OH: Ohio Department of Mental Health.

Latimer, E. A. (2001). Economic impacts of supported employment for the severely mentally ill. *Canadian Journal of Psychiatry, 46*(August), 496–505.

Lehman, A. F., & Steinwachs, D. M. (1998). Patterns of usual care for schizophrenia: Initial results from the Schizophrenia Patient Outcomes Research Team (PORT) client survey. *Schizophrenia Bulletin, 24*, 11–23.

MacDonald-Wilson, K., Rogers, E.S., Massaro, J., Lyass, A., & Crean, T. (2002). An investigation of reasonable workplace accommodations for people with psychiatric disabilities: Quantitative findings from a multi-site study. *Community Mental Health Journal, 38*(1), 35–50.

MacDonald-Wilson, K., & Whitman, A. (1995). Encouraging disclosure of psychiatric disability: Mental health consumer and service provider perspectives on what employers do. *American Rehabilitation, 21*, 15–19.

Mancuso, L. L. (1995). Achieving reasonable accommodation for workers with psychiatric disabilities: Understanding the employer's perspective. *American Rehabilitation, 21*, 2–8.

Marrone, J. (1993). Creating positive vocational outcomes for people with severe mental illness. *Psychosocial Rehabilitation Journal, 17*, 43–62.

Marrone, J., & Gold, M. (1994). Supported employment for people with mental illness: Myths and facts. *Journal of Rehabilitation, 60*(4), 38–47.

Marrone, J., & Hagner, D. (1993). Getting the most from VR the system. *Tools For Inclusion, 1*(1).

Marshak, L. E., Bostick, D., & Turton, L. J. (1990). Closure outcomes for clients with psychiatric disabilities served by the vocational rehabilitation system. *Rehabilitation Counseling Bulletin, 33*, 247–250.

McCarthy, D., Thompson, D., & Olson, S. (1998). Planning a statewide project to convert day treatment to supported employment. *Psychiatric Rehabilitation Journal, 22*(1), 30–33.

Mueser, K. T., Becker, D. R., & Wolfe, R. (2001). Supported employment, job preferences, and job tenure and satisfaction. *Journal of Mental Health, 10,* 411–417.

Newman, L. (1970). Instant placement: A new model for providing rehabilitation services within a community mental health program. *Community Mental Health Journal, 6,* 401–410.

Resnick, S. G., & Bond, G. R. (2001). The Indiana Job Satisfaction Scale: Job satisfaction in vocational rehabilitation for people with severe mental illness. *Psychiatric Rehabilitation Journal, 25,* 12–19.

Russert, M. G., & Frey, J. L. (1991). The PACT vocational model: A step into the future. *Psychosocial Rehabilitation Journal, 14*(4), 7–18.

Rutman, I. D. (1994). How psychiatric disability expresses itself as a barrier to employment. *Psychosocial Rehabilitation Journal, 17*(3), 15–35.

Sengupta, A., Drake, R. E., & McHugo, G. J. (1998). The relationship between substance use disorder and vocational functioning among persons with severe mental illness. *Psychiatric Rehabilitation Journal, 22*(1), 41–45.

Torrey, W. C., Mead, S., & Ross, G. (1998). Addressing the social needs of mental health consumers when day treatment programs convert to supported employment: Can consumer-run services play a role? *Psychiatric Rehabilitation Journal, 22*(1), 73–75.

Torrey, W. C., Becker, D. R., & Drake, R. E. (1995). Rehabilitative day treatment vs. supported employment: II. Consumer, family and staff reactions to a program change. *Psychosocial Rehabilitation Journal, 18*(3), 67–75.

Unger, K. V. (1998). *Handbook on supported education: Services for students with psychiatric disabilities.* Baltimore, MD: Brookes.

Van Dongen, C. J. (1996). Quality of life and self-esteem in working and nonworking persons with mental illness. *Community Mental Health Journal, 32*(6), 535–548.

Wahl, O. (1997). *Consumer experience with stigma: Results of a national survey.* Alexandria, VA: NAMI.

Walls, R. T., Dowler, D. L., & Fullmer, S. L. (1990). Incentives and disincentives to supported employment. In F. R. Rusch (Ed.), *Supported employment: Models, methods, and issues* (pp. 251–269). Sycamore, IL: Sycamore.

Wehman, P., & Moon, M. S. (Eds.). (1988). *Vocational rehabilitation and supported employment.* Baltimore: Paul Brookes.

Index